Murder Madness

TRUE CRIMES OF THE TROUBLES

ALAN SIMPSON

Gill & Macmillan

Gill & Macmillan Ltd
Goldenbridge
Dublin 8
with associated companies throughout the world
www.gillmacmillan.ie
© Alan Simpson 1999
0 7171 2903 9
Print origination by Andy Gilsenan, Dublin
Printed by
The Guernsey Press

This book is typeset in Goudy 10 on 12.5pt.

A CIP catalogue record for this book is available from
the British Library.

1 3 5 4 2

CONTENTS

In deepest gratitude to my dear wife, Caroline,
and sons, Adrian and Stephen,
for their unfailing loyalty through many difficult years.
Also with thanks to all my former police colleagues,
especially ex Detective Sergeant Kenneth French
and ex Detective Constable Alistair Newell,
both of whom played a key role in many of these cases.

INTRODUCTION

'Murder madness' was the immediate but appropriate response by Sir Hugh Annesley, the Chief Constable of the Royal Ulster Constabulary, as he and other senior police officers faced the world's press on a drab street corner of South Belfast following yet another bloody chapter in the history of Northern Ireland.

The scene was a bookmaker's shop in the predominantly Roman Catholic Lower Ormeau Road area. It had been crowded with early afternoon punters, most of them unemployed youths and men, whiling away a few hours and hoping to strike it lucky with their small bets on horse and dog races. Suddenly, two 'loyalist' gunmen, one armed with an AK47 assault rifle and the other with an automatic handgun, appeared through the door and opened fire. Chaos reigned within the shop as the gunfire reached a crescendo. To those present this seemed to go on forever but in reality it only lasted a matter of seconds. The gunmen calmly made their retreat to a waiting getaway car, leaving behind five dead and as many wounded. The emergency services were alerted at once and on arrival a few minutes later the police and ambulancemen entered a scene of carnage, where the acrid smoke of gunpowder still filled the air and mingled with the sweet, sickly smell of human blood. At least two of the dead were little more than children. This would be of no consequence to the gunmen so long as they were Roman Catholics.

The police and army had been expecting a revenge attack of this nature. Some few days earlier the Provisional IRA had slaughtered eight Protestant building workers on a lonely stretch of road at Teebane, County Tyrone, eighty miles from Belfast. The men had been engaged for some weeks on construction work at a British Army base in the nearby town of Omagh and were travelling daily to and from home in their employer's minibus. The Provisional IRA regarded these workers as 'collaborators' with the British Army and as such they proved an easy target for attack. The movements of the minibus were obviously watched for a number of days and the paramilitaries planted a massive land mine in an area where they could lie in wait for the workers undetected. They detonated the bomb as the minibus passed, throwing it several feet into the air. It landed in a tangled mass of wreckage. The remains of the eight dead were widely scattered amid their lunch boxes and shattered coffee flasks. In the wild open countryside the killers had no trouble in making good their escape. The terrible irony of both these atrocities is that the thirteen victims were non-combatants in the civil disorder which raged in Northern Ireland for almost thirty years, claiming nearly four thousand lives.

The main responsibility for combating crime of every sort in Northern Ireland, ranging from Chicago-style racketeering to mass murder, rests with the Royal Ulster Constabulary. The RUC is descended from the Royal Irish Constabulary (RIC) which was founded in 1836 by Sir Robert Peel who was then Chief Secretary for Ireland. Peel brought together a disparate number of county and provincial law enforcement bodies and moulded them into a single Constabulary. The newly-formed RIC were trained in Phoenix Park, Dublin and dispersed to no less than sixteen hundred barracks throughout Ireland. Due to the widespread violence experienced at the time they were suitably armed to deal with dangerous situations.

In 1922 at the time of partition many of the RIC members moved into the Garda Síochána, the police force for the Republic of Ireland. The Gardaí are largely unarmed and enjoy a good policing relationship with the population. Other members of the RIC found themselves in the infant state of Northern Ireland. In 1922 the RIC became the Royal Ulster Constabulary (RUC) which today is numerically over twelve thousand strong.

I had the privilege of serving in the RUC, having joined as a uniformed constable in 1970 and retiring some twenty-three years later as a detective superintendent and deputy head of the Criminal Investigation Department (CID) in Belfast. I was stationed in some of the most difficult areas in this city and witnessed at first hand many of the results of the paramilitary violence. On some unforgettable occasions I almost became a victim myself. Many of my colleagues were killed or seriously injured and I estimate I attended the scenes of at least two hundred civilian murders.

Despite being much maligned by frontmen for paramilitary groupings, the RUC is far from being the partisan police force so often portrayed. I have observed with immense satisfaction the dedication of my former colleagues at all ranks and in all departments as they strive to provide a service to society as a whole.

I have often pondered on what the public perception of the average policeman is and as I came to the end of my police career I felt compelled to put pen to paper and set the record straight on a number of issues. I hope that at its conclusion the public will have a clearer understanding of the RUC as a whole and see the human side of policing a divided community.

Also, as a detective for over twenty of my years in the police I became involved in numerous murder investigations, not all of which were related to paramilitaries. I have selected a number of these cases to write about in the belief that they would make interesting reading and demonstrate the work of operational detectives and forensic scientists. I am fully aware of my obligations of confidentiality to the force. However, all the cases that I write about have been openly tried in court so the facts are already in the public domain.

1

TRAINING AND
FIRST POSTING, 1970

I entered the RUC training centre in Enniskillen, Co. Fermanagh on the morning of Monday, 16 February 1970, as a twenty-two year old recruit. I was welcomed by the sight of squads of earlier intakes drilling back and forth across the broad tarmac parade ground to the harsh, barking commands of the drilling instructors.

When all the new recruits were assembled that day the Commandant of the training centre, the formidable District Inspector John Hermon addressed us and outlined the standards required of us during our training period. Altogether the initial training period in Enniskillen lasted three months and each day began with a formal parade and inspection in front of the clock tower, followed by classes in law, physical training, first aid and yet more drill. Although for the most part the training was enjoyable and many good friendships were struck up, everyone looked forward to the passing-out parade when we would be allocated to our stations and be given the opportunity to prove our worth as policemen.

Our big day arrived in mid-May and was a rather grand, formal occasion. The splendid RUC band led us on to the parade ground where we performed a complex drill display in front of our invited families and friends. The inspecting officer was the much be-medalled Sir Arthur Young and he took the salute from the podium as we marched off the parade ground. Later, the atmosphere relaxed a little when we retired to the dining hall to enjoy some refreshments with our families. The following day we bade farewell to the training centre and set off for Glenravel Street RUC Station in Belfast for a two-week swimming and civil defence course. None of us yet had any idea where our final posting would be but during the second week a sergeant instructor assembled the squad in one of the large dormitories, formally called out our names in alphabetical order and gave us our stations.

Many of my colleagues were being dispatched to far-off rural locations throughout the Province but I and three others were allocated to Tennent Street station in North Belfast. At that stage I only had a vague idea where Tennent Street station was, but I was immediately aware that it had often featured in news bulletins when there was public disorder in Belfast. In my youthfulness I was pleased and excited at the prospect of getting into the thick of things. Within the next few days the four of us called at the station to find out our duties for the forthcoming week and where we would be accommodated.

The following Monday I took up my first day's duty as a fully-fledged police officer and began to find out more about the area in which I was to serve. Tennent Street station was in fact linked with Oldpark station to make up C Division. This division had responsibility for policing the loyalist Shankill and Woodvale areas, the republican Ardoyne and the mixed areas of Oldpark and Ligoniel. The division was sandwiched between the much-troubled republican West Belfast and the loyalist Shankill area. The Falls Road had been the scene of much bitter rioting and a corrugated iron peace line had been erected by the army to separate it from the Shankill district. To the north of the division lay the republican New Lodge Road area which had also witnessed much violence. One could not have chosen a more strife-torn area of the city in which to serve as a policeman.

These areas were largely populated by working class people living in endless rows of neat terraced houses. The original inhabitants had been attracted there by the employment provided by the linen mills, now lying derelict, which form an integral part of the history of Belfast.

Prior to the outbreak of civil unrest in 1969 most of these areas had been populated by mixed religions but by 1970 many of the people had retreated into their own clearly defined tribal districts where they felt more secure. As the weeks went by I gradually became familiar with these sectarian interfaces, the most striking of which was a stretch of the Crumlin Road which formed a physical barrier between Woodvale and Ardoyne. It had been the scene of much fierce feuding and it was quite a shock to see rows of streets which had been completely burned out, nothing remaining but the charred shells of the terraced housing. Altogether one would not have been surprised to have seen such dereliction on film footage of Berlin at the end of the Second World War.

In June 1970, within a month of my arrival in the division, serious rioting again erupted in this area but this time guns were produced by the mobs and at the end of it three loyalists lay dead. The police who were endeavouring to separate the rival factions were themselves unarmed and in an effort to prevent further loss of life they had to resort to the unseemly method of tackling the snipers by hurling stones at them. Nevertheless, it was an act of some bravery on the part of the police officers involved and this was later acknowledged by the award of at least one British Empire Medal. It was also a clear indication that the Hunt committee report, which had recommended reconstituting the RUC as an unarmed force, and which the Chief Constable Sir Arthur Young had attempted to implement, had been naïve and unworkable at a time of mounting civil disorder.

At the end of that weekend's rioting the army put in place Belfast's second peace line by sealing off the ends of these streets with eight-feet high corrugated iron. A narrow pedestrian opening was left in each barrier to allow access to the few remaining shops which fronted the road.

In addition, the police divisional commander ordered that the interface should always have a presence of at least two constables. I was one of several officers who spent weeks and months patrolling this short stretch of road in order to give early warning of impending disorder. This simple but effective strategy worked. On several occasions lighted petrol bombs or hails of stones came over the barriers from either side, but the early warning provided by the ever-watchful police on duty quickly brought reinforcements to the scene. At the best of times a sinister atmosphere hung in the air but in the dead of night it took on an added dimension of eeriness as we stood unarmed in convenient doorways to avoid becoming targets for snipers. The army was barracked in many of the old linen mills and I was often glad to see a 'duck' patrol of soldiers with blackened faces moving silently down each side of the road. Invariably they bade us a friendly 'goodnight' before moving on into the streets of Ardoyne, a no-go area for the still under-manned and ill-equipped police force.

The summer is the traditional marching season in Northern Ireland, particularly for the loyalist community as they parade in lodges, accompanied by bands, celebrating important dates in their historical calendar. The summer of 1970 was particularly sensitive and the police and army were fully stretched to keep the peace as the parades passed by nationalist areas.

Although I had only been in C Division for a few months I had grown accustomed to sporadic outbreaks of violence. But I was still unprepared for the events which were to overwhelm me and some of my colleagues on what began as a peaceful Saturday in mid-September 1970. Central to the incident were Unity Flats, which comprised low-rise blocks of dwellings situated at the bottom of the Shankill Road and only a few hundred yards from Belfast city centre. The area, formerly known as Carrick Hill, had been made up of streets of old terraced houses occupied by both religions. These houses had been demolished and were replaced by Unity Flats as part of the urban modernisation plan. Unity Flats were occupied mainly by Roman Catholics and now became a sectarian flash point as loyalist parades moved past them going to and from the Shankill Road.

On several occasions I had done duty at the flats as the police shepherded the parades by, some of which had deliberately slowed down and provocatively increased the volume of the party tunes from their bands. A particular problem was the 'skinhead' brigade of loyalist youths who were supporters of Linfield Football Club. They attended every match played by the team, passing Unity Flats on their way to the match. They always returned en masse and were extremely difficult to handle as many of them by that stage would be under the influence of drink.

On this particular Saturday Linfield were playing at Windsor

Park and the supporters were due to pass the flats at around 4 p.m. on their journey back to the Shankill Road. Chief Superintendent David Chesney was our divisional commander and he was present opposite the flats with approximately eighteen police officers including myself. We were supported by an equal number of Royal Military Police. A small reserve of RUC officers were kept out of sight in a back street.

The football match at Windsor had ended and the RUC Special Patrol Group were moving with the supporters and attempting to control them as they crossed the city centre, heading in our direction. Word came through on the police radio that the crowd of supporters was exceptionally large, numbering around two thousand. We braced ourselves for a difficult situation and within about ten minutes the front of the mob came into sight, having turned off Royal Avenue. Steadily the whole of Lower North Street filled with a mass of 'skinheads' and I could see that the estimate of their numbers had not been exaggerated.

They were in a positively ugly mood and as they drew level with Unity Flats they slowed down and began foot stamping. We did our best to keep them moving but soon the situation degenerated into pandemonium and the first arrests were made. Stones began to fly through the air and Chief Superintendent Chesney ordered us to draw batons and don riot helmets. We baton charged the mob and, remarkably for such a small number of police, we drove them further towards the Shankill area.

At this stage the situation had turned into a full-scale riot and we carried out a running battle with the mob as far as Agnes Street junction, a quarter of a mile up from Unity Flats. However, at the junction the rioters regrouped and hijacked a number of vehicles including a red Belfast Corporation double decker bus. We also took the opportunity to consolidate our position and formed a thin line of police across the road about one hundred yards below the junction.

Between us and the rioters was an area of no-man's land into which strode Chief Superintendent Chesney, alone and unprotected. By this time the hijacked double decker bus was swaying back and forth as the rioters attempted to overturn it. They turned their attention away from the bus and began to throw stones towards Mr

Chesney. In an act of pure defiance and bravery he stood his ground.

The situation was now lost beyond recovery. The divisional commander called us forward and we took the junction, giving the bus back to a rather shaken driver. We kept the rioters on the move until they were in the middle of the Shankill area. But we were still small in number and soon the crowd realised they had the advantage. At the junction of Wilton Street-Shankill Road they cornered and surrounded us, pelting us with stones and anything else which came to hand. They began to pull up and smash the flagstones from the footpaths and the cast iron gratings from the road. Eventually one of my colleagues fell to the ground, unconscious. He had taken a direct blow to the head from a jagged piece of iron which pierced his fibre-glass riot hat. We dragged him round the corner into the side street and once again regrouped. Two army landrovers made a welcome appearance from the direction of the peace line dividing the Shankill and the Falls. We flagged them down and hurriedly lifted our injured colleague onto the rear of one of the open-backed landrovers. His face was covered in blood and he looked a sorry sight indeed as the soldiers sped off with him to the Royal Victoria Hospital.

Meanwhile, more reinforcements of troops arrived and the rioters turned their attention towards them, allowing us to make our way through a maze of side streets, somewhat bedraggled and bruised, back to the station. The army had begun to fire CS gas and even from a distance we felt the stinging sensation in our eyes as the wind carried it in our direction. The rioting continued well into the night and became very intense with an all-out attack on the King's Regiment which was billeted in an old bakery in Snugville Street in the heart of the Shankill.

The following morning I commenced duty at 7 a.m. and the rioting had subsided by then. Constable Raymond Carroll and I were detailed to go on an exploratory foot patrol along the Shankill Road to gauge the mood on the streets. We found a scene of devastation. Practically all of the shop windows had been smashed and the premises looted. The streets were virtually empty of people save for a number of shopkeepers who were vainly trying to secure what remained of their businesses. We turned into Snugville Street which was carpeted with rubble particularly in the vicinity of the army post. Every six feet or so along the street the debris was piled high in almost a straight line and this was the only remaining evidence of where the soldiers, protected with shields, had faced the rioters.

We continued with our patrol and at around 9 a.m. the streets began to fill again with people. I recall John McQuade MP addressing a crowd from the back of a lorry, asking them to return to their homes in peace. They ignored his advice and the rioting flared up again. This brought the army back onto the streets. Constable Carroll and I returned to the station where we reported that the mood was extremely hostile.

As it turned out the rioting on the second day was even more ferocious. Part of the mob eventually broke their way into the bakery by battering down the front door with a heavy piece of wood. Fierce hand-to-hand fighting with the soldiers took place. The rioting did not die down until the following day and by that time the army had fired more than one thousand cartridges of tear gas. Over one hundred troops and police had been injured and the damage to property must have amounted to many hundreds of thousands of pounds.

I was pleased to see Monday morning's daily paper carry a front-page photograph of our seriously injured colleague sitting up in his hospital bed with a heavily bandaged head. Someone had obviously brought the remains of his riot helmet to the hospital to show him how it had probably saved his life. The photograph portrayed him proudly holding it with two of his fingers protruding through a gaping hole.

This particular riot had erupted on a day when a young officer who was to become one of my most enduring colleagues arrived in Tennent Street station, fresh from initial training. With much good humour the two of us have often recalled the amazing events of that weekend and are both in agreement that his first day's duty was a baptism of fire.

During the remaining months of 1970 and the early months of 1971 the overall situation continued to deteriorate and a quiet re-arming of the RUC began in certain hard-line areas. Bullet proof vests were issued to officers on patrol. However, this failed to prevent a major setback for the police in C Division when on the late evening of Friday, 26 February 1971 Detective Inspector Cecil Patterson and Constable Robert Buckley were gunned to death by a hidden sniper as they attempted to separate rival factions in the Etna Drive area of Ardoyne.

Another police officer was seriously injured a few days later at a small police station in Ligoniel on the upper end of the Division. The station, a medium size red brick Victorian style building, had once been fully operational but in the late 1960s it was closed as part of a cost-cutting exercise. In an effort to make the RUC more accessible the station had been renovated and re-opened in late 1970 as a reporting post where the local population could call to have their problems dealt with. Only one police officer was on duty at any given time, detailed from the rota at Tennent Street station. I had my turn there and found it a welcome break from work on the streets particularly in bad weather. However, as I sat alone in the station, thoughts occasionally crossed my mind of how easy a target the lonely station provided for terrorists. These thoughts became reality when the Provisional IRA left a gelignite bomb on the doorstep of the station and rang the doorbell. They drove off and as the officer on duty went to open the door the bomb exploded, hurtling him up the hallway. He was seriously injured but eventually made a good recovery. In due course the damage to the station was made good and it was re-opened, but now a static police guard was placed on duty outside.

Ligoniel had once been a village of linen mills and small houses, separated from Belfast. However, the urban sprawl of the city had gradually grown to meet it. A large part of the area still bordered onto open countryside and on the evening of Wednesday, 10 March 1971 it gained much unwelcome notoriety when one of the foulest crimes committed in Northern Ireland occurred in a quiet by-way known as Squires Hill Lane. In the early evening of that date a man out digging his garden heard five loud bangs. Initially he dismissed them as a car backfiring. A short time later he heard the screaming of children and he ran to the nearby Squires Hill Lane. There he saw the bodies of three young men lying on the ground, apparently having been shot dead. Beer glasses were found nearby. When the police eventually unravelled the details of the crime it transpired that the victims were off-duty members of the Royal Highland Fusiliers. The regiment was based in Belfast on peace-keeping duties and certain sections of the city were still regarded as being safe for off-duty servicemen to socialise in.

The victims were eventually named as brothers Joseph and John McCaig and Donald McCaughey. They had been drinking in a city centre bar and members of the Provisional IRA had pretended to befriend them. On the pretext of going to a party they had lured them into a car and driven towards Ligoniel, turning into Squires Hill Lane. Here they dragged them from the car, produced handguns and cold-bloodedly murdered them. John McCaig was only seventeen years of age at the time. Within a matter of days the military authorities withdrew one hundred and sixty similar aged soldiers from the province, announcing that no soldier under eighteen years of age would serve there in the future.

The violence continued unabated through the spring and summer of 1971 with widespread public disorder on the streets. The Provisional IRA intensified its bombing campaign against commercial targets and for the first time began to blow up the homes of serving police officers.

On the evening of Tuesday, 25 May 1971 a suitcase bomb was thrown into the reception area of Springfield Road RUC station which is located in the heart of Republican West Belfast. The station was also occupied by some members of the Third Battalion of the Parachute Regiment. In earlier IRA campaigns the fronts of police stations had always been heavily fortified against gun and bomb attacks but as part of Sir Arthur Young's effort to transform the RUC into a mainland-style police force these defences had been done away with. When the suitcase bomb landed in the foyer a number of members of the public were present on routine matters and Sergeant Michael Willets of the Paras and RUC inspector Ted Nurse shielded them from the blast with their own bodies. When the bomb went off Sergeant Willets was killed instantly and Inspector Nurse was injured. The civilians escaped virtually unscathed with the exception of a two year old baby lying in a pram parked at the front of the station and it was rushed to the hospital with a suspected skull fracture.

Three days later the funeral of Sergeant Willets began and his coffin, borne on a gun carriage, passed Springfield Road police station where two hundred members of the Parachute Regiment and one hundred and twenty RUC men stood to attention in silent tribute. Buglers on the roof of the station played the Last Post and the flag flew at half-mast. Sergeant Willets was buried in his native England and was posthumously awarded the George Cross. Inspector Nurse also received the George Cross and in years to come I had the honour of serving with this gentle giant of a man.

By August 1971 the violence had become widespread throughout Northern Ireland and the death toll was steadily rising. The joint forces of the police and army were trying to restore order under the normal law of the land but in reality the Province was on the brink of an all-out civil war. The Northern Ireland government was in no doubt about this and Mr Brian Faulkner, the Prime Minister, took the major decision to introduce internment, which in effect meant the arrest and imprisonment of terrorist suspects without trial under the Civil Authorities Special Powers Act.

At this time I had been an operational police officer for about fifteen months but many of my duties had been on the static points throughout the Division where we kept a watch out for possible disorder. To a large extent these duties involved long hours of boredom standing on some street corner, interspersed with periods of high excitement when communal strife flared up again. On rare occasions we were given a normal beat duty to perform and welcomed the freedom this gave us to patrol the streets and bid the time of day to local shopkeepers and other well-disposed citizens.

The Ardoyne area was still largely patrolled by heavily armed soldiers but efforts were being made to re-introduce normal policing. Tentative steps in this direction were taken by the detailing of two constables to work with the army patrols. The duty began by reporting to the Flax Street army base where we would link up with a platoon of soldiers. We then set off through the gate and into the heart of Ardoyne. Normally we would endeavour to walk about one hundred yards in front of the soldiers so as not to appear to be too dependent on them. Nevertheless, we were still unarmed and our presence in the area often brought women to their front doors, hurling abuse at us. Packs of dogs roamed the streets. They too sensed we were unwelcome and snapped and growled at our heels. The threat of snipers was ever-present. Often when we turned a corner we were out of sight of our armed guards for a while and I always kept a weather eye out to make sure they didn't lose contact with us. These beat patrols were purely symbolic, unpleasant experiences, and the return to the ugly old Flax Street army post was anticipated with some pleasure. Here we could relax with our protectors for a few minutes with a cup of good strong army coffee before making our way back to Tennent Street station.

At this stage in the troubles many of my fellow officers were middle-aged, with years of police service behind them. They were gradually replaced by younger officers fresh from the training centre and soon I became relatively senior on my particular turn of duty. In mid-summer 1971, I was assigned full-time to mobile patrol duties in a fast saloon car or landrover. This gave me the opportunity to experience the excitement which I craved. The mobile patrols were primarily responsible for answering the 999 emergency calls. I was normally the driver in the saloon car with the callsign 'Charlie One'. We took our instructions from the central control room for Belfast at Castlereagh in the East of the city. The callsign there was 'Uniform'.

Internment day came on 9 August 1971 when mass arrests took place across the Province. I commenced duty at 7 a.m. that day and because of the level of violence overnight we were issued with .38 revolvers. I began my mobile patrol in Charlie One with another colleague and after we left the station we did a general tour of the Division. We could see palls of smoke hanging over a large part of Ardoyne and many other parts of the city. Barricades had been erected in side streets and gunbattles raged in almost all of the hardline republican areas. Radio traffic on the police network was constant and before long we received a flood of emergency calls from families who were being intimidated from their homes.

The first calls took us to the large loyalist Highfield housing estate where the few remaining Roman Catholic families were evacuating their homes and loading their furniture onto all sorts of lorries and vans. A menacing mob of loyalist youths was roaming the streets and the best we could do in the circumstances was to keep circling in the patrol car to give the fleeing families time to load their belongings and escape. In retrospect it may seem a poor response to the distress of these families but manpower was stretched to the limit and most of the city was engulfed in violence.

As soon as we were finished at Highfield we were directed to attend a similar situation in the mainly loyalist Alliance Avenue area, adjacent to Ardoyne. On arrival we found another assortment of lorries and vans loaded with family possessions. Once again we did our best to maintain the peace as the Roman Catholic families evacuated the area. Before departing, some of them smashed the interiors of their homes to make their anticipated occupation by Protestant families as difficult as possible.

The control room then asked us to take a call to Mountcashel Street which was just off the Springfield Road and a short distance outside the boundary of C Division. The local police at Springfield Road were under siege by snipers and rioting mobs and could not send a patrol to Mountcashel Street. On arrival we found three soldiers at each end of the street doing their best to control mobs of angry loyalist youths. About half a dozen of the now familiar lorries and vans were being loaded by the last remaining Roman Catholic families. We moved into the street and left the patrol car to aid the soldiers as best we could. I noticed three mature men walking up and down the street in a very suspicious manner and every time I approached them they cunningly melted into the crowd of youths. However, I got the clear impression they were behind the intimidation of the Roman Catholic families and I logged their faces in my memory for future use.

At 3 p.m. we handed over the vehicle to a fresh crew. However, we were retained on duty and were sent out to monitor activity in Twaddel Avenue, a neat avenue of well-kept houses linking a large loyalist estate with a row of shops at Ardoyne. Prior to leaving the station my colleague had to surrender his revolver as guns were scarce and had to be distributed as widely as possible to other officers. However, I was allowed to retain mine and had a total of ten rounds of ammunition.

We set off for Twaddel Avenue on foot and took up position at a corner of a street where we would be out of sight of snipers.

Several hours passed relatively uneventfully although the rattle of gunfire and the sound of explosions could still be heard throughout the city. At around 7 p.m. things began to change for us when a mob of about one hundred loyalist youths appeared in the avenue, walking in the direction of Ardoyne. We knew this spelled trouble and my colleague and I went out into the middle of the road and stopped them. When asked where they were going they replied that they were heading for Ardoyne as they had heard some of the loyalists living on the edge of that area were under siege. My colleague and I remonstrated with them and warned them that if they went any further some of them would not come back alive. We appealed to them to go back to their own areas. About half of them listened to us but the remainder arrogantly brushed past us. Within seconds a sustained burst of rifle fire broke out from the direction of the Ardoyne shops. I could hear the whiz of bullets pass over our heads and the 'brave' loyalist mob which had just passed us stampeded back. In their rush they knocked us to the ground and several of them actually trampled on us. Very soon they were nowhere to be seen. I was lying in the middle of the roadway and I recall digging my fingers into the tarmac as I desperately pulled myself to the cover of a gatepost.

A rival mob was now beginning to appear out of Ardoyne and the shooting continued. I drew my revolver but did not fire as I was anxious to conserve my meagre ten rounds in the event of the situation further deteriorating. Meanwhile, my colleague used his pocket radio to call for assistance and within minutes an army landrover appeared with five armed soldiers. They casually drew to a halt, which surprised me somewhat, but I later found out that they had only been assigned to assist us with stone-throwing mobs. A further number of shots rang out and the sergeant in-charge quickly took command. The soldiers advanced on each side of the street by darting from gatepost to gatepost. They quickly identified the source of the gunfire as a butcher's shop and immediately opened up on it with their self-loading rifles. They released a thunderous volley of shots and no doubt the hidden gunmen beat a hasty retreat out towards the back where they could lose themselves in the maze of alleyways.

When the situation was more or less back to normal the soldiers left with our thanks and we remained in position but well under cover until 11 p.m. Occasionally the odd shot rang out from the direction of the shops and we could hear the bullets smack off the tarmac. Our relief patrol turned up and we both made it back to the station to find that we were heavily bruised from the earlier stampede. We learned with much sadness that a soldier, Private Hatton of the Green Howards, had been shot dead in Ardoyne. Also, Patrick McAdorey, a long-time suspected member of the Provisional IRA had been killed by the army. His position was confirmed in subsequent newspaper death notices where he was named as a Staff Captain in the 3rd Battalion of the Provos. Prior to his funeral he 'lay in state' for some days in Ardoyne. During my earlier beats through that area with the army I had often seen him sullenly watch us from street corners.

The violence continued all through the night and in my bedroom in Tennent Street station I was frequently awakened by the sound of gunfire. I began duty at 7 a.m. on the following day, 10 August 1971. Sergeant Dan O'Connor informed us that the death toll was steadily rising and that a large part of Upper Ardoyne had been burned out. I resumed mobile patrol with a colleague. We were instructed to go to the scene of the fire at Upper Ardoyne, work with the army to keep the peace, and prevent looting as best we could. When we arrived in the area we were met with the most incredible sight. Two streets, Farringdon Gardens and Velsheda Park, were almost completely burned out. These streets had been occupied by Protestant families, but the events of the previous twenty-four hours had left the people feeling too vulnerable to stay any longer. As a result there had been a mass evacuation overnight. But prior to leaving, some of the more extreme loyalists had set fire to the houses to prevent them from falling into Catholic hands. Over 200 houses had been burned and some of them were still smouldering. The fire brigade had had difficulty in getting to them because of the risk of sniper attack but the army was now strong on the ground and the firemen were dousing the last of the flames.

The final death toll in Belfast for the period was fifteen and the cost of the damage to property was incalculable. In addition to the flames which damaged buildings a number of political fires were ignited. The reverberations from these events continued for many years.

The mass arrests on internment day were intended to remove the hard core of paramilitaries, both republican and loyalist, off the streets. However, the aftermath proved that someone had got it wrong because, if anything, the violence over the following weeks intensified. With the benefit of hindsight it is now widely accepted that the police and army intelligence prior to the mass arrests was not of the highest quality. Many non-activists were swept up and detained. This led only to a greater depth of bitterness if such a thing were possible.

On the evening of Friday, 17 September 1971 I was on mobile patrol in the Division with a fellow officer when at around 11 p.m. we received an emergency call to attend the scene of a reported shooting incident in Downing Street, off the Shankill Road. As I turned our patrol vehicle into the street I saw a small crowd of people gathered around a Vauxhall car. We both got out of the patrol car and moved the crowd back. I could see the body of a man in the driver's seat with his head slumped to one side. The driver's door was open and a man was massaging the chest of the person in the driver's seat. I shone my torch on the body and saw what appeared to be a number of gunshot wounds to the head. When I looked closely at his face I instantly recognised him as one of the three mature men I had kept under observation in Mountcashel Street on internment day some weeks previously. He was obviously dead and we summoned the Criminal Investigation Department (CID). While awaiting their arrival we did our best to preserve the scene by keeping the crowd well back. No one was ever charged with this killing.

More deaths were soon to follow, and one of the most traumatic incidents I have ever been involved in during my entire police career occurred about two weeks after the killing in Downing Street. I had completed my eight-hour tour of duty in the patrol car but was retained on duty and, with one other officer, was given an area of the Upper Shankill to patrol on foot. It was a typical damp evening in early Autumn and we patrolled back and forth through the maze of side streets, occasionally stopping cars to check their occupants and pausing for a chat with some of the local people who were pleased at the visible presence of police in their area.

Around 10 p.m. we emerged from one of the side streets onto the Shankill Road and, almost immediately, a massive explosion took place about one hundred yards away. A great cloud of black smoke and dust billowed into the air followed by the sound of crashing glass as shop windows fell onto the pavement. Many of the street and shop lights were blown out and in a scene of almost total darkness I heard the ringing burglar alarms set off in the shops by the shock waves from the blast.

We ran in the direction of the blast and out of the cloud of dust and smoke which filled the air emerged the figure of a man staggering towards us. I grabbed hold of him but he was unable to speak. One side of his head was raw flesh and a great flap of skin which had once covered it now grotesquely hung below his chin. He was obviously in deep shock and I shouted at him to keep moving. Civilians were now gathering in the area and I knew that they would take care of him.

We continued deeper into the area of the explosion and could see that the main blast had occurred in the bar known as the Fourstep Inn. I stumbled my way through the rubble and tripped over the body of a man who lay on the floor apparently lifeless.

I could hear the screams of others somewhere in the darkened premises and I shone my torch through the cloud of dust. Eventually, I picked out the face of a man sitting dazed behind the bar counter with a great wooden beam lying at a crazy angle just above his head. I tried to grab him by the hand but instead took hold of a warm soggy mess, his hand apparently having been blown off or severely mutilated. I led him over the rubble and handed him into the care of civilians.

By this time the clubs and pubs on the Shankill had emptied and a great crowd of people surrounded the bar in a very ugly mood. Other police soon arrived at the scene and we began to pull away the rubble in search of more victims. One dead body was found and by this time the crowd on the street watching us had swollen to about a thousand.

The mortuary van with which I was to become so familiar was

slowly reversed through the crowd to the pile of rubble. We assisted the attendants in wrapping the two victims in body bags and placing them on stretchers. These were passed over the rubble to the waiting mortuary van. The crowd were being held back by a thin line of police but they roared with anger as we placed the bodies into the van. They showed no signs of dispersing and one could sense that they were planning immediate revenge, perhaps by invading a Roman Catholic area. This was just what the Provos who planted the bomb had hoped for. However, the Reverend Ian Paisley and the local MP John McQuade made an appearance and addressed the crowd, eventually persuading them to disperse. The following day a number of innocent Roman Catholic building workers paid the price when groups of angry loyalist youths ordered them off the many building sites in the Shankill area.

The increase in the number of deaths in the Province, particularly in Belfast, was now unrelenting and on the afternoon of Friday, 15 October 1971 I lost two more of my colleagues from Tennent Street station. They were Constables Cecil Cunningham and John Haslett, who on that Friday had been detailed to work in plain clothes, keeping observations from a car on local banks and post offices which were being repeatedly robbed to fund paramilitary organisations.

Just after twelve noon they were parked on the Woodvale Road at a point where they could monitor activity at the Ardoyne shops but they had obviously been seen and recognised by some members of the Provisional IRA. Suddenly, a hijacked car pulled in behind them. A gunman leapt out and ran to the passenger window of the police car. He immediately opened fire with a sub-machine gun, killing both officers. The hijacked car drove back into Ardoyne and the driver and gunman made good their escape.

When the news of the killings reached us at Tennent Street station we were stunned and could not believe that we had lost two more colleagues, much respected officers.

Cecil Cunningham was a heavily built mature man who had served in C Division for many years and was well known in both sides of the community. He had a friendly word for everyone and often kept the more junior policemen in the station on the right tracks with his sound advice. His loss was greatly felt among his colleagues and family.

John Haslett was only twenty-one years old and had arrived in the station just a few months previously, fresh from initial training. He was a young man with impeccable manners. He turned out for duty in an immaculate uniform and still kept the mirror-like polish on his boots more usually seen on the training centre parade ground at Enniskillen. As a result he had become affectionately known to us as 'Bootsie'. He was still in that early phase of service in C Division where one was required to stand for long periods of duty on static points. He found this frustrating and often asked me if I would collect him during his forty-five minute mealbreak and allow him to come on mobile patrol for that short period before returning to his static point. I obliged him when I could but as I recall nothing exciting happened during these brief sojourns. His funeral took place from Saint Dorothea's Church in East Belfast and I was one of the pallbearers who carried his coffin in front of the RUC band to his final resting place in Roselawn Cemetery.

The murders of Cecil Cunningham and John Haslett were followed by many more killings across the Province and in the final two weeks of October 1971 one soldier was murdered in Ardoyne, one in Ballymurphy, West Belfast and three in Londonderry city. RUC Sergeant Dodds from Toomebridge station also died when he was ambushed by the Provisional IRA, having been lured to his death by a bogus fire call. He was the passenger in a police car being driven by one of my friends. My friend was wounded in the attack but survived. When I met him on duty some months later and enquired after his health he showed me one of his lower wrists which had a bandage on it. He peeled it back and I could see a bullet head protruding from his flesh. He explained that the surgeons who operated on him had left it in place temporarily because to remove it would cause more serious damage to the nerves and tendons. In the neighbouring Division, in North Belfast, Inspector Alfred Devlin was killed when the Provisional IRA blew up Chichester Road police station.

There was to be no let up in the killings in C Division when in mid-November the Grim Reaper returned and cut down two more of my police colleagues. They were Sergeant Dermot Hurley and Constable Walter Moore both of whom were stationed in Oldpark. The crime occurred on a Thursday afternoon when the two officers went to visit an off-licence premises at the rear of Oldpark station. They were friendly with the owner and she had invited them into her rear kitchen for a drink out of public view. Members of the Provisional IRA had obviously been watching them and two gunmen entered the shop a few minutes later. They first took the contents of the till. Then they entered the rear kitchen and opened fire on the two policemen, killing them instantly. As the two bodies were carried from the shop at the end of the scene examination, local women stood weeping. The post-mortem examination of the dead policemen showed bullet holes in their hands which were sustained when they tried to protect their faces from the hail of bullets.

I had known both officers well. Walter Moore, who was the son of a retired policeman, was a genial man who had a friendly greeting for everyone. He was an honourable and fair policeman, well respected in the area and a real loss to the RUC.

Sergeant Dermot Hurley was a perfect gentleman in every respect and a person whom I admired greatly. He was a tall, thin man with a kindly face. I was always struck by the fine row of medal ribbons on his police uniform which had been won during wartime service with the Royal Navy. When Sir Winston Churchill died Dermot Hurley was one of four RUC officers selected to represent the force at the state funeral, an honour which is indicative of the high regard in which he had been held. His funeral service took place at the St Vincent de Paul church on the Ligoniel Road and was attended by many representatives from both sides of the community.

The RUC remained the favourite target of the gunmen and on the early morning of Thursday, 22 January 1972 two police officers were ambushed and killed by gunmen in Londonderry. They were Sergeant Peter Gilgun and Constable David Montgomery who had gone through initial training with me at Enniskillen.

The following day C Division suffered yet another major setback when my good friend Constable Raymond Carroll was murdered by the Provisional IRA. It was he who had walked the beat with me during the riotous weekend on the Shankill Road in September 1970. We had performed many duties together and some months previously I had seen him through his stag night just a few days before he married his lovely wife Shirley. He was a car rally enthusiast and on the day of his death he was off duty and had gone to work at a car service bay in a garage on the Oldpark Road. He had been spotted by a sympathiser of the Provisional IRA who quickly took details of the sighting back to members of that organisation in the nearby Ardoyne. They hurriedly put a murder team together, drove to the garage, and pumped nine bullets into him at close range from an M1 carbine.

Raymond died instantly but within a few days a William Bates from Ardoyne appeared in court charged with his murder. As he left Tennent Street station on his way to court I got my first glimpse of Bates and immediately recognised him as a mechanic who worked in a backstreet garage, off Crumlin Road, not too far from the station. He had serviced my car a number of times and on at least two occasions had taken me for a test drive afterwards. I recalled him driving me up the Crumlin Road, through republican Ardoyne, down the Oldpark Road and back to the garage. He certainly knew I was a policeman and with that knowledge he had deliberately driven me into hostile areas. I found this somewhat disconcerting at the time and had put it down to naïveté on his part but when he was charged with Raymond's murder things began to fall more clearly into place for me.

At his trial some months later Bates admitted that he had spotted Raymond in the service bay of the garage when he himself had pulled in for petrol. Bates claimed that another man in his car had remarked to him that the person in the service bay was a policeman. The two men drove back to Ardoyne and some time later an IRA hit squad arrived at the garage and shot Raymond Carroll dead.

Bates was convicted of the murder and sentenced to life imprisonment but on appeal was allowed a re-trial and was acquitted on the grounds that he acted under duress. Raymond lies buried in the shadow of a tree in a quiet churchyard in his native Enniskillen.

The bombings continued unabated through the early months of 1972. In March a huge car bomb went off in Lower Donegall Street in the city centre killing six people and injuring ninety-seven others.

Two of the dead were Constables Ernest McAllister and Bernard O'Neill, both of whom normally worked in the Belfast control room but when not on their eight hours shift there volunteered for extra duty patrolling the city centre. On many occasions I had conversed with them on the police radio as I patrolled C Division in Charlie One.

In an effort to combat the bombings, unattended vehicles were banned from a large part of the centre of Belfast but this did nothing to save Major Bernard Calladene, an army bomb disposal officer, who was killed trying to defuse a large car bomb in Wellington Street.

In the meantime much political activity was taking place, and it was decided that internment would be phased out. By 7 April 1972 the first of the internees were released from prison. However, this did little to quell the unrest. The Provisional IRA continued with their bombing onslaught and in one day alone set off eighteen explosions across the Province. Meanwhile, loyalist paramilitaries were becoming increasingly active. 1972 was to become the worst year for sectarian killing as sections of the Protestant community embarked on a series of senseless murders.

Throughout the final half of 1972, hardline republican districts, particularly in Londonderry, became semi-permanent no-go areas for police and soldiers, with the entrances to many streets blocked off by barricades. The loyalist UDA had now become a large organisation and its leaders were threatening to close some of their areas to the security forces unless steps were taken to return the forces of law and order to all parts of the Province.

The Secretary of State, William Whitelaw, responded by giving the army the go-ahead to clear away three main barricades in Londonderry which opened up some main routes again to traffic. The UDA compromised by declaring that they would keep main roads open, but they set about closing off the loyalist pockets of Woodvale, Shankill and Oldpark, all of which were located in C Division.

Work began almost immediately. The entrances to many streets were dug up by the UDA and large metal spikes cemented into the roadway. Other streets were blocked off by lorries or barricades and all were manned by hard-faced youths or men. To all intents and purposes we had lost control of these areas and police and army patrols were confined to the main roads.

On Tuesday, 4 July 1972, the UDA attempted to set up a barricade in Ainsworth Avenue, one of the main routes linking republican West Belfast with the loyalist Shankill Road. This was in contravention of the earlier pledge by the UDA not to block off arterial routes. The army physically confronted them on the evening of that day and the UDA assembled eight thousand men in battle dress, some of whom were carrying iron bars, sticks and stones. The scene was set for a bloody battle but senior Army officers negotiated a peace with the UDA leaders and persuaded them not to erect the barricade.

The other barricades remained in position all through July. As police officers we found the situation bizarre and frustrating but realised we were just on the brink of a total collapse of law and order and carried out our duties sensitively.

On 31 July the situation came to a head when the Army mounted operation 'Motorman' by sweeping away the barricades in Londonderry and regaining control of the area. The loyalists responded by voluntarily removing their barricades and this most difficult period for the security forces came to a close.

One of the areas in C Division which had remained accessible to the police during all of this period was the middle-class district of Lynhurst and Westway, just off the Ballygomartin Road and in between the large loyalist housing estates of Highfield and Glencairn. On a Saturday morning at the beginning of July we were informed by the Belfast control room that a body was reported to be lying on waste ground in Westway Gardens. We drove to the scene immediately and a number of the local people who had gathered directed us to a steep bank which led down to a small stream running off the nearby Blackmountain.

I could see what appeared to be the body of a young man lying just over the edge of the banking. His head was covered with a hood and the stillness of the body certainly gave the impression that he was dead. I approached it and felt for a pulse but could detect none. His wrist was cold and the police doctor, who arrived a short time later, confirmed death.

The CID were quickly in attendance and in due course the hood was lifted off his face. None of us recognised him. Subsequent enquiries revealed that he was a nineteen year old Englishman named Paul Jobling who came from Seaham in Durham. He was a student at Loughborough College and had come to Northern Ireland apparently without the knowledge of his parents.

It later transpired that he had been staying with a classmate in Unity Flats and was working voluntarily in a play school in the Republican Moyard district. He came to Belfast on 25 June 1972 but went back to England for a job interview on 29 June. The day before his body was found he had returned to Belfast by plane and was given a lift from the airport into Belfast. It appeared he was unfamiliar with the tribal districts of Belfast and it was later concluded that he had probably wandered into a loyalist area where he would quickly be spotted and challenged as a stranger. When questioned the mention of Unity Flats and Moyard would be sufficient to incense some of the loyalist paramilitaries. No doubt he had fallen into such hands who had then murdered him and dumped his body.

The gun attacks on the police by the Provisional IRA also continued and on a Sunday evening in mid-July 1972 I had just driven out of Tennent Street station to go on patrol with two of my colleagues. The police radio was switched on and before we reached the junction of Tennent Street station and Crumlin Road we heard the patrol car, Delta One, from the neighbouring D Division calling Belfast control to report they had been hit by gunfire. The officer using the patrol car radio was in an agitated state but we were able to make out that he was on his way to the Mater Hospital on the Crumlin Road with one of his crew who had been injured.

We immediately set off for the hospital which was just half a mile away and as we reached the front entrance Delta One screeched to a halt and almost collided with us. My colleagues and I jumped out of our vehicle and ran to the other police car. The driver was in a very distressed condition and a young policeman lay slumped across the rear seat of the car. I pulled him upright and saw that he had sustained a serious head wound. Some of my colleagues had by this time run into the casualty department and reappeared with a number of nurses and a trolley. I tried to lift the injured policeman out of the car but his feet had become crossed under the driver's seat. I placed him back in the police car and untangled his legs. Again I bodily lifted him out and another officer grabbed hold of his legs. We placed him on the trolley and wheeled him through the casualty waiting area. In the treatment room we lifted him onto the table and started to cut away his uniform as the nurses applied oxygen. Within seconds a surgeon appeared in a gown and cap and gave the impression he had been engaged in an operation in some other part of the hospital. He quickly examined the young policeman and the only wound appeared to be to his head. The medical staff continued with their frantic fight to save his life but minutes later the surgeon announced they had lost and the young policeman died in front of our eyes. We found out that he was Constable Robert Laverty from Glenravel Street RUC station. He was aged eighteen. The driver of Delta One explained to us that they had been travelling along the Antrim Road when a burst of gunfire raked the car. I returned to Tennent Street station shocked by the sight of the dying policeman and changed my blood-stained shirt and tunic. Some days later I attended the funeral of Constable Laverty on the north Antrim coast.

During the Friday of that same week the Provisional IRA planted twenty-six no-warning car bombs across Belfast, killing eleven people and injuring 130 others. That day of infamy went down in history as 'Bloody Friday' but in due course several of those involved in the attacks were brought before the law.

The loyalist killing machine also continued in full motion and on the morning of Monday, 14 August 1972, the body of Roman Catholic Thomas Madden was found in the doorway of a shop on the Oldpark Road. The post mortem examination revealed one hundred and ten stab wounds, strangulation, broken ribs and extensive bruising. There was no doubt that he had met such a hideous death at the hands of loyalist killers. The cruel nature of these crimes epitomises the depth of hatred which existed on both sides of the sectarian divide.

In August 1972 we attended yet another murder scene on a grass verge at Glencairn Road just across the stream from where the body of Paul Jobling had been found. A man who lived in the Lynhurst area heard what he thought were two shots during the night. He arose at daybreak and took a walk along the Glencairn Road where he discovered a man lying on the verge face down. The police were then contacted and on arrival I turned the body over and saw his face which was very badly beaten. He groaned faintly: quite remarkably, considering the state of his injuries, he was still alive. We summoned an ambulance by means of the police radio and he was removed to hospital but died on the way. He was subsequently identified as fifty-year-old James Lindsay who resided in Danube Street in the Shankill area. He was a Protestant but it later emerged that he was keeping company with a Roman Catholic woman and had been warned by loyalist extremists to keep away from her. This now appeared to be the motive for his death.

The Glencairn Road, a narrow tarmaced stretch of country road leading from the Glencairn housing estate to the foot of Blackmountain which overlooks Belfast, became a favourite place for murder gangs to dump their victims and we began to patrol it more frequently. One morning towards the end of September 1972 I left Tennent Street station at 7 a.m. with a colleague to commence a turn of duty in Charlie One. We decided to head straight for Glencairn Road and I cruised along its full length but saw nothing of interest. When on returning we reached the area where the unfortunate James Lindsay had been found a few weeks earlier, my colleague asked me to stop and reverse a few yards. He thought he had seen something in the tall grass close to the little stream. We moved back and sure enough a knee was visible just above the top of the grass. We got out of the car and went over to the spot where we found the body of a man lying on his back. He too had been badly beaten and was quite obviously dead. This was soon confirmed when all the various scene examination agencies arrived, including the police doctor. The man was later identified as forty-seven year old William Mathews who lived alone in the Lower Falls Road area. As far as I am aware no-one has been brought to justice for his murder. He had most probably been picked up by a loyalist murder gang and the post-mortem examination revealed he had been stabbed to death.

The summer of 1972 had seen another season of traditional band parades by both sides of the community but by early autumn these were drawing to a close, much to the relief of the police and army. Scores of loyalist parades had been escorted safely past the flashpoint of Unity Flats. However, on one particular Sunday afternoon in late September I was on duty at the flats with a number of other police and troops. We were there in connection with a small loyalist parade which was due to pass on its way back up the Shankill, returning from a church service in some other part of the city. As it passed by there was some minor agitation but we kept the parade on the move and soon it was out of sight as it continued up the Shankill. The bulk of police and army at the flats were then stood down but a colleague and I were asked to remain behind and keep a watch in case some of the followers of the parade should drift back towards the flats.

We stood in the doorway of a shop across the road from a long stretch of advertising hoarding which formed a convenient barrier between the main road and a large area of waste ground in front of the flats. Through gaps in the hoarding I could see groups of children begin to gather and soon stones came over the top of the hoarding. Some of these landed harmlessly on the roadway but others struck passing cars. I sensed that the stone throwing was a build up to something else. We ignored this as best we could, hoping the parents of the children would soon appear and assume responsibility for their offspring. But this was not to be.

The stone throwing continued and as an ambulance passed by it was hit. This to me was the last straw. I made my way across the road and entered the waste ground through a gap between a red brick building and the end of the advertising hoarding. As I appeared the children scattered and ran off into the flats. I ventured on into the waste ground and when I had gone about sixty yards I heard the sharp crack of a rifle shot. The bullet raised a small amount of dust and small stones into the air as it smacked off the ground some six feet in front of me. The whole affair with the stone throwing children had been part of a carefully laid plan by the Provisional IRA and I had fallen for it.

I took cover by running back to the corner of the red brick

building, drew my revolver and fired three shots in quick succession over the roof of the flats. I could not see where the sniper had fired from but I wanted him to know that I was still in business. A few minutes later an elderly man approached me across the waste ground from the direction of the flats and accused me of shooting at the children who had long since disappeared. I tried to explain the true situation to him but he had closed his mind to any views except his own and became aggressive. Some people passing by had witnessed the true events and joined me at the corner of the red brick building confirming that I had had a close shave with a sniper. The man by now had become abusive and I grabbed him by his coat collar and pointed him back towards the flats. He headed off across the waste ground, muttering obscenities.

Almost one month later I experienced another horrible incident. I had been on normal patrol in Charlie One when the control room asked us to go to a shooting incident in the Glencairn housing estate. We went there immediately and saw a small crowd of people around a black London-style taxi. I cleared a passage through the crowd and saw the taxi driver sitting bolt upright in the driver's seat. He had the most ghastly bullet wound in the middle of his forehead but incredibly he was still alive. His eyes were wide open and he stared at me. He was obviously in deep shock and confused about what had happened. I tried to speak to him but he simply stared at me, unable to answer. In the belief that he could possibly hear I offered him some words of comfort. Very soon the ambulance arrived. I tried to ease the driver out of his seat but both his hands had a vice-like grip on the steering wheel. He refused to let go and I had to unfold each of his fingers one by one until I got his right hand free. My colleague took hold of it and firmly held it down while I repeated the same procedure with his left hand. The ambulance men had now joined us and between us we managed to pull the injured man out of the taxi and onto a stretcher. He was placed in the ambulance and taken to hospital but not surprisingly he died three weeks later.

The man was identified as forty-five year old William Clarke, a Protestant, who ran a legitimate taxi service from the city centre area. The CID eventually solved the murder and it turned out that his killers had hired him to drive them to Glencairn and shot him in the mistaken belief that he was a Roman Catholic.

At this stage in my police career I had been on the streets for almost two and a half years. I had seen much violence and had attended the scenes of several murders. My duty at a murder scene had mainly been to preserve the scene intact, pending the arrival of members of the CID. The nature of their work held a certain fascination for me as they had the opportunity to follow a case through to a conclusion. The CID was steadily expanding because of the increase in its workload. I made an application to join that department and was accepted following a selection procedure at RUC headquarters. I could have been sent anywhere in the Province but within a couple of weeks I received official notification that I had been appointed to the CID in B Division in Springfield Road station, situated on the other side of the peace line, in the heart of republican West Belfast and about one mile from Tennent Street station.

2

THE STORY OF ANN OGILBY

In mid-December 1972 I arrived at Springfield Road station dressed in my best suit, hoping to create a good first impression and looking forward with some trepidation to my new role as a trainee detective. The station itself is a modern three-storey building. At that time it had ugly fortifications all round it, some of which had been put in place following the suitcase bomb which killed Sergeant Willets.

As with Tennent Street, the station had a strong army presence although it too was only a tactical headquarters with the majority of troops based in several old linen mills throughout the area.

The police division was comprised of the three sub-divisions of Hastings Street, Springfield Road and Andersonstown. There was a separate CID for each but all were based in adjoining offices on the top floor of Springfield Road station. I was welcomed by the detective chief inspector in charge of the divisional CID and allocated to the Andersonstown office but in fact we all had to help out where the need was greatest.

I quickly settled into my role and enjoyed the camaraderie of my new-found friends. With the advent of Christmas the first few weeks were relatively uneventful. Even the paramilitaries took some time off from their nefarious activities to be with their families. I used the time productively, clearing up reports from my last station so that I would have a clear desk at the beginning of the new year.

Once Christmas had passed the paramilitaries wasted no time in getting back into action and on 2 January 1973 they fired a Russian made RPG7 anti-tank rocket into the station sergeant's office on the ground floor. The outer defences of the station absorbed most of the blast but the station sergeant and his civil service typist were badly shaken by the incident as fragments of the rocket and other debris fell around them.

On Sunday, 18 February 1973 at around 2 p.m. I found myself virtually alone in the CID offices. The phone rang and when I answered it the officer on duty in the station enquiry office informed me there had been what appeared to be a double murder in Divis Street, some half mile from the station.

I went to the enquiry office and a fresh-faced young uniformed constable, who was later to join the CID and become one of my closest friends, led me out to a military armoured personnel carrier. It was manned by soldiers whose function was to patrol the area with uniformed police. This was the only relatively safe way for officers to move around the Division.

The uniformed constable took the front passenger seat and we headed out through the front gate of the station and made our way to Divis Street. A crowd had already gathered there. We quickly established that two Roman Catholic post office workers from a nearby sorting office had been walking towards their homes in the Clonard area when a hijacked car pulled up. A man with a sub-machine gun stepped out and shot both men in the back. They had been removed to hospital but were dead on arrival. In due course I had the scene photographed and examined for evidence. We collected several 9 mm spent cartridge cases. I soon found out that the car used by the killers had been hijacked in the Shankill area and was now parked in a side street in the same general location.

Soon I was joined by the detective inspector in charge of crime investigation in the area where the murders occurred. In due course he was able to link one suspect with the car, by means of forensic evidence. This person had the rather grandiose name of Winston Churchill Rea. At trial stage it could not be proved that he had actually been in the car at the time of the murders. He was convicted only of the crime of assisting offenders and was sentenced to eight years imprisonment.

In early March I assisted with investigations into one of the most harrowing crimes committed during my service in West Belfast. The Queen's Lancashire Regiment were based in Lower Falls and most of them were billeted in the Albert Street Mill. On a Sunday afternoon a patrol left the base in two armoured personnel carriers to search a lock-up garage in McDonnell Street following a shooting incident. While some of the soldiers carried out the search others took up vantage points to protect them from snipers. A hostile crowd of women gathered and began to harangue the soldiers. The search was concluded but nothing was found so the soldiers clambered back into their vehicles to return to Albert Street Mill.

Unfortunately, they mistakenly left Private Gary Barlow behind and he was quickly surrounded by the crowd of women. He still had his self-loading rifle but obviously didn't use it as the women kept him hemmed in until a gunman was brought to the scene. The soldier was cruelly shot in the head and his rifle was then stolen. The part played by the women in this was horrible but some human decency shone through when two of them ran to Albert Street Mill and shouted to the guard, 'There's a soldier down the road being beaten up — come quick.' A patrol was immediately sent out and they went to McDonnell Street where they found Private Barlow lying on the ground. He was immediately removed to hospital but died a short time later.

His body was removed to the primitive city mortuary on Laganbank Road for a post-mortem examination. The following morning I had the most unpleasant duty of taking Private Barlow's company commander to the mortuary where I pulled back the sheet from the body and he officially identified him to me. Before I replaced the sheet the company commander took one pace back and movingly saluted the dead soldier. I attended the examination of the body and the pathologist recovered a .45 bullet from the soldier's head.

The Roman Catholic bishop of Down and Connor, Doctor Philbin, later visited the colonel of the regiment and expressed his sympathy. Some days later Private Barlow was buried with full military honours in his native Wigan. He was only nineteen years old. It is one of the murders which remains in my mind as I remember the cruel manner in which he met his death.

That year ended with yet another sad note for Tennent Street station when one of my former colleagues was lured to a robbery in the Glencairn housing estate where he was cut down by a hail of gunfire from members of the UDA. This was a reprisal attack in response to an incident the previous night when an army patrol shot a man dead on the Shankill Road. The dead policeman was twenty-one year old Michael Logue. Some days later I attended his funeral in the Roman Catholic church at Ardmore, near Londonderry. In due course the CID at Tennent Street arrested a number of men for this crime and they were sentenced to life imprisonment.

Also, on 24 June 1974, Sergeant Dan O'Connor, who had been my supervising sergeant in Tennent Street, was gunned down and killed by the Provisional IRA on the Crumlin Road as he was making his way on foot to help keep order at a loyalist band parade. Once again I found myself attending a mass in a Roman Catholic church when Sergeant O'Connor's funeral took place in Ballycastle. One man was brought to book for his involvement in the crime and was sentenced to ten years imprisonment.

At around the same period I assisted with the investigation into the murder of a young woman, the details of which depict the depravity so endemic in all of the paramilitary groups. The events for the CID commenced just after 9 a.m. on Monday, 29 July 1974 as two motorway maintenance men were tidying up the grass verge on the city-bound carriage way of the M1 about half a mile from where it terminated at the Broadway intersection. The actual motorway formed the boundary between B Division in which I was serving and the adjoining A Division.

The grass verge was level and about nine feet wide and then fell sharply away into a ditch which contained about eighteen inches of stagnant water. As one of the workmen trimmed the grass on the verge he noticed with horror the body of a young woman wearing a red jumper and grey slacks lying in the ditch, partly submerged in the water. His fellow workman joined him and the police were immediately notified.

A uniformed patrol initially attended the scene and quickly notified the CID. Several of us left Springfield Road station and went to where the body had been found. We were joined a short time later by the police doctor who went through the necessary formality of certifying that the woman was indeed dead.

The body was actually lying on its back, face upwards, with both arms outstretched. She appeared to be about thirty years of age and of slight build. One of the shoes was missing from the body but was lying a short distance away at the top of the ditch. A large brown sack also lay nearby. The whole scene was photographed and mapped by officers from the CID support services.

The area was thoroughly searched for other evidence and we then summoned the undertaker's van. And as the motorway traffic roared by we placed the woman in a body bag and had her removed to the city mortuary under police escort. A scenes of crime officer collected the shoe and sack and placed these in exhibit bags. The grass on which they had been lying had turned yellow, indicating that these items had been in position for some considerable time.

Death had therefore probably occurred some days earlier and this was confirmed during the post-mortem examination which revealed a horrendous catalogue of injuries. There were ten deep lacerations to her scalp and the pathologist gave the opinion that these could have been caused by something like a brick. Her skull had been fractured and this was the main cause of death. In addition her face, arms, hands and legs were heavily bruised by something like a shod foot or a wooden pole.

There was no evidence of identification on the body so her physical description was issued to the press together with details of a number of rings on her fingers. The local radio and television news bulletins carried details of the incident and within a few hours we were contacted by a social worker who told us she had been looking after a Miss Ann Ogilby who was the mother of a six year old child named Sharlene. The social worker informed us that Ann Ogilby and her child had arrived late for an appointment in the social service offices in Lower Crescent, Belfast on Wednesday, 24 July 1974 but had left for some unknown reason before she had a chance to speak with her. Sharlene later turned up alone that same day at the Young Women's Christian Association hostel on the Malone Road where they had been staying. Her mum had not been seen since and the child had been taken into care. On arrival at the hostel on that day Sharlene appeared red-eyed from crying and said, 'Where's my mammy? Where's my mammy?'

We took the social worker along to the mortuary to view the murder victim and she confirmed that it was indeed the body of Ann Ogilby. Ann originally came from the small County Tyrone village of Sion Mills. Later that same day I took one of her brothers along to the mortuary and he confirmed that the bruised and blackened face was that of his sister.

Enquiries into the background of Ann revealed that she was twenty-eight years of age and was the mother of four children, all of whom had been taken into care with the exception of Sharlene who was the eldest. Ann had moved to Belfast some six years previously and had resided at a number of addresses. She had more or less been under the constant care of the social services who had recently placed her in the YWCA hostel on the Malone Road.

Later that same day a uniformed police sergeant from A Division contacted the murder squad at Springfield Road station to report that on the evening of Tuesday, 23 July 1974 he had dealt with an incident involving Ann Ogilby. He was asked to come to our offices at once and when he did he explained that on the Tuesday evening he had been called to the scene of a row at the nearby Glengall Street bus depot. On arrival he had spoken to one of the staff who explained to him that some minutes earlier a young woman had been pulled off a bus by a number of women and driven away in a car. The sergeant circulated details of the car by radio. A police mobile patrol saw it on the Upper Malone Road some three miles away and stopped it. The sergeant made his way to where it was located and found that there were no fewer than ten women in the car.

When asked where they were going some of the women said they were on their way to a party. The sergeant asked who had been pulled off the bus and some of the women pointed to a girl who identified herself as Ann Ogilby. She seemed somewhat distressed and the sergeant arranged for all of the women to be brought to Queen Street police station for further investigation. At the station he confirmed each of their identities. Most of them had addresses in the loyalist Sandy Row area. He took Ann Ogilby aside but she declined to make any formal complaint despite her apparent nervousness. As a result all of the women were released from police custody and the sergeant arranged for Ann Ogilby to be taken home by taxi. The following day, Wednesday 24 July he saw her again by arrangement but she reiterated that she did not wish to make a complaint. The young woman asked the sergeant to give her and little Sharlene a lift to the social services offices in Lower Crescent and he kindly did so. The timing of this coincided with her late arrival for the appointment with the social worker.

The main question to be answered now was where Ann Ogilby had been from the time she was seen at the social security offices and the finding of her body on the motorway. With the help of the social services we located Sharlene in a children's home and had her sensitively interviewed by one of my female colleagues. She turned out to be a bright little child and could recall going with her mum to the social services office on Wednesday, 24 July. Sharlene described how a man had called for them and taken them away in a blue van before they had a chance to speak with the social worker. They were driven to Hunter Street in the Sandy Row area. They stopped outside a big building which the man opened with a key. He led Sharlene and her mum into the building and they were quickly followed by a number of women wearing masks. Sharlene said she was then put out of the building and given ten pence by the man to run to the shop and buy sweets. She returned to the big building some minutes later. The man placed her back in the van without her mum and took her to the YWCA hostel. He left her on the doorstep and rang the doorbell before making off.

The woman detective then arranged for two of our male colleagues to take her and Sharlene to Sandy Row in a CID car. She wanted to see if Sharlene could direct them to the big building where she had last seen her mum. Sharlene directed the driver through a number of side streets into Hunter Street where she pointed out the building she was referring to. In order to test her credibility the detectives drove away from Hunter Street and approached Sandy

Row from an entirely different direction. Again Sharlene accurately took them back to Hunter Street and the big building which turned out to an old bakery converted into a UDA club.

The detective inspector in charge of the investigation decided to move quickly and the following morning arranged for the arrest and interviews of the women who had been in the car with Ann Ogilby on the evening of 23 July. In addition he ordered that the old bakery in Hunter Street be examined by a scenes of crimes officer and one of my colleagues.

The next morning we turned up for duty at Springfield Road station at 6 a.m. In a fleet of police cars and landrovers we went to the home addresses of the women and brought most of them in for questioning.

The examination of the old bakery also went according to plan. The officers ascended a set of stairs which led into a large first-floor room. This room was in a state of near dereliction. There was an old bench-type wooden seat and on the floor close to it was a matchbox, some pieces of wood and an old sack, all of which were bloodstained. The officers found, under the sack, five very significant pieces of paper each of which was bloodstained. These were a National Insurance card in the name of Ann Ogilby, a Ministry of Health and Social Services card also bearing her name, a paper with the name of a children's home written on it, a piece of paper which had on it, 'Change pass from Monday to Tuesday, Compound 9, W.J. Young, 182784' and an envelope addressed to W.J. Young, No. 40, Maze Prison, Lisburn.

A large area of bloodstaining was found on another part of the floor, some distance from the bench, and efforts had been made to conceal it by spreading debris over it. In that same area a makeshift punchbag hung from the ceiling, the room apparently once having been used as a gym. When the stuffing was removed from it, the old sack seemed to be similar to the one found beside the body on the motorway. Two masks were also found and some evidence of bloodstaining was discovered on the stairs leading up to the room. There seemed no doubt now that this was the room where Ann Ogilby had met her death. The news was conveyed to us at Springfield Road where the interviews with the suspects were well under way.

The items found at the old bakery were submitted to the Forensic Science Laboratory and the expert who examined them soon reported that the grouping of the blood staining matched that of Ann Ogilby. The expert had by then also examined the sack found near the body and discovered several small cuts in the bottom of it, apparently caused by a blunt instrument.

The first of the admissions soon came and it was revealed that the murder had been carried out by female members of the Sandy Row UDA, assisted by a man named as 'Bumper' Graham. Ann Ogilby had been living for some months with a William Young, whose name was on some of the documents found in the old bakery. He was then in prison. Young was a married man and Ann Ogilby had been visiting him regularly in prison. She was allegedly causing trouble by spreading a rumour that his lawful wife was not sending food parcels to Young, despite finance being made available for such by an organisation known as the Loyalist Prisoners Association. Mrs Young had been able to prove that she was in fact using the money properly and the whole situation had caused a great deal of resentment within the UDA.

On the evening of Tuesday, 23 July Ann Ogilby had been questioned about these allegations and had been asked if she was receiving threatening letters. This took place in a club near Sandy Row and at its conclusion she had been dropped off by car at Glengall Street bus depot to catch a bus home. On getting out of the car she had allegedly passed a sarcastic remark which incensed the others and it was this which led to her being dragged off the bus. But whatever plans the women then had for Ann Ogilby that evening, they were thwarted when the police intercepted the car on the Upper Malone Road.

The following day several of the women gathered in the Elm Bar and Elizabeth Douglas, the self-confessed leader of the Sandy Row women's UDA, had decided that Ann Ogilby should be 'Rompered'. The expression 'Rompered' is peculiar to Northern Ireland and is derived from a children's television programme called 'Romper Room' in which persons dance about. This term had been adopted by the paramilitary groups when they wanted to punish someone. It usually took the form of a beating.

The women had somehow got to know that Ann Ogilby was due at the social security offices in Lower Crescent at half past three the following day, Wednesday, 24 July. Elizabeth Douglas assembled her 'Heavy Squad' which consisted of three teenage girls named Etta Cowan, Christine Smith, Joey Brown and the twenty-six year old man named Albert 'Bumper' Graham. They were instructed to detain Ann Ogilby, take her to the old bakery in Hunter Street and give her a punishment beating.

The 'Heavy Squad' went to the lounge bar of a hotel near Lower Crescent and had a drink by a window which overlooked the social security offices. Graham kept his blue minibus parked nearby. Ann Ogilby turned up on time and went into the offices but the 'Heavy Squad' grew impatient. Graham called her and Sharlene out of the social security offices before they had had a chance to see the social worker. He told Ann Ogilby that she was required by a UDA commander and she and Sharlene willingly got into the minibus with Graham while Cowan, Smith and Brown made their way round to Hunter Street on foot.

On arrival at the old bakery Graham led Ann Ogilby up the set of stairs to the derelict room, leaving Sharlene on the footpath outside. Cowan, Smith and Brown appeared, wearing masks, and ordered Ann Ogilby to take a seat on the wooden bench. Cowan then put a blindfold over Ann's eyes and placed a sack over her head and shoulders. She punched Ann on the face, knocking her off the bench. Meanwhile Graham had given Sharlene ten pence and sent her to a corner shop to buy sweets to keep her out of the way. Cowan and Smith began to kick Ann about the face and stomach. Then, in an act of pure savagery, both girls began to crash bricks down on her head. She by this time had put her hands up inside the sack to try and protect her face. Graham returned to the room and he and Brown began to panic at what was taking place. They tried to remonstrate with Cowan and Smith but to no avail. Graham and Brown left the room and according to Cowan's admission she and Smith then stopped the beating to have a cigarette. At that point they could hear Sharlene knocking at the door outside and calling for her mammy. The two assailants were totally unmoved by the cries of the child and resumed the beating of Ann who by this time was probably fatally injured. When Cowan had finished the beating she removed the sack and saw that Ann appeared to be dead. They wrapped her in a second sack and carried her to the bottom of the stairs after which they went for a drink with Elizabeth Douglas and gave her an account of what had taken place.

Meanwhile Graham collected Sharlene from outside the old bakery, drove her to the YWCA hostel and dropped her off where she was received by the staff until taken into care by the social services.

The only problem now left for the UDA was the disposal of the body. Elizabeth Douglas admitted that she made the arrangements for this but refused to tell the CID who carried it out. This aspect of the crime was never satisfactorily resolved and it is presumed that the gruesome business was handed over to male members of the UDA. This they had done by taking it in some form of vehicle onto the motorway and dumping it.

Eleven women and one man, which included all of the 'Heavy Squad', were charged with the crime and their trial was listed to begin on 6 February 1975. Lord Justice McGonigle sat on the case and he presented an imposing figure in his red gown and wig as he entered Belfast Crown Court that morning. All twelve accused were in the dock and the public gallery was filled to capacity.

Each of the accused was arraigned and Cowan and Smith pleaded guilty to the murder of Ann Ogilby. At the time of the crime they were both under seventeen years of age so the court was unable to pass a sentence of life imprisonment but instead ordered them to be detained at the pleasure of the Secretary of State.

Elizabeth Douglas pleaded guilty to manslaughter and on the grounds that she had not intended her 'Heavy Squad' to kill Ann Ogilby the charge of murder was withdrawn. She received a sentence of ten years imprisonment.

Graham and Brown pleaded guilty to being an accessory after the fact and to causing grievous bodily harm to Ann Ogilby. Their attempts to stop Cowan and Smith from continuing with the beating were recognised when the Crown withdrew the murder charge.

The remainder of the accused pleaded guilty to intimidating Ann

Ogilby and most of them were sent to prison, the only exception being a sixteen year old girl who received a suspended sentence.

During the sentencing Lord Justice McGonigle summed up the case by saying, 'In this case again the UDA is condemned in the persons of the accused who stand before me. I do not know what constitutes a paramilitary organisation. What appears before me today under the name of the UDA is gunlaw, a vicious and brutalising organisation of persons who take the law into their own hands, and who, by kangaroo courts and the infliction of physical brutality, terrorise a neighbourhood through intimidation and rule an area of this city.'

When dealing with Elizabeth Douglas the judge said, 'You organised and directed the punishment of this girl. You chose and chose well those who were to carry out your directions. When you heard what had happened you organised the cover-up and disposal of the body. Your concern was to ensure that these happenings should not come to light. You were the commander of these women; your responsibility was great. You are no stranger to crime. You have a record of smuggling, forgery, assault and actual bodily harm and aiding and abetting the keeping of a brothel. Though the last of these was in 1961 it is an indication of your character.'

Turning to Cowan and Smith the judge commented, 'You were well chosen for what you did and maybe the fact that you both have convictions for disorderly behaviour and possession of offensive weapons made you a suitable choice. Cowan, it has been said you had a mad look in your eyes when you brought the bricks down on Miss Ogilby. You both stopped in the course of this terrible punishment to have a smoke and restarted when you heard Miss Ogilby's daughter outside. Afterwards you went for a drink and then to a disco. You are without feeling or remorse.'

Lord Justice McGonigle closed by saying that it was an indication of the power such a gang possessed that Ann Ogilby did not attempt to seek the protection of the police and made no complaint to them on 23 July when she was rescued from a car into which she had been forced, although she must have then known that physical force was intended. Even more significant was the fact that she did not attempt to escape or seek help even when taken to the UDA 'Romper Room' in Hunter Street but sat quietly on the bench and submitted to being blindfolded and hooded. When first hit she collapsed passively onto the floor and lay there, taking all the brutality offered and dying under the blows. The judge concluded that this was not an association of decent hard working respectable people represented before him. He urged the people of Sandy Row to recognise the evil they had among them and drive out those associated with it.

Not long after we had wound up the Ogilby investigation in the summer of 1974 and had all twelve of the accused charged and remanded I experienced one of the most frightening incidents in my police career through my own carelessness. It occurred in early August 1974 when the army shot dead a Provisional IRA man in the Lower Falls. Subsequent death notices in the newspapers described him as a member of D company, 2nd Battalion of the IRA and claimed he died on active service against British imperialist forces in occupation.

There had been many IRA funerals in the earlier years of their campaign, invariably attended by large numbers of people. On several occasions men dressed in paramilitary uniforms with black berets and sunglasses had marched beside and behind the hearse and it was common for volleys of shots to be fired over the coffin at some stage.

At that time we as CID officers could move relatively freely through the Division in unmarked cars although it was always wise to have a back-up companion and to look well ahead to avoid riots and any other trouble which could erupt without warning.

On the day of this particular funeral I had completely forgotten about it as events like the shooting of an alleged gunman were quickly overtaken by other matters. I had arranged to see someone at Andersonstown police station and left Springfield Road alone in my own car to keep the appointment. There were several routes I could have chosen and decided to take a shortcut through the Beechmount area and onto the Falls Road which leads to Andersonstown. As I drove further into Beechmount I got caught up in a traffic jam at the junction of Beechmount Avenue and the Falls Road. A lot of people were milling about and the part of the Falls Road that I could then see was lined by people approximately six deep on each side. It dawned on me now, somewhat late, that the funeral of the alleged gunman was under way and I found myself in a very difficult situation. I was well jammed in by other cars and was acutely aware that Provisional IRA members attending the funeral would recognise me as I had interviewed many of them about their suspected involvement in terrorism.

If I was now spotted alone in my car they would soon take advantage of the situation. Hatred for the police and army was such that I envisaged the crowd attacking me and I would have suffered a severe beating, probably death. Unfortunately, such a situation did develop many years later when two army corporals in plain clothes inadvertently ran into an IRA funeral in Andersonstown and the whole world saw on their television screens man's bestiality when they were savagely dragged from their car, beaten and shot.

I discreetly locked each of my car doors on the inside, pulled down my sun visor and put my hand on my chin to conceal my identity as much as possible. The traffic remained at a standstill and in due course the funeral cortege passed slowly by on the Falls Road followed by a large crowd of people on their way to the burial at Milltown cemetery. After what seemed an eternity, but in reality was only twenty minutes, the traffic emerged from Beechmount Avenue onto the Falls Road and I followed the cortege at a snail's pace for about half a mile.

The footpaths on the Falls Road were solidly lined with people and any potential escape route for me through streets to the left or right were blocked off by the crowds. My luck had so far held and my car was regarded simply as one of many following the funeral. Eventually I came to the major junction of Donegall Road and Falls Road and to my immense relief the crowd had not blocked it off. I turned sharply left and breathed a sigh of relief that I had been so lucky. But I was also angry at myself for being so careless. I didn't stop until I reached the safety of the city centre where I parked my car and went for a quiet cup of coffee to ease the flow of adrenalin running through my body. I made a solemn promise to myself to avoid such complacency in future.

The spiral of sectarian killings continued ever upwards and on a Friday morning in late November 1974 a car with three loyalist gunmen on board drove into The People's Garage on the Upper Springfield Road. The garage had been so named as part of the republican element's image of a thirty-two County Socialist Republic but it was just a typical filling station with a shop attached. At least one gunman opened fire killing one of the female employees, Geraldine Macklin, and injuring the manager Seamus Mac Seáin.

The following day members of the Provisional IRA drove into the Edenderry filling station on the Crumlin Road and shot dead a young man and woman, both of whom worked there. This was typical of the tit-for-tat killings which went on in Northern Ireland at the time. However, I am pleased to say the killers in both cases were brought to justice and sentenced to life imprisonment.

Although I was heavily engaged in my work as a CID officer with very few off-duty periods I somehow found time to study for and pass the police examinations which made me eligible for promotion to the rank of sergeant. I attended an interview selection board at which I was successful and in the spring of 1975 I was promoted to the rank of detective sergeant. Normally such a promotion brought a transfer to some other area but I remained with the CID in West Belfast.

The murder rate throughout the Province was now so high that Sir Jamie Flanagan, who was then Chief Constable of the RUC, accepted proposals to set up a specialist team of detectives to try and make further in-roads into the killer gangs. In June 1975 a team of thirty-six detectives from various stations was pulled together and given the title 'A' Squad to represent its anti-assassination role. They were supported by the Special Patrol Group. The idea was that any police division within the Province suffering from an increase in its murder rate could call upon the squad to reinforce the local CID for the period until the problem was resolved.

The autumn of that year saw the start of one of the many feuds which broke out between republican factions from time to time. This particular one was between the Provisional IRA which grew out of the violence beginning in 1969 and the old guard of the Official IRA which had traditionally represented republicanism down through the years and was now referred to as the Republican Clubs Movement. It erupted into violence on the evening of Wednesday, 29 October 1975 when the Provisional IRA launched a co-ordinated attack against alleged members of the Republican Clubs by carrying out a series of shooting attacks around 6 p.m. I arrived into Springfield Road at about 6.30 p.m. and received word that a number of persons had been admitted to the nearby Royal Victoria Hospital with gunshot wounds. I collected a colleague and went to the hospital who were bound by law to disclose details of persons admitted as a result of shooting incidents. A total of twenty-six persons had been received into the casualty department from across the city and I took note of their names and addresses. I then returned to Springfield Road and recorded the details of the victims. The feud continued for several more weeks and many people died as a result.

As we moved into 1976 the RUC suffered two major setbacks. Inspector Bell of the Special Patrol Group and Detective Constable Cummings of Donegall Pass CID were killed when a booby trapped shotgun exploded in their faces. The Provisional IRA were behind the atrocity. They converted a shotgun into a bomb and placed it in a loyalist area of the city. Someone telephoned the police about the weapon and it was brought into the station. The two officers were in the process of examining it when it exploded, killing them instantly.

A few weeks later my former colleagues in C Division were hit again when Inspector Murtagh and Sergeant Blakely were gunned to death as they walked the beat a quarter of a mile or so from Oldpark RUC station. Two Provisional IRA men crept up behind them, shooting the officers dead before running off.

The A Squad was by now in existence almost a year and had enjoyed considerable success in bringing terrorists to justice from both sides of the community. In May 1976 the Chief Constable of the RUC, Sir Kenneth Newman, a former member of the London Metropolitan Police, decided to build upon this success by expanding the squad and I was one of several detectives transferred into it. However, in the weeks before my transfer I became involved in a most unfortunate case which brought dishonour to the otherwise distinguished and famous Scottish regiment of The Black Watch.

They were based in Andersonstown on a four-month peace-keeping tour of duties. At that time if soldiers detected anyone engaged in activities such as carrying arms or explosives, the procedure was that the Royal Military Police would go to the scene and ensure that items of evidential value were not lost. They would then bring the prisoner and whatever had been found to Springfield Road. We, as CID officers, would interview the suspects, formally charge them, prepare the necessary papers for submission to the Director of Public Prosecutions, and see the case through court. During the weeks prior to my transfer a number of prisoners, about six in all, had been brought to the station after small quantities of ammunition had allegedly been found in their vehicles at army checkpoints. Each of the suspects was interviewed by the CID. On every occasion we exercised our discretion and did not issue criminal charges as something did not ring quite right about the cases. Instead, the prisoners were released from police custody on the understanding that a file would be sent to the DPP and a prosecution might well follow.

As these cases kept arriving in we had a feeling of unease about them and we sat down to closely analyse the manner in which they occurred. We discovered that on each occasion the finds had been made by a foot patrol of soldiers headed by Lance Corporal Alexander McKay. This raised suspicions, especially as each of the detectives who had processed these cases was spoken to and all agreed that the arrested persons they had interviewed were quite convincing in their claims of innocence.

The situation was brought to the attention of our CID authorities at a high level and they in turn spoke to the Army Command in their headquarters at Lisburn. They were sufficiently convinced on the face of it that something was badly amiss. A decision was reached that the following day, which was a Saturday, the Army's Special Investigation Branch and the CID at Springfield Road would join forces and take some members of the patrol into custody for the purposes of interviewing them.

The matter was kept well under wraps. The Black Watch received no prior warning of the operation and knew nothing until a fleet of army and CID cars arrived at their main base on the Saturday morning. The situation was explained to the adjutant and we discovered that Lance Corporal McKay and a patrol were actually at that moment guarding Andersonstown police station, a duty which fell to each platoon by rota.

We received maximum co-operation from the adjutant and his fellow officers. They quickly assembled a relief platoon and we drove to Andersonstown police station where each of the suspect soldiers was relieved from his guard post, placed in one of the cars and driven to Springfield Road police station.

Within a short time some of the soldiers began to admit they had been engaged in planting ammunition on innocent motorists. They explained that they were very much acting under the influence of Lance Corporal McKay and generally lived in fear of him.

In due course McKay also admitted to the crimes. I recall him sitting in the interview room with his self-loading rifle across his lap. He refused to give it up, even to the army SIB officers. This was a matter of some considerable concern to us. For obvious reasons we were not keen on dealing with armed interviewees.

At the end of that day all of the soldiers involved admitted their part in the crimes. We discovered that McKay had instigated the whole affair. He had been a month late in arriving with the regiment in Andersonstown as he had been in some form of trouble back in Scotland and wanted to re-establish himself by making as many arrests as possible.

The soldiers were handed over to their own authorities. I vividly recall their grim-faced regimental sergeant major arriving down to collect them. He ordered McKay to hand over his rifle, which he then did.

The soldiers involved were eventually charged and tried at Belfast Crown Court before Lord Justice McGonigle who had sat on the Ann Ogilby case. He had been a much decorated wartime soldier himself and was a founder member of the Special Air Service. The soldiers pleaded guilty and the judge took a very dim view of their activities. They had brought disgrace to the peace-keeping forces. He sentenced McKay to seven years imprisonment and the others on a descending scale of punishment depending on their degree of involvement.

It was a sad note on which to leave Springfield Road b.
impressed by the integrity and judgement of my colleagues i
CID. On each occasion they had correctly measured the situatio.
and released the motorists for report to the DPP in preference to
charging them which would have meant a period in custody
pending bail applications.

3

THE BOMBING OF BALLYMENA

My transfer to A Squad came on a Monday in mid-May 1976 when I reported to its offices at RUC Headquarters, Brooklyn, located in the comparatively peaceful Knock area of East Belfast. The main building of the complex where the chief constable had his office had once been a gentleman's residence. A modern three-storey wing had been added on to accommodate administrative staff together with other police departments such as the fingerprint branch, criminal records office etc.

The buildings are set in mature well-trimmed gardens. A section of the lawns had been surrendered to make way for a row of large but neat portable offices which were required for the extra staff resulting from the steady expansion of the force.

The squad was housed in one of these offices and the overall pleasant surroundings and ease of access were in stark contrast to the heavily fortified stations of Tennent Street and Springfield Road. These, although modern in design, were now beginning to show the signs of wear and tear from the continuing violence.

However, this was simply a base for the squad to operate from. As I entered the large general office that morning I was warmly greeted with handshakes from colleagues old and new. Several other detectives arrived on transfer also and at nine o'clock sharp the detective superintendent-in-charge arrived into what was to become a regular Monday conference. Here the successes and failures of the previous week were formally analysed and the duty for the present week was detailed.

The Squad was sub-divided into nine investigative units, each consisting of a detective sergeant and three detective constables. I was placed in unit number five. This pleased me because one of my best friends and former colleagues from Springfield Road was already attached to it. I was acquainted with the other two members, both of whom were fine detectives, and the four of us went on to develop a firm bond of friendship which has continued down through the years.

The detective superintendent was a mature man with many years of CID experience behind him. He had a well-deserved reputation of being a very shrewd and able detective. He had a magnetic personality with a well balanced sense of humour and as he listened to the detective sergeant-in-charge of each unit recounting details of the investigations they were involved in he occasionally interjected to offer congratulations on successful operations or to suggest some alternative route for those cases which were not yet on course.

The conference closed with the duty detail and my unit was tasked to assist the CID at Dunmurry in South Belfast which was suffering from an increase in paramilitary murders. We reported to the local detective inspector, brought ourselves up-to-date with the problems of the area and agreed upon the most productive lines of investigation to follow. I was also very conscious of the A Squad philosophy which was to provide a much-needed boost to the cutting edge of the local CID during times of increased paramilitary activity, rather than taking over investigations.

My unit remained in Dunmurry for the next six weeks. We enjoyed moderate success against the paramilitaries mainly through long hours spent at Castlereagh Detention Centre where most suspects were taken for interview. On one memorable day we obtained an admission from a Provisional IRA suspect about his involvement in a sectarian killing. Shortly afterwards we were asked to move onto a UVF suspect then in custody who was believed to be involved in the bombing of a Roman Catholic bar on the Antrim Road in which two people were killed on Grand National day the previous year. We questioned him right through the night and I recall returning him to his cell at around 7 a.m. after he had made his full written confession to the crime. Such successes were hard earned but the round-the-clock working produced enough adrenalin to keep us going.

Within a month of joining the squad I had another narrow escape. It occurred when my former Springfield Road colleague and I were on our way by police car from Castlereagh to Dunmurry. We were tuned into the police radio network and heard patrol cars being sent to the scene of a shooting incident in Orpen Drive which is in the residential Finaghy Road South area. I contacted the control room and told them that we would also proceed to the scene. Seconds later, as we turned into Orpen Drive, we met an ambulance just leaving the street with flashing blue lights and sirens blaring. I could see uniformed police further along the street. We stopped, got out of the car, and spoke to the officer-in-charge who explained that a local businessman had been seriously injured. Gunmen had knocked at the front door of his home and shot him several times before making their escape in a hijacked car.

A number of uniformed police officers were now on duty round the house, preserving the scene for examination. My colleague and I looked up the hallway and saw a trail of 9 mm spent bullet cases leading as far as the rear kitchen. We did not enter the house but walked round to the back window where we saw some more spent cases and a pool of blood on the kitchen floor. I decided to leave the scene intact for expert scientific examination and my colleague and I went to the house next door where the injured man's wife was being comforted. As I pressed the doorbell a large explosion went off in the house where the shooting had taken place and a number of uniformed police guarding it were blown into the street. Apart from being shocked we were also confused, until we realised that in addition to shooting the businessman, the terrorists had left a bomb in the front downstairs room of the house. This was set to go off just when the scene should have been undergoing examination.

We rushed to the aid of the police officers and brought three of them to hospital in our squad car. The dust from the explosion was now beginning to settle and I could see that a large section of the front of the house was blown out. The room was totally wrecked and a dividing wall had been blown into the hallway where the spent bullet cases were lying. Had we not decided to leave the scene totally intact for the experts we would have caught the full force of the blast probably with fatal consequences. The injured businessman and the injured policemen all made a good recovery in due course but the incident was a further sharp lesson in how treacherous the Provisional IRA could be.

Meanwhile, the UVF were taking advantage of the situation, in several normally quiet parts of the Province, by placing bombs at Catholic-owned premises or engaging in other forms of gangsterism such as robberies. Several units of the Squad had been investigating these and had now reached the stage where arrest and interview operations were the next logical step. My unit was drafted in to assist and over the following four or five weeks we spent many long hours at Castlereagh Detention Centre interviewing suspects. Much success was achieved and the squad together with the local CIDs locked up virtually all of the UVF units from Carrickfergus, Ballyclare and Coleraine, returning these areas to normality.

Later, we were called to Londonderry to assist the local CID with their enquiries into the murder of a young policewoman who had been callously shot in the back while on foot patrol. A number of Provisional IRA suspects were in custody. Most of them went on to admit their part in the crime. The trial later took place before Lord Justice McGonigle who convicted almost all of them.

The pace of work for the squad was now almost frenetic and on a Saturday afternoon in mid-October 1976 I was relaxing at home when someone from the office telephoned asking me to assemble my unit and go at once to the large town of Ballymena, County Antrim. The Provisional IRA had launched a bomb blitz in the main shopping area of Ballymena, killing a young woman. I contacted my colleagues at home, all of whom readily responded, and we met at RUC Headquarters before setting off for Ballymena police station.

On arrival we went to the local CID offices and learned that several members of the Provisional IRA had arrived in the town around lunchtime. Although a number of bombs had been planted, causing widespread damage and death, things had not gone quite according to plan.

The first indication of what was taking place occurred around 12.30 p.m. when an explosion went off within an orange coloured Toyota car in an area of the town known as Fairhill. This is an open market place and on that day it was crowded with thousands of shoppers. When the explosion occurred an off-duty policeman ran to the scene where he found a man with a blackened face and bleeding eyes standing by the driver's door of the car. A short distance away he saw another man lying on the ground, his clothes in tatters and his left leg missing. Close by were two other men, both obviously seriously injured, and very soon uniformed police and ambulancemen arrived to give assistance.

The off-duty policeman had a look inside the car, saw a large hole in the floor of the vehicle and noted that the roof bulged upwards. All of the windows had been blown outwards and it was apparent that an explosion had gone off inside the car. Later, when it was more thoroughly examined by an army bomb disposal officer, a number of unexploded incendiary devices were found together with the remains of one which had exploded. There was no doubt now that the four injured men were members of a Provisional IRA bombing team. They had been priming the devices in the car when one went off prematurely, causing the injuries and associated damage.

However, they were only part of the overall bombing team. Other members had already successfully planted devices in a number of shops throughout the town, some of which were now starting to explode. Altogether ten shops had been attacked but the most serious incident occurred at the Alley Katz Boutique in Bridge Street which was being looked after by twenty-six year old Yvonne Dunlop and her eight year old son, Denis. Two women had entered the boutique. One of them had taken a dress off a rack and had gone into a small changing cubicle apparently to try it on. The second woman hung around the shop looking at other clothes until her companion emerged, placing the dress back on the rack. Both women then left the shop. Some few minutes later young Denis entered the cubicle and saw what appeared to be a shopping bag. He called his mother and she looked inside the bag. It exploded immediately, engulfing the shop in flames. A number of people ran to the premises just in time to see the young child stagger out onto the footpath through the flames and smoke. He cried that his mother was still inside the shop. Several people tried to beat their way in but failed because by now it was a raging inferno. When the flames were eventually extinguished by the fire brigade Yvonne Dunlop's charred remains were found in the area where the changing cubicle had been.

Fortunately no-one had been injured in any of the other explosions. The police by now had received a warning via the telephone operator and were in the process of clearing all people from within the town centre when the blast at the Alley Katz Boutique went off.

Some other members of the bombing team must have panicked on hearing the explosions as five incendiaries were found unexploded and apparently dumped in a street leading from the town's commercial centre.

It was also disclosed that a uniformed constable engaged in clearing the town centre had arrested a young woman who had been identified as twenty year old Ann Marie Bateson, a member of a well-known South Londonderry Republican family.

The overall briefing we received was thorough in its detail and was attended by several senior police and army officers including the local divisional commander and detective chief inspector. Our own detective superintendent was also present and several other members of the A Squad had now arrived to assist.

At the end of the briefing we were all given specific tasks. A colleague and I were asked to interview Miss Bateson and establish details of her suspected participation in the bomb attacks. We brought her from the cells to a quiet interview room at 9.30 p.m. She was an attractive dark-haired young woman who appeared outwardly calm and collected. We began by asking her if she had been involved in the bombings. She denied that she had and claimed she had come to Ballymena from her home some twenty miles away merely to do some shopping. She had got caught up in the evacuation of the town and a policeman had arrested her for no apparent reason.

Miss Bateson maintained this attitude for some time but bearing in mind that she had been arrested around 1 p.m., and had more or less been held in isolation in the cell block since that time, we believed she should probably be unaware of the premature explosion which had injured four of the paramilitaries and also of the death of Yvonne Dunlop.

My colleague and I then began to release some of these details to her. We told her first of the explosion in the Toyota car. She reacted with a measure of disbelief until we added the names of the four injured men. We knew that if she was involved in the bombings she would know the four men and would see we had to be telling the truth. She was taken aback by this and we knew then that we were definitely on the right track.

However, she continued to deny involvement in the bombing operation. But when we told her of the death of Yvonne Dunlop in the boutique, she was visibly shaken and sat silent and motionless for a few minutes. It was apparent to us that Miss Bateson was now beginning to realise the enormity of what she had been involved in. We pressed her further and she then conceded she had taken part in the bombings but had not intended that anyone should get hurt. She was most anxious to be assured that Yvonne Dunlop had been killed in a boutique and not in some other shop. This was either to ease her own conscience if she had not planted that actual bomb, or to distance herself from it if she had.

Miss Bateson went on to admit involvement in the planting of devices in three shops. These she identified as a discount store, a china shop and a hardware store. She stated that she had arrived in Ballymena with others in a blue Volkswagen car. They had bombs with them and prior to leaving the vehicle one of the team had primed the devices to go off in one hour. She also conceded that she was aware that other members of the bombing team had arrived in town in the orange Toyota car. It became apparent that at least one other, and probably two, bombing teams had been active.

In order to clarify beyond doubt which bombing she was accepting responsibility for we asked Miss Bateson to accompany us in a police car and point out the shops where she had assisted in placing the devices. She agreed and identified the three shops she had earlier referred to. We brought her back to the station and she made a full written confession. We returned her to her cell at around 7.30 a.m.

The cell block corridor of the station was a hive of activity. The cells were actually filled to capacity with other prisoners and a number of males were also under guard by uniformed police in the corridor. When we asked what was going on we were told that during the night some of the local loyalists had murdered a Roman Catholic in the town by pouring petrol on him and setting him alight. The victim's name was Seán Patrick McCrystal. It appeared he had been put to death in retaliation for the bombing of Ballymena. When the details of his murder were later unravelled it turned out that McCrystal was an entirely innocent person. As a result of information obtained, the killers were identified and arrested. Two were subsequently convicted of murder and one of manslaughter.

My colleague and I went and had some breakfast at the police canteen and at around 8.30 a.m. our detective superintendent arrived at the station. We fully briefed him on the results of the interview with Miss Bateson. Other detectives who had been to the hospital where the men injured in the premature explosion were being treated were also present. All of the intelligence gained was collated and plans were laid to arrest a number of other suspects. The detective superintendent also ordered the remainder of A Squad to come to Ballymena to assist in the interviews of the suspects for the murder of Seán McCrystal. My colleague and I departed for some rest in the certain knowledge that a hard day lay ahead for the local CID and our fellow detectives in the squad.

We returned to Ballymena police station at around 7 p.m. and had difficulty finding a car parking space. This was the first confirmation that it had indeed been a busy day. On entering the CID offices we saw that the walls were covered with evidence flow charts. Empty coffee cups and full ash trays were strewn across normally tidy desk tops. We were informed that several people had admitted involvement in the murder of Seán McCrystal and were about to be charged.

The investigations into the bombings were also progressing satisfactorily and the post-mortem examination of Yvonne Dunlop had been carried out by Professor Marshall, the State pathologist.

Unfortunately, owing to the condition of the body, normal identification was impossible and dental records were called on for verification. The pathologist then found the cause of Yvonne Dunlop's death to be the combined effects of the explosion and burns. He concluded that death had been very rapid. This was the only crumb of comfort one could offer to her family.

In the days which followed four more people were charged with the bombings, including one of the women who had planted the device in the Alley Katz Boutique. In addition to the four men injured in the premature explosion and Miss Bateson, this now made a total of nine.

The place where the actual bombs had been manufactured was identified as a farmyard a short distance outside the village of Toomebridge which is about fifteen miles from Ballymena. The farm was immediately sealed off and a team of expert scene examiners began an inch-by-inch search of the outbuildings. In a tractor shed they found the remains of five rolls of black electric insulating tape. Each roll had been almost entirely used up with only a small amount still attached to the standard cardboard spools. Three short strips of red plastic electric wire sheathing were also found. Later when all of these items were examined by forensic scientists they found that the cut end of insulating tape on one of the cardboard spools was a perfect physical match with the cut end of similar tape found on one of the unexploded bombs inside the orange coloured Toyota car. Remarkably, two of the cut ends of the red plastic sheathing matched similar covering on wires on two of the unexploded devices also recovered from the car. This indisputable evidence confirmed that the farm had indeed been used as a base by the bombers.

Almost a year later the trial of the Ballymena bombers began at Belfast Crown Court before Mr Justice Murray. At its conclusion most of the accused were found guilty of causing the death of Yvonne Dunlop insofar as they had all acted together and for a common purpose. Accordingly, Mr Justice Murray handed down severe sentences, the maximum of which was twenty years imprisonment.

The sheer futility of terrorism was demonstrated clearly in the bombing of Ballymena. An analysis of the crime portrays nothing but a trail of human misery, beginning with the incineration of Yvonne Dunlop in front of her eight year old son, the injuries sustained by the four young terrorists in the premature explosion, the cruel murder of Seán McCrystal, the damage caused to property, and the final lengthy imprisonment of approximately twelve people in connection with both killings, which in turn condemned their families in some instances to two decades of trekking to far-off prisons on weekly visits.

Altogether my unit's involvement in the investigations into the bombings lasted just over three weeks, into early November 1976. Much success was achieved but the commitment required from us was quite demanding and we were looking forward to a few days relaxation before moving on to some other case yet to be decided.

The pleasant prospect of a few days off was quickly shattered when I was summoned to the general CID office in Ballymena to take an urgent call from my detective superintendent who was telephoning from Springfield Road RUC station in Belfast. In grave tones he disclosed to me that one of my best friends from my days in Springfield Road had been shot dead by the Provisional IRA in a side street about a quarter of a mile from the station. He was Detective Constable Noel McCabe and I was devastated by the news of the loss of yet another close friend. I was asked to assemble my unit and proceed immediately to Springfield Road to assist in the murder investigation.

We left Ballymena at once and needless to say my colleagues and I were somewhat silent and grim-faced on the journey to Belfast. Noel and I had worked and socialised a lot together and my thoughts were with his young wife, Helen, who by now probably had the tragic news broken to her by senior police officers.

On arrival at Springfield Road we went straight to the CID offices and one could sense that the overall atmosphere within the station was distinctly subdued. Our detective superintendent was present and he briefed us on what had occurred. We learned that Noel had been keeping observations from a car on a number of suspected terrorists in some of the side streets off the Falls Road. In order to remain as unobtrusive as possible he had been in the car by himself although there was a back-up crew at another location some few minutes away. Noel had driven round a number of the side streets several times and had obviously been spotted by the terrorists. They had collected a handgun from one of several hides in the area and two of them waited for the observation car to reappear. Unfortunately, Noel turned into that side street once again and as he did so one of the terrorists stepped out in front of the car, slowing it down almost to a halt. A second man leapt onto the bonnet of the car and fired several shots into Noel from a .38 Special revolver, killing him instantly. The gunmen then ran off into the maze of side streets and made good their escape.

A full scale murder investigation was now under way and later that day the detective superintendent and I called at Noel's home to offer our condolences to Helen. A number of relatives had of course by now assembled in the grief-stricken house and on entering I met Helen in the hallway. She knew how close I had been as a friend to Noel. I embraced her and offered what words of comfort I could muster. Some few days later Noel's funeral took place and was attended by hundreds of mourners including several senior police and army officers. Helen led the cortege with great dignity and the coffin was lowered into the ground in a quiet churchyard near Lisburn.

During the next two months the local CID and members of the squad worked almost constantly on the investigation into the murder. In crimes of this nature local people who could offer some assistance remained silent, so great was the fear generated by the gunmen. The main suspects were arrested and interviewed in due course but denied involvement and, in the absence of any other evidence, had to be released. Having said that, no investigation remains closed forever. Often in cases of murder some unexpected turn of events occurs even years after the crime, opening up new avenues of enquiry. I certainly subscribe to the theory that the arm of the law is indeed long.

4

AT WORK IN CASTLEREAGH
DETENTION CENTRE

The year 1977 began in a more relaxed atmosphere for me when during January and February I attended a CID course at the Metropolitan Police Training Centre at Hendon in North London. The course was designed to benefit detectives who had some experience behind them by consolidating their knowledge of criminal law and studying more advanced practical aspects of investigation. The class was made up mainly of police officers from several of the English constabularies. Most of them displayed a keen interest in the situation in Northern Ireland and the work of the RUC.

So far in my own police career I had been engaged almost exclusively on investigations into terrorist-related killings but the crime of murder held a certain fascination for me so I welcomed the opportunity to attend lectures from eminent forensic scientists and pathologists such as the world-renowned Professor Keith Simpson. The interpretation of injuries and scenes were of particular interest to me and I endeavoured to absorb every piece of knowledge imparted by these gentlemen, most of whom delivered their lectures with a well-honed sense of humour essential in their otherwise morbid profession.

During those weeks I was frequently interrupted in my studies to attend courts back in Belfast. Many of the investigations I had been involved in were now at trial stage and for a while I seemed to be constantly shuttling by air between London and Belfast. As a consequence I probably did not gain all that I could have from the course. Nevertheless it was a pleasure to meet other detectives from quite a different police background and to listen to their experiences.

I returned to normal A Squad duties in early March and as if to compensate for my period of 'relaxation' in London I was plunged almost immediately into the interviewing of terrorist suspects at Castlereagh Detention Centre.

The killings continued throughout the Province, but the event that really hit the headlines was the abduction and murder of British army Captain Robert Nairac. Captain Nairac was abducted from the car park of a public house in South Armagh close to the border with the Irish Republic. It is an area where many police and soldiers have been killed by means of large landmines. The patrols which moved through it did so heavily armed and access to most of the military bases was by helicopter only. In fact, the large army base at Bessbrook had so many helicopter movements each day that it was regarded as the busiest heli-port in the United Kingdom.

Captain Nairac was engaged in intelligence work and had on occasions been seen in plain clothes in some of the hard-line villages along the border. He cut a somewhat enigmatic figure as he talked or attempted to talk to the local people, practically all of whom were fiercely anti-British. Since his disappearance there has been much speculation as to his true role and many people have labelled him as a member of the SAS, a view which I do not subscribe to, given his subsequent actions.

On the Saturday evening of his abduction he had gone alone and in plain clothes, though carrying a concealed personal-protection handgun, to the Three Step Inn public house in open countryside close to the border.

The bar was filled to capacity with customers and it is alleged that Captain Nairac tried to pass himself off as a Belfastman by adopting the distinctive Northern Ireland accent. This must have proved difficult given his background of an upper-middle class English family, his education at Ampleforth Public School, followed by a period at University, and rounded off with his officer training at Sandhurst which produces graduates with a standard-issue upper-class accent.

During his time in the bar that evening Captain Nairac spoke to a number of local people and at one point even ventured onto a small stage where he sang a traditional Irish ballad, probably in an effort to convince those present that he was indeed a true Irishman.

Many people on both sides of the sectarian divide in Northern Ireland tended to engage in an obsessive form of 'stranger watching', constantly alert to someone from the opposing side infiltrating the security of their own camp. The inhabitants of South Armagh were considered to be particularly adept at this as many of them engaged in smuggling goods across the border; even during peaceful intervals in our history they have always been alert to the possible presence of the excise man.

The customers in the bar that evening were no exception and among them were a number of men who had links with the Provisional IRA. As Captain Nairac moved around the bar, socialising, they quietly kept him under observation but were careful to do nothing in the presence of the other customers. Instead, they drifted into the car park at closing time where they hung around waiting for the 'stranger' to appear. When he did the gang pounced on him and wrestled him to the ground. During the struggle Captain Nairac managed to produce his gun but it was kicked from his hand and soon he was completely overpowered. He was bundled into a waiting car which sped off towards the border followed by another car containing the remaining members of the gang.

The cars drove directly to Ravensdale Forest which lies several miles inside the Republic of Ireland, approximately mid-way between Dundalk in County Louth and Newry, County Down. In total darkness Captain Nairac was hauled from the car and taken to a small clearing where the process of interrogation began. In short, he was beaten to within an inch of his life and questioned about his true identity. Despite this savage treatment Captain Nairac gave nothing away. This was confirmed during the subsequent police investigation when it was revealed that one of his abductors cynically resorted to pretending to be a priest in a last-ditch effort to extract a confession.

Several of the men remained with Captain Nairac in the forest while one of their number went to Dundalk in an effort to notify more prominent members of the Provisional IRA about their capture. Dundalk had gained considerable notoriety over the years as a safe haven for Republicans on the run from security forces in Northern

Ireland. Its attraction lay in its close proximity to the border, placing it within an hour's drive of Belfast. It had often been likened to a wild-west frontier town and I am sure many of the decent local inhabitants viewed its reputation with some disdain.

By the time the messenger had arrived in Dundalk from the forest it was well into the early hours of Sunday morning and the town was practically deserted. The only prominent terrorist around was a Liam Townson who by all accounts was somewhat under the weather with drink. When told of the events up to that point he obviously smelled blood as he readily agreed to come to the forest, collecting a handgun on the way. On arrival Captain Nairac appears to have been senseless and Townson finished him off by shooting him in the head. His body was later secretly buried and to this day has not been found. Captain Nairac was not listed as missing by the army for several hours until his normal reporting-in time had passed. The local police were alerted and soon they found his car outside the public house where it had remained overnight. As the hours wore on the disappearance of Captain Nairac became a matter of grave concern and senior police and army officers reluctantly agreed that the worst must have happened.

A full-scale murder investigation was launched and several weeks afterwards police and army made a dawn swoop on a number of suspects who were brought to Castlereagh Detention Centre for interview. My unit had not been involved in the investigation up to that point but we were then drafted in to assist with the interviews. We spoke with a Gerard Fearon and on the first day of his detention he admitted his part in the abduction and subsequent killing. Several other men also confessed and when the events at the forest were revealed the Garda Síochána were notified. They too immediately set in motion a murder investigation. They found the clearing where the killing had taken place and later arrested Liam Townson who also confessed to his part in the crime.

The case proved an interesting one from a legal point of view insofar as the abduction had taken place in Northern Ireland and the murder in the Republic of Ireland. In addition the dead body of the victim had not been found. Fortunately there have been precedents for this in British law and the production of the body is not necessary for proving a crime of murder.

Some months later the persons arrested within the Northern Ireland jurisdiction were tried at Belfast Crown Court before Lord Justice Gibson, a small man with a very sharp mind. The prosecution was led by Mr Brian Hutton QC, later lord chief justice for Northern Ireland. In order to prove the case members of the Garda Síochána and their forensic experts travelled to Belfast where they gave essential evidence about the scene in Ravensdale Forest. At the end of the case the accused were convicted and sentenced to lengthy terms of imprisonment. The authorities in the Republic of Ireland tried Liam Townson within their own legal system. He was convicted of the killing and sentenced to life imprisonment.

Although the crime was somewhat sensational at the time it was quickly overtaken by other events and relegated as simply another statistic. However, I still retain memories of Captain Nairac's elderly and genteel parents appearing on television emotionally appealing for the return of their son's body. His father was an eminent eye surgeon who undoubtedly had done much to alleviate the suffering of others. I felt his life's work had been poorly rewarded by the loss of his son, and especially when he was deprived of the opportunity of giving him a proper burial. Not all of those involved in the crime were brought to justice. As they were being sought by police in both parts of Ireland, they had no hiding place, and it is believed they fled to America which is a traditional route taken by such fugitives.

Some nine years after the trial of the accused members, the Provisional IRA had their revenge when they murdered Lord Justice Gibson and his wife, ironically just a few miles from Ravensdale Forest. The judge and his wife had been holidaying in England and had travelled to Southern Ireland by car ferry on their return journey. They had been escorted most of the way from the ferry port by the Garda Síochána but these police officers could go no further than the border with Northern Ireland. Their RUC escort was waiting at a security post set about half a mile back from the border. The area in between had become something of a no-man's-land. Many policemen and soldiers had lost their lives on this dangerous stretch of road as the result of terrorists being able to keep watch on their movements from vantage points in the surrounding high ground. It was here that the Provisional IRA had placed a large landmine. As Lord Justice Gibson and his wife drove along, the landmine was detonated and both were killed instantly.

Judge Gibson was a great loss to the Northern legal system. I had often appeared in his court to give evidence and had admired his fairness and his ability to get to the core of a case by wiping away the irrelevancies sometimes raised by loquacious barristers.

As soon as my unit was released from the Captain Nairac investigation we were moved on to the interview of James 'Tonto' Watt who was suspected of being the top UVF bomb maker in Belfast and therefore responsible for many deaths, including the murder of a ten year old boy on the Falls Road some weeks earlier.

This particular crime had occurred on Easter Sunday which was the day various branches of the Republican movement held a traditional parade along the Falls Road to commemorate the Easter uprising in Dublin in 1916. This was a vast parade composed mainly of people who supported the Provisional IRA, but also some who were members of the Official Republican Movement, known later as the Worker's Party – a group who earned the reputation of genuinely trying to unite working class people for a common purpose across the sectarian divide. The parade was watched by large numbers of spectators, not all of whom supported terrorism but were there mainly for the sights and sounds of the occasion.

The leadership of the UVF saw the 1977 parade as an opportunity to launch an attack, hoping to hand back some death and destruction to the Provisional IRA. They agreed to set a bomb on the route, timed to go off when the Falls Road would be crowded with marchers and onlookers.

James 'Tonto' Watt was ordered to make the explosive device and he and other members of the UVF reconnoitred the area to see best how it could be done. Watt noted that part of the Beechmount area in the central Falls had been sealed off by metal beer barrels filled with concrete and this had been done by some of the locals to restrict traffic and reduce the risk of sectarian attack.

Watt decided to make a large bomb in a beer keg and several hours prior to the start of the parade a UVF gang placed it inconspicuously among the security barrels in Beechmount. The parade began after lunchtime and the bomb exploded as the Official Republican contingent was passing. Several people were seriously injured and tragically a ten year old boy was killed.

Watt was now in Castlereagh Detention Centre and was already under interview by other detectives to whom he had admitted the murder. We concentrated our questioning around a booby-trap device which had been discovered at The People's Garage on the Springfield Road, the same premises where Geraldine Macklin had been murdered by the UDA during my time as a detective in West Belfast.

This particular device had been the subject of considerable ingenuity as the maker had cunningly placed it inside the tyre of a wheel of a car. The electrical circuit of the bomb was somehow held open by a nail which had been pushed through the tread of the tyre and the UVF placed it at the garage on the pretext of it being a punctured tyre left in for repair. Prior to doing so the bombers went as far as circling the nail with a chalk mark to ensure that some unfortunate fitter's attention would be drawn to it in the certain knowledge that when it was pulled out the bomb would explode, causing death and serious injury to those in the immediate vicinity. Some members of the bomb team must have had a pang of conscience about the device and a telephone warning was received by the police who immediately went to the garage, located the spare wheel and notified the army bomb disposal officer who defused it.

During our interviews with Watt he made a detailed confession to this crime. He described in graphic detail how he had spent a whole day making the booby trap in the rear yard of a bar on the Shankill Road. He had first to lever one side of the tyre off its rim, then insert the explosives. He hammered the nail into the surface of the tyre and made up the electrical circuit, placing it also inside the tyre. The major difficulty was getting the tyre back onto the rim without setting off the bomb prematurely. He told us how he did not stop working on it even for a refreshment break as he did not want to lose his concentration.

Watt went on to admit to several other killings and at Belfast Crown Court some months later he was sentenced to nine terms of life imprisonment.

The intense pace of work within the squad continued and as a result of the successes achieved by all of the investigative units the requests for assistance from the divisional CIDs was rapidly increasing. Personally, I was thriving on the buzz generated by this side of police work and was well and truly addicted to the intrigue which each new day brought.

Our next case was no exception and began for us in August 1977 when the CID at Tennent Street asked us to help in the interviews of thirty year old Kenneth McClinton, a suspected member of the UFF, who was believed to have been involved in two killings in North Belfast.

The case turned out to have many twists and turns along the way. For me, it has typified the complex nature of policing in Northern Ireland and amply demonstrates the duplicity and deception faced by those involved in the investigation of crimes committed by terrorists.

The first of the victims believed to have been killed by McClinton was thirty-two year old Daniel Carville. This crime occurred in the early evening of 17 March 1977 at Cambrai Street. Mr Carville was a Roman Catholic living in republican Ardoyne. Just before 6 p.m. he left his home in his car accompanied by his ten year old son, Francis, intending to travel to West Belfast.

Cambrai Street leads onto Ainsworth Avenue, both of which are situated in the Upper Shankill area and are therefore loyalist dominated. They form a convenient route linking Ardoyne with West Belfast and Roman Catholics traversing these streets were exposed to a certain degree of risk, particularly during times of civil unrest. However, on most occasions traffic flowed back and forwards unimpeded.

As Mr Carville drove westwards along Cambrai Street he remarked to his son that he felt uncomfortable about a red coloured car in front of them which, for some reason, he believed to have UVF connections. This car eventually turned off into a side street and Mr Carville continued on his way but was required to slow down almost to a halt at a series of ramps. The killers used the ramps to their advantage. Two gunmen stepped out and fired a number of shots into Mr Carville who courageously threw himself across his young son in an attempt to save him from injury. As a consequence of this action Mr Carville sustained a number of gunshot wounds to his back and was found to be dead on arrival at hospital a few minutes later. His son escaped with a minor laceration to his leg but was deeply shocked and one can only imagine the psychological scars this incident has had on him.

The killers escaped from the scene in a waiting car which was soon located by police abandoned in a side street about half a mile from the killing. It turned out to be a taxi. Its driver had taken a bogus call to a pub on the Shankill Road where he had been hijacked and held in another bar under guard until the murder had been committed. This was the favourite terrorist method of obtaining transport for a crime. It provided them with a cover story should they be arrested soon afterwards and forensically linked to the vehicle. In these circumstances they could always claim they had legitimate access to it perhaps on a Friday night run home from the pub and any evidential case against them was therefore considerably weakened.

The forensic examination of Mr Carville's car revealed four bullet holes in the windscreen and one in the pillar of the driver's door. A .38 bullet head was recovered from the passenger door panelling and a .45 head was found under the passenger seat, both of which had been fired from revolvers. Their position further emphasised how close the child had been to death or serious injury. At the post-mortem examination of Mr Carville the following day a total of four bullet heads were recovered from his body and these too were of .38 and .45 calibre.

A major investigation into the crime was set in motion and a check on Mr Carville's background revealed that he was a hard-working family man with a completely unblemished character. There seemed no doubt that he had been selected at random and this was confirmed when the crime was eventually solved. It transpired that some members of the murder gang had been keeping observations from a car on the main traffic exit from Ardoyne. This was probably the red coloured car Mr Carville had commented on to his son. It had UFF, not UVF, connections. Unknown to him it had flashed its headlights to the gunmen at the ramps, signalling that the car immediately behind had just left Ardoyne and was therefore most probably being driven by a Roman Catholic.

The first significant development in the investigation came on a Sunday some ten days after the murder. At around 6.30 a.m. two youths were walking down the Shankill Road on their way to carry out an early morning newspaper delivery round when a number of shots were directed at them from an upstairs room of the loyalist Salisbury Bar. Fortunately, the two youths were uninjured. They immediately notified the police who quickly responded and surrounded the bar. Two officers gained entrance through a broken upstairs window which led into a lounge area. Just beside the window they saw a small table with glasses on it containing fresh beer. Close by lay a loaded M1 Carbine, two spent bullet cases and one live round. The officers then carried out a cursory room by room search to establish if any person was present on the premises, but no one was found.

A minute search of the bar lasting several hours was then carried out and at the end of it the police had found two .38 and two .45 revolvers. Several other articles of a terrorist nature were also located such as microswitches. When these items were sent to the forensic science laboratory word soon came back that tests on two of the revolvers proved they had been used to kill Mr Carville in Cambrai Street.

Often in criminal investigations an initial development like this seems to trigger off other events. Soon intelligence was received by the local CID to the effect that the man who had fired the shots from the Salisbury Bar on the Sunday morning was a local thug named as twenty-five year old Samuel McCaw and that he had also been involved in the murder of Daniel Carville. Thorough investigation was carried out into his background and a few days later, at the end of March 1977, police raided his home in the heart of the Shankill area. He was brought to Tennent Street police station under arrest. That same evening, during interview, McCaw admitted his involvement in the murder of Mr Carville. He described in detail how he and other members of the murder gang summoned a taxi to the Horseshoe Bar on the Shankill Road in order that it could be hijacked. After the car had been seized the driver was taken to the Salisbury Bar where he was held under guard. McCaw said he got into the hijacked car with two other men, one of whom he knew was armed with a .45 revolver. He was then handed a loaded .38 revolver and they drove up the Shankill Road, turning right into Cambrai street. They drove over the ramps and stopped adjacent to a side street which they intended to use as an escape route after the crime.

McCaw stated that they hung around for about ten minutes and a car which they now knew to have been driven by Mr Carville came along Cambrai Street from the direction of Ardoyne. As it approached the ramps McCaw and the other gunman got out of the hijacked taxi and both began firing into Mr Carville's car. When the shooting ceased the two gunmen got into the hijacked taxi and abandoned it where it was later found by police. The three of them made their way on foot through a maze of side streets back to the Salisbury Bar and the taxi driver was released. His written confession ended with the words, 'It was after this I felt desperate about it and I realised what I had done. I now feel sorry I had anything to do with it.' I have seen so many apologetic phrases of this nature at the end of confessions that they have become totally meaningless to me. In my cynical view they are merely self-serving and not worth the paper they are written on.

McCaw went on to admit being the gunman who had fired the shots from the Salisbury Bar as the two young boys passed along the Shankill Road on the Sunday morning some few days previously. He offered no rational explanation for doing so and one can only presume it was a drunken escapade in which he couldn't resist letting off some of the firearms so close at hand. He was charged with the murder of Daniel Carville and the attempted murder of the two boys. He was remanded in custody while the case papers were prepared for submission to the Director of Public Prosecutions.

The local CID maintained the momentum of the investigation and now in August 1977 they detained McClinton on suspicion of having been the second gunman involved in the murder of Mr

Carville. In addition he was also believed to be the lone gunman who stepped on board a city bus at a halt on the Crumlin Road on 10 May 1977 and shot dead the driver, forty-six year old Harold Bradshaw, a Protestant who came from Newtownabbey in the north east of the city.

The crime occurred during a loyalist workers' strike, a weapon frequently used by politicians since the troubles began. They usually arose as the British government at Westminster attempted to break the political stalemate in Northern Ireland by introducing some new initiative, often to the displeasure of certain loyalist politicians. Their response was to bring the country to a standstill by calling a general strike. The method was quite effective, particularly when the electricity power stations were closed down, and on occasions the government caved in as a result. The strikes caused major inconvenience to everyone and they were steadily losing support among the local population who found it difficult enough to obtain employment, without this added problem.

In the spring of 1977 such a strike was called and in the heartlands of certain hard-line loyalist districts it was reinforced by the hijacking of vehicles and the erection of barricades. The police were determined to maintain law and order on the main arterial routes through the city to ensure that those who did not want to take part in the strike could go about their daily business as freely as possible. One of the routes kept open was the Crumlin Road and the city bus services continued to operate along it. This angered the hard men in the loyalist paramilitary groups. They decided that the murder of a bus driver would soon ensure their compliance with the strike and ordered that such a killing should go ahead.

On the afternoon of 10 May 1977 Harold Bradshaw was on this route, his final destination being Ligoniel, and he stopped every few hundred yards or so to set down or pick up passengers. He pulled into the stop at the junction of Crumlin Road and Queensland Street where a small queue had formed. Among them skulked a gunman armed with a 9 mm automatic Walther pistol. A number of passengers alighted from the bus while others got on, including the gunman. He produced the handgun and shot Harold Bradshaw twice in the head. The victim slumped dead over the steering wheel. The killer, who was wearing a cap, ran off along Queensland Street and escaped into the back alleyways.

McClinton was now in Castlereagh Detention Centre and we prepared ourselves well for the forthcoming interviews with him by studying every known aspect of the killings. This preparation is essential and puts the interviewers in a confident position where they can more easily catch out the suspect should he choose to lie about anything, thereby increasing the chances of an admission.

As McClinton came into the interview room, escorted by his uniformed jailers, he immediately struck me as being somewhat cocky and self-assured. It did not seem that the killings we believed he had been involved in were weighing heavily on his mind. We commenced by carrying out the usual formalities such as introducing ourselves and explaining to him that we wanted to talk to him about the murder of Harold Bradshaw. It had been agreed earlier on that we would concentrate initially on this crime in view of the fact that he appeared to have been acting alone. If pressed he might wish to spread the blame among others. We decided that we would keep the details of the killing of Mr Carville in reserve.

When I put the accusation to McClinton he smiled and denied involvement in the crime. We asked him if he clearly identified in his mind the crime we were referring to. He said he did and that he could recall people 'slabbering' about it in the bars afterwards. He said he had his own views on the killing but would prefer not to talk about it. McClinton maintained his self-confident attitude for several hours and even went so far as to accuse me of trying 'to pull a CIA frame-up' on him. However, every indication to then tended to show that he was indeed the right man.

Our interviews with him lasted through the morning and afternoon. He continued to deny involvement, so during the evening period we handed him over to the other two members of my unit who were very able and astute interviewers. My assessment of McClinton to that point was that his bold front was patently false and that the truth of his involvement in the killing lay just under the surface. My instincts were well founded and during the course of that first evening he confessed to the murder of Harold Bradshaw. He began his admission by first of all agreeing that he was a member of the UDA. He went on to explain how, on the afternoon of the murder, he had been approached by a UDA officer in a bar on the Shankill Road. This officer asked him to kill a bus driver in order to persuade the others to cease operating the buses.

McClinton, in a not untypical manner, attempted to ease his own culpability by claiming he at first refused to do the shooting but that, under threat of being shot himself for disobeying an order, he carried out the murder. Once again my well-nurtured cynicism shone through and I regarded his claims and many similar ones made by other terrorists as unadulterated hogwash.

McClinton described how he was given the 9mm Walther pistol and walked through the side streets to the bus stop on the Crumlin Road where he joined the bus queue. He was disguised only with a cap. A second man was placed in a street nearby to take the gun from him after the killing, thereby removing any incriminating evidence should he be pursued immediately after the crime. This second man was a Hugh Black and he was now also in Castlereagh under interview by another team of detectives. He too went on to admit his part in the murder. McClinton continued by saying that after standing in the queue for a few minutes a bus appeared. The driver pulled in at the stop where some passengers got off and the persons in the queue got on. McClinton said he followed the last of them on and pulled the pistol from his waistband, released the safety catch and pumped two rounds into the driver's head. He then ran from the bus, into Queensland Street, and along the alleyway where he met the other man who took the weapon from him as arranged. He made his way back to the bar on the Shankill Road where he reported to his officer that his instructions had been carried out.

When asked by the interviewers how he had felt since the murder he said he hadn't slept well and was glad he had now got it off his conscience. He went on to vividly describe how Harold Bradshaw had looked straight at him just before he killed him and as the bullets entered his victim's head everything seemed to go into slow motion. He recalled that a few nights after the killing he was watching television when he saw a news film clip from the Vietnam War in which a plain clothes police officer in Saigon summarily executes a north Vietnamese insurgent by shooting him in the temple with a revolver. This particular piece of film, which has been shown on television many times, reminded McClinton of how he had killed Harold Bradshaw and according to him, caused him to flee from the room in distress at the thought of what he had done.

As soon as McClinton's confession to the murder of Harold Bradshaw was recorded in writing we moved on to his suspected involvement in the killing of Daniel Carville. McClinton accepted that he had been one of the gunmen at the ramps in Cambrai Street. He described how two cars had come from the direction of Crumlin Road, the one in front having flashed its headlights. He was armed with the .45 revolver and as the second car slowed at the ramps he and the other gunman ran to the driver's side and began to fire into it. The driver slumped over. Then he and his accomplice ran to their getaway car and drove off into the side streets where they abandoned the vehicle and escaped on foot.

McClinton was charged with the murders of Daniel Carville and Harold Bradshaw while Hugh Black was charged with possession of the firearm used in the latter killing. Both appeared at Belfast Magistrates Court where they were remanded pending their trial which would take place at Belfast Crown Court.

The number of persons awaiting trial was abnormally high during that period, owing to the considerable successes achieved by all operational units of the security forces. A backlog of cases was steadily building up in the court's system. It was therefore not unusual for an accused person to wait well over a year for his case to be heard and it was not until May 1978 that Samuel McCaw appeared before Lord Justice Kelly. He was tried on charges of murdering Daniel Carville and of shooting at the two youths from the Salisbury Bar. McCaw contested the charges on the grounds that his confessions were obtained unfairly by the interviewing detectives. However, the judge rejected this defence and sentenced him to life imprisonment.

The McClinton and Black trial began in January 1979 before Lord Justice O'Donnell. Black pleaded guilty and was put back for sentence. McClinton, however, tendered pleas of not guilty and his trial then commenced. It soon became apparent that he had not wasted his time on remand and had been studying the law on the admissibility of confession evidence. When the formal aspects of the crime had been proved he came to the witness box to lay his defence. Mr Thomas Cahill QC, his very able defence counsel, led him through his version of events which in effect was that he was innocent of the crimes alleged and that he had made his false confessions as a result of having been assaulted by me in Castlereagh. To say that I was surprised at these allegations would be untrue. Such are an occupational hazard of being a working detective. However, I personally abhor violence of any kind and would only resort to such to defend myself or in a public order situation.

McClinton's performance in the witness box was outstanding and it soon became apparent to those seeing him for the first time that he was a wily and intelligent man. He certainly impressed us all by quoting passages from his new-found knowledge of the law. At all times he maintained a respectful and restrained attitude, continually addressing the judge as 'my lord'. It seemed almost as though he had undergone a course of instruction in evidence-giving. One of the tell-tale signs of this was his unusual ability to adopt correct court etiquette by looking at the barristers as they posed their questions but answering by turning directly towards the judge, a skill which one normally sees only in experienced witnesses. In fact, on one occasion the judge raised this point with McClinton but he denied he had made a special study of giving evidence.

McClinton's main allegation was that during the early interviews I had become frustrated with his denials of the killings and had hauled him from his chair and crashed him against the wall. He said that this so frightened him that he made his false confession to my two colleagues later on in the hope this would prevent my re-appearance in the interview room.

When his defence counsel had finished drawing this out of McClinton piece-by-piece, it then became the turn of the Crown lawyers. They cross-examined him at great length but he remained perfectly in control of himself. However, they gently but devastatingly guided him down the road of his background in crime.

It was revealed that he had no less than eight previous convictions for violence, some of which were gained during his life as a merchant seaman. He was pointedly asked by Crown counsel if he was seriously suggesting that with a history such as this he was so frightened by my alleged assaults that he admitted to two murders. He replied that he was. At the end of the cross-examination everyone was impressed by the effort McClinton put into the preparation of his evidence. It was clear that he was not going to be convicted without a good fight.

McClinton did not play all his cards in the witness box but kept what he believed to be his masterstroke up his sleeve when on the eighth day of the trial he called the convicted Samuel McCaw to the witness box. McCaw was of course now serving his term of life imprisonment for the murder of Daniel Carville. He was brought into the courtroom in handcuffs and flanked by prison officers.

In a hushed courtroom his handcuffs were removed and he stepped into the witness box. The prison officers remained close at hand. McClinton's defence counsel began to elicit from him the evidence he wished to give. This was essentially that he had been convicted of the murder of Daniel Carville and that McClinton had not been involved in the crime. Lord Justice O'Donnell asked McCaw if he had pleaded guilty at his own trial on the murder charge and he answered that he had not. When asked who the trial judge had been McCaw said Lord Justice Kelly had heard his case. Lord Justice O'Donnell asked McCaw if he was now saying that his conviction had been a correct one and he agreed that it had. The Lord Justice then wryly commented that Mr Kelly no doubt would be pleased to hear that he had adjudged his case correctly. Altogether McCaw was in the witness box no more than fifteen minutes. He cut the pathetic figure of someone who could not be relied on in any way.

At the conclusion of the trial Lord Justice O'Donnell accepted into evidence the confession made by the accused. However, he added the rider that he could not be totally satisfied that I had not assaulted him in the manner alleged, but that even if I had it would have caused McClinton little or no upset given his violent background and certainly not to the extent that he would have falsely confessed to two murders. Needless to say, I was annoyed that the judge chose this particular course but such slings and arrows from certain members of the judiciary are a further occupational hazard.

In his final summing-up of the case the judge found McClinton guilty of the two killings and described him as a ruthless assassin. He was sentenced to life imprisonment with a stipulation that he not be considered for release until the expiration of twenty years. As he was led from the court McClinton screamed abuse at me and my colleagues, but we remained impassive to his insults. Hugh Black was then brought forward and his relatively minor role in the killing of Harold Bradshaw was acknowledged with a much lighter sentence.

As soon as McClinton was sentenced and removed from court he was taken by underground tunnel back to his remand cell in HM Prison, Crumlin Road. Here he collected his belongings and was transported to the much more modern HM Prison, The Maze, near Lisburn and about fifteen miles from Belfast.

The Maze houses a large number of dangerous republican and loyalist paramilitaries and there had been a long-running dispute with the government over what was known as special category status. This was a status granted to paramilitaries in the early phases of the troubles when certain crimes were regarded as political and those convicted were, to a certain extent, treated in the style of prisoners-of-war. This had led to a steady erosion of authority from the prison staff as each group set up its own rank structure within the prison and, by and large, ran its own affairs. The government had called a halt to this and declared that persons convicted after a certain date would be regarded as ordinary criminals and therefore accorded only the appropriate privileges. A number of prisoners had engaged in an extreme form of protest by refusing to wear prison uniform and some were now isolated in cells clothed only in a blanket. In addition, they exacerbated the situation by spreading their own excrement on the cell walls. Not long after his arrival McClinton, who was still in a very hostile mood, decided to join the protest. He remained for several months 'on the blanket', as it was known. In effect he was virtually held in solitary confinement due to his non-acceptance of prison rules. I have no doubt he was still festering at being sentenced to twenty years imprisonment.

One of the few items he was allowed in his cell was a Bible. It was later revealed that even during his period of hostility he had begun to read it and was finding solace in the scriptures. He seemed to undergo a religious conversion. In mid-August 1979 he came off the blanket protest and entered into normal prison life which in Northern Ireland is quite progressive. He became a model prisoner and tried to encourage others to cease their protest. This incurred a certain degree of displeasure from the more hardened prsoners. In fact they became so incensed at his actions that a group of them attacked him, beat him up and poured boiling water over his body causing severe burns, as a result of which he spent many painful months in hospital.

I personally heard nothing from McClinton until May 1982 when I returned to Tennent Street station but this time as the detective chief inspector-in-charge of the CID. I was contacted by a police inspector who was a committed member of the Christian Police Association engaged in voluntary welfare work within the prisons. He informed me that McClinton and he had had a meeting in the Maze Prison during which McClinton disclosed to him that he had been involved in several other crimes prior to his arrest. He had not confessed to these crimes in Castlereagh Detention Centre back in August 1977 and now, as a result of his religious conversion, he wished to make a clean breast of everything.

Although I was pleased to hear that McClinton had chosen a path which would result in several more crimes being cleared up in my books, I was somewhat sceptical of the motivation behind this course of action. Almost three years had elapsed since he announced his religious conversion and it seemed odd to me that he should wait so long to cleanse himself of these matters. His timing did, however, coincide with the advent of the supergrass era in which a number of paramilitaries from all of the organisations offered their services as witnesses against their former accomplices in crime. Many hard men had been swept up as a result and were now in prison awaiting trial. This development caused nervous ripples within the paramilitary groups. It did cross my mind that perhaps McClinton feared being 'grassed' by some of his former friends and was now getting in first by clearing his slate. If I am wrong in this theory perhaps he will forgive me and understand that the nature of my work breeds an unhealthy degree of scepticism. In any event McClinton laid down only two conditions before making his admissions. These were that he would not be mentioning the names of his accomplices and that he would wish to have the admissions recorded by a detective who was a committed Christian.

A close friend of mine was appointed to the task and he spent two full days with McClinton at the Maze prison, recording admissions to a further nine crimes. During these interviews McClinton conceded that he had been a member of the outlawed UFF. He admitted causing a number of explosions by making and sending parcel bombs through the post to several leading republicans. One of these was intercepted by staff at the postal sorting office. The army were called in to deal with it but unfortunately as it was being moved to a safe area it went off and a soldier had his left hand blown off.

McClinton also admitted causing an explosion at a bar in North Belfast so that it would have to close down and hence more business would be directed to a local UDA drinking den. This smacked of Chicago-style gangsterism. In addition he confessed to hijacking a car used in a car bomb at a factory in West Belfast and to setting fire to a clothes manufacturing premises which were being kept open in contravention of the loyalist workers' strike. McClinton disclosed he had moved explosives and firearms on a number of occasions and had hijacked commercial delivery vehicles so that he could steal their loads.

The most serious crime he revealed to his interviewers was the disposal of the dead body of a suspected member of the UDA who had been killed by that organisation on suspicion of being a police informer. The deceased was a Jackie Hutchinson from the Shankill Road area. On 14 July 1977, about one month before McClinton's arrest, his body had been found in a shallow grave just off the quiet Glencairn Road where so many of the other murders I have referred to had taken place. According to McClinton, about five days before the remains of Hutchinson were discovered he had been instructed by his officers in the UDA to go to the scene of the killing and bury the body. He found the body in a field in a crouched position with an apparent bullet wound to the back of its head. McClinton said he recognised the deceased as Jackie Hutchinson and he then dug a grave in which he placed the body, poured lime over it and covered it with soil.

The wording of these fresh admissions contained many religious quotations and on several occasions McClinton referred the reader to particular Biblical passages. However, he still declined to offer the names of any of his accomplices on the basis that this would be a breach of trust and impede his Christian ministering to other members of the prison population. I took the opposing view that it would be morally more appropriate to let the police have the names so that other terrorists could be removed off the streets, perhaps preventing further death or serious injury.

The case papers concerning these new admissions were prepared and forwarded to the Director of Public Prosecutions. It was recognised by all that if McClinton was charged and convicted on the fresh evidence he would most likely receive a sentence to run concurrent with his twenty years term of imprisonment. A prosecution was therefore considered a waste of taxpayers' money and the DPP ordered that the crimes be left on file and regarded as solved.

On receipt of written confirmation of this I went with one of my detective inspectors to see McClinton in prison and to give him the result. He greeted me warmly enough and when I disclosed that he was not to be prosecuted for the additional crimes he exclaimed, 'Praise the Lord!' I could see that prison life had taken its toll on him as he was much thinner and had aged considerably since I had last seen him. After a few minutes he relaxed a little and began to reminisce about his trial and how life had changed since then. I remarked to him that he had put a lot of effort into his defence and he explained that all of his many months on remand had been spent preparing for his court appearance. He apologised for making the false allegations of assault against me.

At the end of this meeting we shook hands and he invited me and my colleague to join in a short prayer. I suspected that he was trying to manipulate us so I declined his offer and we went on our way. During the return journey to Tennent Street station we passed through an area of West Belfast where we had a brick thrown through the rear window of the police car, striking my colleague on the hand. We have often humorously remarked to each other that the incident was the result of McClinton calling the wrath of God down upon us.

One could well be forgiven for thinking this was definitely the last I could possibly hear of McClinton but not so. He came to the fore again in 1984 when he asked to see the Christian Police Association officer who had recorded his additional confessions back in 1982. McClinton told him that during his own murder trial he had coerced McCaw into giving the evidence that he, McClinton, had not been involved in the killing of Daniel Carville. He now proclaimed that he had indeed been one of the killers and that McCaw had nothing to do with it. McClinton maintained his vow of secrecy in respect of the others involved in the murders. Once again the papers were re-submitted to the DPP but the police investigation was not re-opened.

McClinton was released from prison in due course, having served out a large proportion of his sentence. He now refers to himself as Pastor McClinton and one of the duties he carried out in this capacity was to give the graveside oration at the funeral of LVF leader Billy Wright who was shot dead within the Maze prison by suspected members of the INLA.

The events concerning McClinton which have been described in the preceding pages stemmed from our interviews with him in August 1977 and we spent much of the remainder of that year interviewing other suspected terrorists or attending trials at Belfast Crown Court. I rounded off the year by passing the qualifying examination for promotion to the rank of Inspector and as we entered 1978 there was no let-up in the workload as the paramilitaries on both sides continued to wage their campaign of violence.

The first significant investigation for us occurred in late March when two middle-aged men were observed circling the sidestreets adjacent to Tennent Street police station. A patrol was sent out and apprehended them. The car was being driven by a man named Henry McCavana and the other person was a Francis Maguire, aged about forty years, who was seated in the rear. He was wearing heavy duty rubber gloves and cradling a loaded Armalite rifle. The rear windows had been wound down and a check on the car revealed it had been hijacked a short time earlier in Ardoyne. When all of the evidence was assessed it was noted that the car had been stopped at a time when the morning turn of duty was due to terminate for the day and the afternoon shift would take over. This caused a fair degree of movement around the station as early foot-patrols returned and others left to replace them. There seemed no doubt that the two men were cruising the streets waiting for a suitable target to appear but fortunately they were apprehended before any lives were lost.

Maguire was known to the police. McCavana, however, was of a slightly different mould. He in fact had his own reasonably thriving building business and owned his house in the residential Glengormley area on the suburbs of Belfast. When questioned in depth he explained that he had a number of building contracts in Ardoyne but could only proceed with these if he had the approval of the Provisional IRA. He felt the need to ingratiate himself with them and as the weeks went by he had become more deeply involved with them until he ended up driving on a murder mission.

Two of my colleagues then shrewdly recalled that a few weeks earlier a gang of Provisional IRA terrorists, posing as builders, had taken over the home of an elderly woman approximately half-a-mile from Ardoyne. They had used her rear upstairs bedroom as a vantage point from which to launch a machinegun attack on an army foot patrol in Cliftonpark Avenue. The weapon used by the killers was an M60 machinegun of the type carried by American soldiers in Vietnam. An M60 has a devastating fire power and is capable of bringing down a helicopter but on this occasion the gunmen killed a young soldier named Gunner Shepherd. When asked about this killing McCavana nervously denied it. He began to whistle softly to himself and tap his foot on the interview room floor. Psychologists could probably put a label on such body language but my two colleagues were in no doubt that it was an indication that something was deeply troubling McCavana.

He was pressed further on the matter and eventually admitted complicity in the murder of the soldier. He explained that when the house had been taken over by the killers posing as building workers, he had assisted by wheeling in the machinegun wrapped in sacking on a builder's barrow. At his trial many months later he pleaded guilty to several charges including the murder of the soldier and he was sentenced to life imprisonment. Maguire was also convicted of possession of a firearm with intent to endanger life and related offences surrounding his arrest and was given a lengthy term of imprisonment.

Many of the cases I have referred to were brought to a successful conclusion due to the dedicated work which took place in Castlereagh and other detention centres. However, many long hours were spent talking to suspects from whom nothing was obtained. The principal role of the A Squad, and of the Regional Crime Squads which by now had been formed in the North, South and Belfast areas of the Province, was the interviewing of suspects. Many dangerous paramilitaries were removed from the streets by this method and much intelligence on their activities was obtained.

There is strong evidence that during the mid to late 1970s the squads were winning the war of attrition against the paramilitary groups, much to their chagrin. These groups realised that they would soon have to do something to reduce their losses. They settled on a campaign of propaganda, a subject in which they were well practised. Efforts were made to discredit the detention centres by claiming that suspects were being subjected to widespread physical abuse by interviewers. A number of leading politicians and churchmen joined in the campaign. It is true to say that a worrying number of suspects were leaving the detention centres showing signs of bruising. However, there was also unequivocal evidence that some of these were self inflicted. Also it was not uncommon for suspects to wait until they had seen their solicitor at the end of their period of detention, before making allegations. They would turn these into the foundation for a possible defence, in the way McClinton had done.

There was some evidence that a small number of suspects were being ill-treated. With the benefit of hindsight it is not difficult to see how this came about. Hard-pressed detectives were placed for hours on end in the same rooms as terrorist suspects, some of whom had carried out the most hideous crimes imaginable. Human nature being what it is, tempers were bound to fray at times, particularly when the suspects became verbally abusive to their interviewers; sometimes suspects lay on the floor, and even urinated into the box-like metal ashtrays. However, prior to leaving the detention centres either on release or on their way to court, each prisoner was given the opportunity of a medical examination. If a complaint was made at that time the details would be forwarded to the Complaints and Discipline Branch of the RUC who would investigate the matter thoroughly. On some occasions this resulted in detectives being prosecuted. Nevertheless, I can categorically state that there was no policy of ill-treating persons in custody. Those cases which did come to court were the result of isolated incidents.

In June 1978 the government was becoming so concerned at the mounting propaganda that the Secretary of State for Northern Ireland, Mr Roy Mason, MP, set up a committee of inquiry to examine police procedures and practice relating to the interrogation of persons suspected of terrorist crimes. The committee was chaired by His Honour, Judge Bennett QC, a leading English County Court judge and he was assisted by Sir James Haughton, CBE, QPM representing HM Inspectorate of Constabulary and Professor John Marshall, MD, FRCP, DPM, a leading neurologist and psychologist.

The committee sat for several weeks and heard evidence from a number of interested bodies and individuals. In view of my lengthy experience of interviewing suspects I was nominated by the head of the CID to represent the Detective Sergeant ranks and I spent an afternoon giving evidence to the committee.

Some months later they reported the findings and stated that, in the course of their enquiry, they had seen abundant evidence of a co-ordinated and extensive campaign to discredit the police. They did, however, take note that a number of prisoners leaving police detention were showing some medical evidence of violence, not all of which could be regarded as self-inflicted.

As a result the committee made a number of recommendations, the majority of which were accepted by the Chief Constable. The most significant of these was that each interview room should have two closed circuit television cameras installed. These would relay pictures back to a monitor room which would be manned by at least one inspector who would be in a position to watch all activity taking place within the rooms.

I and my colleagues welcomed these steps. They primarily protected us from false allegations of assault and also put a stop to those few occasions where prisoners were being assaulted. I firmly believed that such isolated incidents were eroding confidence in the police and were pushing some people deeper and deeper into terrorism.

The involvement with the Bennett Committee of inquiry was almost my final act for A Squad, which, incidentally by now had its name changed to Headquarters' Crime Squad. On 2 October 1978 I was promoted to the rank of detective inspector and was transferred to the post of deputy head of the Belfast Regional Crime Squad.

5

HERR NIEDERMAYER

The Belfast Crime Squad was based in offices in Castlereagh RUC station and close to the detention centre where terrorist suspects are held for interview. Their duties were little different from those of A Squad, the only exception being that it was intended, so far as was possible, that they should confine their activities to assisting CIDs within the Belfast region.

The duties of my new rank were therefore quite similar except that I had responsibility for a larger number of personnel and could play a more leading role in the decision-making processes involved in criminal investigations.

The morning of Monday, 11 March 1980 brought one of those turns of events which makes CID work so fascinating when the driver of a mechanical excavator uncovered badly decomposed human remains at Colin Glen in West Belfast about half a mile into the countryside from the republican estates of Lenadoon and Andersonstown. I was asked to go along to the scene with other senior detectives and on arrival we were met by a patrol of uniformed police from the local Woodbourne RUC Station. They had so far established that the area in which the remains had been found had once been a beauty spot. Over the years the locals had turned it into an eyesore by indiscriminately dumping all sorts of household rubbish there. There was also some evidence that building-contractors had been using it as a convenient place to dump loads of rubble and soil. What had once been a lovely Irish wooded Glen, falling away to a gently flowing river, had gradually been transformed into an unsightly health-hazard.

The area came under the responsibility of Lisburn Borough Council and they had embarked on a clean-up scheme intending to return the Glen to its former glory. They erected a high steel fence to prevent further tipping but gave pedestrian access for the locals who wished to enjoy its natural amenities.

The contractor carrying out the clean-up operation had now been on site for four weeks and the mechanical excavator had been working non-stop loading a fleet of three tipper lorries which were transporting the rubbish to an approved dumping-site approximately two miles away. Overall, it was estimated that two thousand tons had been removed. This phase of the project was nearing completion and the original top soil and contours of the Glen were now visible again.

On this particular Monday the excavator driver was tidying up the final few yards of ground. He was digging a hole into which he intended to bury the last remnants of the rubbish when he noticed bones protruding from a pair of trousers in the bucket of his machine. He immediately switched off his engine and examined the trousers, confirming that each leg contained a large bone. He then examined the hole he had just excavated and saw a white, putty-like substance at the base. The driver was in little doubt that he had uncovered human remains. He informed his employer who immediately notified the police.

The local police had by now cordoned off the area which, owing to the constant movement of the excavator and lorries, was a sea of mud. They had rightly allowed no further interference with the scene. My CID colleagues and I carried out a cursory examination of what had been found and saw that the heavily mud-stained trousers were of a cavalry-twill material. I had attended sufficient post-mortem examinations to know that the parts of the bones so far exposed seemed to be those of the human lower legs. We also examined the hole in the ground without disturbing any evidence and could see sections of a great deal of other material partially exposed. It was not unusual for excavators to unintentionally disturb ancient burial sites but the material the trousers were made of confirmed that the remains were comparatively modern.

We therefore felt it essential to have the remaining evidence expertly examined. We asked the Belfast Regional Control Room to notify the Forensic Science Laboratory and the Department of Pathology that we required their services. Within an hour a biology expert and a pathologist arrived at the scene and we gave them details of the events up to that point.

They began their examination by sifting through the contents of the excavator bucket and they carefully laid out the trousers and their contents on a plastic sheet. The pathologist noted that the pelvic bones were present, together with the right femur or thigh bone. The left femur was missing but both sets of tibia and fibula, or lower leg bones, were intact. Significantly the lower trouser legs and the bones therein were loosely tied together with some type of heavily stained cloth material.

The two experts then turned their attention to the excavation and carefully began to scrape away the muddy soil. Inch-by-inch the back of a human skull appeared. As they progressed along the ground from the direction of the skull more large bones appeared and were immediately identified by the pathologist as being the forearms. Gradually the trunk of the body was uncovered and the upper arm bones and rib cage became clearly distinguishable.

The pathologist paused in his work at that stage to explain to us that the body was buried face down. The position of the arm bones above and behind the torso tended to indicate that they may have been tied behind its back at the time of burial.

As further soil was removed a man's necktie appeared from the neck area but it had been knotted in a clove hitch and formed a large loop, indicating it may have been used as a mouth gag.

All aspects of the examination were carefully photographed and sketched by our own staff and after several hours the two experts concluded that nothing more could be learned from the scene until the body was removed from its grave.

We brought a broad wooden board to the side of the excavation and with the aid of spades and trowels gently eased the head and torso from its resting place. Not surprisingly, the head came free and we only managed to keep the rib cage intact. It was carefully laid on the wooden board. The pathologist lifted the skull and placed it alongside the torso.

The full extent of the grave could now be defined and its depth varied from eighteen inches to twenty-four inches. It had been dug at right angles and about fifty feet into the Glen from the roadway. It was at the bottom of a steep slope and the excavator driver confirmed that he had removed a large quantity of rubbish from the spot. The grave was undoubtedly in the original top soil of the Glen.

The two experts then carefully sifted through the soil in the bottom of the grave and I noticed with interest a considerable quantity of crumbly, whitish material. I asked the pathologist what it was. He explained that its proper biological name was 'adipocere' and was composed of body fat which could persist for very long periods in cool moist conditions such as those which existed in the present grave. He continued with the excavations and interestingly uncovered a pair of men's bedroom slippers. These were carefully placed in plastic exhibit bags and labelled.

The remains were removed to the city mortuary for more scientific examination and by now a battery of pressmen had arrived at the scene sensing a good story. One of the detective chief superintendents present gave them an interview about the developments to date but I was left with the less glamorous task of trying to find the missing thigh bone. I retained a small team of detectives with me and armed with rakes and shovels we began to sift through the mud and remaining rubbish. After several hours of work in most unpleasant conditions one of my colleagues uncovered it and we bagged and delivered it to the mortuary.

It hardly needs stating that the evidence then, particularly the binding of the arms and legs, the possible gagging of the mouth and the secret burial place left us in no doubt that we were dealing with a murder. There was widespread speculation as to who the victim could be.

At a very early stage following its discovery the CID strongly believed that the body could well be that of Herr Thomas Niedermayer, OBE, who had been the manager of the West German Grundig Electronics factory at Dunmurry on the fringes of West Belfast. Herr Niedermayer was also honorary West German consul to Northern Ireland and on the late evening of Thursday, 27 December

1973 he had been kidnapped at his home at Glengoland Gardens, Belfast by three men. He had not been seen or heard of since.

The case of Herr Niedermayer was a sensational news story at the time. Down through the years the crime was never far from the headlines as speculation grew about the reasons for his disappearance. Many theories were put forward including one that he had carefully staged his kidnapping and had run off to some foreign parts or that he had been engaged in gun-running for loyalist terrorist gangs.

The reality of the situation was that Herr Niedermayer had been abducted and murdered by the Provisional IRA. The events which led to the crime began on Thursday, 6 March 1973 when the group planted three massive car bombs in central London. The first explosion occurred outside the Old Bailey court buildings and many people were injured in the no-warning blast. The second explosion ripped through Great Scotland Yard just off Whitehall and was aimed principally at an army recruiting office. Unfortunately, one man was killed in this blast and over two hundred persons were injured. A third bomb was found in Dean Stanley Street, Westminster not far from the Conservative Party Central Office, but it was successfully defused, avoiding further loss of life and injury.

The Criminal Investigation Department of the London Metropolitan Police were quick to respond to these atrocities. They received word that a number of suspicious young persons had just boarded an aircraft at Heathrow airport bound for Dublin and Belfast. The police boarded the aircraft and took three women and seven men into custody, all of whom had Belfast addresses.

The suspects were removed to Ealing Police Station and during the days which followed sufficient evidence was found to link them to the bombings. On the morning of Tuesday, 13 March 1973, all ten appeared before Bow Street Magistrates Court and were remanded in custody on charges of conspiracy to cause explosions. The charges attracted a great deal of publicity and the police had difficulty restraining a large crowd of onlookers who had gathered outside the court building. Among the accused were two sisters, Marion and Dolores Price, both of whom came from Andersonstown in West Belfast.

In early June 1973 all ten accused appeared at Lambeth

Magistrates Court for committal proceedings and were returned for trial to Winchester Crown Court. The actual trial began on 23 October 1973 and the Crown case was presented personally by the Attorney General, Sir Peter Rawlinson, QC. The case continued through until 15 November 1973 when the jury returned a verdict of 'guilty' against eight of the accused including the Price sisters.

They were sentenced to terms of life imprisonment and another of the accused, who had pleaded 'guilty' at the outset of the trial, was sentenced to a lesser term of fifteen years imprisonment. A third girl in the case, Róisín McNearney, who had been reasonably helpful to the investigation team, was acquitted by the jury and spirited away by the police.

As the nine prisoners were led from the dock to begin their sentences there were unruly scenes in the courtroom. Relatives and friends shouted and waved from the public gallery. Almost immediately those convicted demanded that they be moved to prisons in Northern Ireland where they would, of course, be granted the privileges of special category status. The British government refused to accede to the demands and Robert Carr, the Home Secretary, officially made this public in a Commons written reply.

In an attempt to force the issue the Price sisters then went on a hunger strike. This is a tactic which has been favoured by those engaged in Irish republicanism down through the years, with those who saw it through to the bitter end being regarded as martyrs. Consequently, it is a highly emotive subject and on this occasion the British government attempted to neutralise its effect by having the sisters force-fed. However, this only served to heighten feelings.

The Price sisters became a cause célèbre in Ireland and placed the Provisional IRA in something of a dilemma. After all, they had dispatched the ten members on a murder mission. These had now been caught and most of them were serving lengthy terms of imprisonment, with two of its members attempting to starve themselves to death. They obviously felt compelled to do something to demonstrate to their members that should they find themselves in a similar situation they would not be forgotten by the organisation and would be afforded every possible support. On this occasion the

Provisional IRA agreed at a high level that the only possible way forward was the kidnapping of a VIP who could be held to the ransom of having the Price sisters removed to a Northern Ireland prison.

The major difficulty in this plot was kidnapping someone of sufficient status to make the British government sit up and take notice. Some months earlier the Provisional IRA became aware that a Herr Niedermayer who seemed to be of some importance resided in the small development of luxury bungalows at Glengoland which is located on the edge of Andersonstown. How they became aware of his presence was never satisfactorily resolved. The most favoured theory is that some months prior to his disappearance an attempt had been made to hijack his car during one of the many episodes of civil unrest in the Andersonstown area when vehicles were suddenly seized, placed across the roads as barricades and set on fire. When Herr Niedermayer was stopped he apparently managed to talk his way out of the situation by proclaiming his West German nationality and diplomatic status. It is believed he also produced official documents to verify his identity. After being allowed to proceed the hijackers passed the information concerning Herr Niedermayer onto the Provisional IRA intelligence officers.

I am sure they could hardly believe their luck when some elementary research revealed that living in their midst was the manager of the giant Grundig electronics factory, who, as well as being a foreign national with diplomatic status, also held the 'Order of the British Empire'. He seemed the perfect candidate for kidnapping as the Provos could apply pressure to both the West German and British governments to bargain for his release.

The die was then cast around mid-December 1973 when the case of the Price sisters was receiving constant publicity. However, with Christmas looming the Provisional IRA decided to let this holiday period pass and set Thursday, 27 December 1973 as the date for the kidnap. They recognised that this would be one of the most important operations they had embarked upon and would undoubtedly grab the world's headlines. They kept the details a closely guarded secret and placed a small selected group of their most trusted volunteers on stand-by to see it through.

Herr Niedermayer had first arrived in Northern Ireland with his wife Ingeborg, in 1961, and they quickly settled into their strange but friendly surroundings. They had two daughters and lived at a number of addresses convenient to the factory before moving to Glengoland Gardens in 1968.

The factory, which employed around fifteen hundred people, was in full production manufacturing tape recorders for world-wide distribution. In years to come the premises were to close as the Japanese began to dominate that market.

Christmas 1973 was not to be a happy one for the Niedermayer family because on Christmas Eve Ingeborg was unexpectedly admitted to hospital. Herr Niedermayer visited his wife each day and did what he could at home to make life as normal as possible for the children.

On the fateful evening of Thursday, 27 December Herr Niedermayer again visited Ingeborg, leaving the hospital ward at around half past eight. Neither realised that this was the last time they would see each other.

Herr Niedermayer arrived home in his Ford Granada car at a quarter-to-nine, parked it on the roadway outside and retired to his room where his fifteen year old daughter, Renate, had brought him a light supper. At around ten o'clock Renate went to bed and at a quarter-to-eleven heard her father settling down for the night.

The peace of the household was suddenly disturbed by the ringing of the doorbell. Renate got out of bed, pulled on a dressing gown, and went to answer it. She found two men on her doorstep and one of them said, 'We've crashed into your car. Is your father or somebody in?' Renate went to her father's bedroom and informed him what had happened. He quickly got dressed in casual clothes and wearing bedroom slippers went to the front door and spoke to the two men.

Across the road from Herr Niedermayer's home lived another senior employee of Grundig, Herr Herbert Hoech. From his living room window he could see the events taking place outside on the roadway. He saw Herr Niedermayer's car parked in its usual spot but also observed a second car parked at an angle across the driveway. There was obviously someone in the driver's seat of this car as the brake lights were on. These cast an eerie atmosphere on the scene, but allowed him to see Herr Niedermayer with two other men kneeling down and examining the side of the Granada car. The three men then straightened themselves and Herr Niedermayer walked back towards the driveway of his home and waved his hand. With the benefit of hindsight we now know he was signifying that everything was all right with his car. The time was around a quarter past eleven.

However, things were far from all right. Herbert Hoech watched as the two men grabbed Herr Niedermayer from behind. A brief struggle ensued and, according to Hoech, Herr Niedermayer seemed to put up little resistance and was pushed into the waiting car. Herr Hoech, who had been in night attire, donned some outer clothing and ran out to the front of his house, but the car sped off.

Meanwhile, Renate had gone back to her bed, leaving her father to deal with the two callers. Herbert Hoech was still uncertain as to what he had just witnessed and for a while thought perhaps Herr Niedermayer was being dragged off to a Christmas party against his will. He waited a few moments but was now very concerned about what had happened in front of his eyes. Following a brief telephone call to Renate, who confirmed she was unaware of the present whereabouts of her father, he contacted the police.

The local police and the CID immediately responded to the call by going to Glengoland Gardens. As the night wore on without the reappearance of Herr Niedermayer all thoughts of him having been reluctantly dragged off to a party were dismissed. There was little doubt that a serious crime had occurred.

A major incident room was set up by the CID. The security forces across the Province were alerted and given descriptive details of the missing man. The world's press gave full attention to the crime but as Friday, 28 December wore on there was still no clear indication as to who had taken Herr Niedermayer. The senior CID officer leading the investigation attended a news conference at which he briefly said, 'We will not know why Herr Niedermayer is being held until his captors make contact — until then we can just speculate.'

The West German government were by now deeply concerned about the abduction of their Consul. Mr Francis Pym, the then Secretary of State for Northern Ireland, announced that the German

Foreign Minister in Bonn and the West German Embassy in London were being kept fully informed of developments. Mr Pym also issued a press statement saying, 'The abduction of the German Industrialist, Mr Niedermayer, is greatly to be deplored and regretted. The security forces are sparing no effort to find him. I am keeping in the closest touch and I have discussed the matter with the German Ambassador. We must all hope it will not be long before Mr Niedermayer is released safe and well.'

In addition to the inter-government exchanges the Grundig company were also becoming very anxious about the fate of the manager of their Belfast plant and the company's chairman, Herr Adolf Wohlrab, flew into Belfast from their head offices at Nuremburg to assess the situation.

The weekend passed with the police still receiving no word from the kidnappers. They maintained the momentum of the investigation in the only way possible by ensuring that the house-to-house enquiries in the Glengoland area were thorough, by determining that uniformed police and army patrols across the Province kept up their vehicle check points in the event that attempts would be made to move Herr Niedermayer, and by following up snippets of information supplied by well-intentioned members of the public, all of which led nowhere.

The family of the missing man were now distraught with anxiety. Ingeborg Niedermayer was released from hospital and did what she could to comfort her two daughters. Their friends, both German and local, rallied round them and the CID kept in constant touch in the event that the kidnappers should contact them first.

The days steadily wore on into weeks and on 9 January 1974 a member of the Grundig management board flew to London to seek assurances from the British government that everything possible was being done to find Herr Niedermayer. In a follow-up press conference the company representative stated that he was sure the kidnapping of Herr Niedermayer was connected with his Consular activities and not with his private or business life. He disclosed that the West German Chancellor, Willy Brandt, had personally written to the British Prime Minister, Edward Heath, about the situation.

Meanwhile back in Belfast, the police investigation team were finding it extremely odd that there had been no contact whatsoever from the kidnappers. In any criminal investigation the primary factor to be established is the motive. Although the detectives working on the case favoured the view that the crime had been carried out by the Provisional IRA to further the cause of the Price sisters, why had there been no public demands or threats from the kidnappers? If the crime was not connected with the Price sisters then the alternative was political assassination. Herr Niedermayer could so easily have been shot dead on his doorstep like so many other unfortunate victims of the troubles. The police had a distinct feeling of unease about the case and were certain that a vital piece of the jigsaw was missing.

Three weeks had elapsed since the crime was committed but it stayed firmly in the news headlines. At that point a quite unusual step was taken. The heads of the four main churches in Ireland got together and issued the following statement which was countersigned by Cardinal Conway on behalf of the Roman Catholic Church, Doctor Simms representing the Church of Ireland, Doctor Orr, Moderator of the Presbyterian Church and The Very Reverend Harold Sloan, President of the Methodist Church:

> Anyone who can throw light on this mysterious case, in the name of Christian compassion and of common humanity, do what they can to relieve the agony of suspense and near despair with which the missing man's wife and family are afflicted. Amidst so much suffering and tragedy in Ireland at the present time the disappearance of the German Consul constitutes an altogether special case.

The abductors were totally unmoved by this impassioned plea. It was not until the end of January 1974 that the first firm indication of what had befallen Herr Niedermayer began to emerge when the well-known Ulster politician, The Reverend Ian Paisley, MP asked the Northern Ireland Office to confirm that the Provisional IRA had offered to release Herr Niedermayer if the Price sisters were transferred to Armagh Women's Prison. The Northern Ireland Office denied that such a demand had been made but to add pressure the Reverend Ian Paisley made it publicly known that he had also been in touch with

Herr Willy Brandt seeking similar confirmation. Paisley then expanded his original claim of Provisional IRA involvement by stating that the British government had refused to bargain with the kidnappers and that Herr Niedermayer had subsequently been murdered.

The police investigation team were obviously interested in the scenario now being presented but had to consider the denials by the Northern Ireland Office. There was a deafening silence from the Provisional IRA on the affair. The history of that organisation to date showed that they were not shy about claiming responsibility for atrocities. If the allegations of their involvement in this case were true they would surely have produced the body to demonstrate that they meant business should such a situation arise again.

Altogether, the facts did not quite add up. However, the air began to clear to some extent soon afterwards. The Home Office in London conceded that after the abduction of Herr Niedermayer the Provisional IRA contacted 10 Downing Street demanding that the Price sisters be moved to Northern Ireland, or that otherwise their kidnap victim would be killed. The Home Office stated that the government felt compelled to re-affirm their determination not to negotiate under threats which could lead to an encouragement of kidnapping as a weapon in Northern Ireland.

These late revelations by the government were really quite sensational. The Reverend Paisley accused the government of 'hypocrisy and duplicity'. He said the Home Office knew perfectly well that the IRA had Herr Niedermayer and that, after a deadline given by the Provisional IRA had passed, the government had second thoughts and tried to re-establish contact with the terrorists but failed.

When asked by the press, RUC headquarters stated that they had no knowledge of any demand having been made by the Provisional IRA. The detectives who had worked so hard on the case rightly felt that by being deprived of this vital information they had been treated somewhat shabbily by the British government.

However, the non-production of the body of Herr Niedermayer continued to nag the investigation team and it cruelly kept his family in hope that he could somehow yet be returned alive. In early March 1974 Ingeborg Niedermayer publicly demonstrated this when she issued the following heart-rending statement:

> My daughters and I appeal directly to the people who took my husband from our home on 27 December. Ten weeks have now elapsed and we have had no definite news of him. You, or the people holding him, are the only ones who can tell exactly what happened. I beg you from the bottom of my heart to let me know one way or the other. I have not known a day in which I have not prayed for the safe return of my husband or some news about him. Every day I await the news reports on the radio, TV, and in the newspapers in the hope that someone, somewhere, had finally decided to put me and my family out of this unending agony — but still no news. Please let me know what has happened to my husband. Give me peace within myself. Have pity and let me know. No one can appreciate the agony and strain you are putting me and my daughters through. Do not close your hearts against my desperate appeal to you. I pray every day that you will show me some human compassion. Please let me know soon.

This appeal brought no response whatsoever from the Provisional IRA and as 1974 wore on the Price sisters continued with their hunger-strike. They had now been joined in their fast by some of the male paramilitaries convicted of the London bombings. By the end of May the Home Office admitted that the condition of the two girls was giving cause for concern as the policy of force-feeding had been abandoned and they were taking only water. The Provisional IRA recognised that if the sisters were allowed to die they would have achieved a massive propaganda coup. They warned the British government that if such should happen, the consequences would be devastating. However, at the beginning of June, there were some welcome signs that the sisters were pulling back from the brink when they received a visit from their parents. Some of the male hunger strikers began to take food at around this time and within days the sisters gave up their fast. Some of the national papers reported that the girls had quietly been given an undertaking that within three months they would be moved to a Northern Ireland prison. This proved to be only slightly inaccurate as in March 1975 they were transferred to Armagh Prison.

In July 1974 there was still no sign of Herr Niedermayer and the police investigation team knew in their hearts that there was now no hope of finding him alive. The detective-in-charge of the case spoke to the press and conceded that his team were no further on now than on the night he disappeared. He added that his detectives had followed up four hundred and forty leads. It was, he conceded, one of the most perplexing and baffling cases in British criminal history and might never be cleared up. As if to seal this depressing news it was revealed that Ingeborg Niedermayer had begun to draw a widow's pension.

Almost seven months of dedicated detective work had now gone into the case and gradually the investigation was wound down. However, the public interest in the crime never waned. Over the following years the CID would on occasions temporarily re-open the case to explore some new theory or piece of information but none of these led anywhere.

Now, in March 1980, some seven years after the crime, I found it oddly exciting to play a part in the solving of the mystery. When I arrived at the mortuary with the missing femur it required little persuasion for me to stay for the full post-mortem examination which was about to be carried out.

The remains had by now been carefully laid out in order on an examination table and when the missing femur was added one could easily define the outline of a human being. Fragments of clothing still adhered to the body and the pathologist explained that it would be logical to first try and salvage these. The remains of a red check sports shirt were visible and these were carefully peeled away. A belt, the remains of a cardigan and pieces of underwear were also located in the torso area and the forensic scientist, who already had possession of the trousers and the slippers, carefully placed all of these items in separate plastic bags.

The pathologist then turned his attention to the skull. The eye sockets, nose and mouth cavity were filled with mud and when this had been removed the teeth became visible. They were in good general condition but a great deal of dental work had been carried out in the form of fillings, gold inlays and a gold crown. This was very important to the investigation team as it probably would be the only reliable means of having the body identified. Remarkably, an examination of the back of the skull revealed a quantity of short dark hair which was showing evidence of turning grey.

On a more detailed examination of the skull two quite distinct depressed fractures were found behind the left ear. The pathologist pointed out to us that the depressions had not been caused during the recovery of the body as their edges were deeply stained by age and decomposition. The upper of these fractures was of a quite distinct crescent shape and the pathologist gave a preliminary opinion that it may have been caused by a severe blow from the butt of a handgun.

The two experts then turned their attention to the torso and found that the rib cage and spine were totally intact and undamaged. Moving further down the body the pathologist drew attention to damage of the pelvic bones but stated that the injuries were fresh and had undoubtedly been caused by the scooping action of the mechanical excavator. The legs and arms were undamaged but sinuous tags of connective tissue were visible on all of the joints. It was noted that the bones of the hands and feet were missing but the pathologist explained that this was not significant. He had now taken his visual examination of the body as far as possible and he asked the forensic scientist to scan the remains with a metal detector to establish if there were any bullet heads lodged in the body. The metal detector gave no reaction so it therefore seemed unlikely that the victim had died from gunshot wounds.

Before arriving at a positive conclusion the pathologist informed us that he would require to have certain scientific tests carried out. He asked us to try to locate the dental records of Herr Niedermayer as the first step in the identification process. In fact this was already underway but was causing complications as, unknown to the police, Herr Niedermayer had had treatment from two local dentists and the records from the first did not quite match the dentition in the skull.

The Niedermayer family had continued to reside in Glengoland Gardens during the seven years which elapsed since the crime. Ingeborg's health had understandably suffered as a result of her ordeal and senior CID officers now called to prepare her for the news that the body found at Colin Glen, which in fact was no more than two miles from her home, was probably that of her husband, Thomas.

The forensic scientist had now gone back to his own laboratory to begin work on the items of clothing found with the body. He carefully washed and dried each item and found that the trousers and slippers were in good condition. The remains of the cardigan, when dried out, revealed that its original colour had been brown and a single button was still attached to it. The pattern of the fragments of the check shirt became more easily discernible and an examination of the trouser belt revealed it was of leather. The metal buckle had rusted away. However, the forensic scientist shrewdly noted that of the series of buckle holes in the belt number five had been the one in common use, giving a waist measurement of thirty five inches. The underwear material turned out to be the remains of a pair of underpants and a string vest revealing nothing of evidential value. The tie, when washed and dried, revealed a floral pattern, and it formed a circle which measured seventeen and a half inches in diameter. The clove hitch knot was certainly unconventional and there seemed little doubt that it had been used as a mouth gag. The heavily stained cloth material which had seemed to bind the lower legs turned out to be a pair of ladies woollen tights.

All of these items, with the exception of the tights, were made as presentable as possible and carefully mounted inside clear plastic exhibit bags. They were removed to a quiet office within RUC headquarters at Brooklyn and at the request of a senior detective, Ingeborg Niedermayer agreed to come and view them. It was an emotionally-charged moment as she cast her eyes over the fragments of clothes. Without hesitation she identified the items as being similar to the clothing worn by her husband at home and verified that these same items were missing from his wardrobe after his disappearance. However, quite significantly, she was emphatic that the floral tie did not belong to her husband.

Meanwhile, the pathologist was working on a more scientific analysis of the remains and he concluded that the bones were certainly those of a middle-aged male. He succeeded in gauging the height as five feet ten inches. He used a method devised in 1958 by Trotter and Gleser, two medical experts who deduced that, using their formula, together with the careful measurements of the main skeletal bones, the true height of a human when alive could be established. The only injuries detected were the two depressed fractures to the left side of the skull and he gave an opinion that these would not necessarily be life threatening if proper medical treatment was applied within a reasonable time. However, if no medical treatment was forthcoming the victim would lapse into an ever-deepening state of unconsciousness with death eventually occurring. The pathologist added a word of caution by advising that the death could have resulted from some other means which could not now be detected because of the decomposition of the vital organs. He did, however, state with certainty that the body had been in its crude grave for a period of some years.

The pathologist was still intrigued by the two indented injuries to the skull, particularly as one displayed a distinctive crescentic outline. He felt they could have been caused by the butt of a handgun. In order to clear up this point he enlisted the help of a forensic firearms expert who, on initial examination of the injuries, tended to agree with him. The firearms expert made casts of the injuries using the simple but effective method of dental impression material. When he returned to his laboratory he compared these with the butts of several types of handguns and found that the impression of one of the injuries perfectly matched the bow shaped butt of a 9mm Browning automatic pistol with the rounded toe of the magazine being particularly distinguishable.

Although Ingeborg Niedermayer had identified the remnants of clothing as being similar to her husband's, the evidence had inherent weaknesses and certainly would not be strong enough to convince a criminal court that the body was indeed that of Thomas Niedermayer.

The detectives were still having difficulty locating accurate dental records for the deceased but the scientific experts working on the remains came up with a brilliant answer to the problem when they noted that the front teeth on the skull had a quite distinctive pattern of fillings and that the biting edge of the teeth showed some evidence of wear to the left front. In addition, a pre-molar was missing. They recalled that at the time Herr Niedermayer disappeared a good quality head-and-shoulder photograph had been issued to the press. Insofar as they could recall, it portrayed him smiling and displaying his teeth. The experts now asked us to obtain the original of this photograph and Ingeborg Niedermayer without hesitation handed it over to us. The experts noted with considerable satisfaction that it did indeed depict a broadly smiling Herr Niedermayer with his front teeth clearly visible.

The pathologist then arranged for one of his laboratory technicians to make a transparent photograph of the portrait, as close as possible in size to the skull. When this was developed the pattern of defects on the front teeth remained clearly visible. It was carefully superimposed on the photograph of the skull. Incredibly, the borderlines of the fillings, the wear pattern, the missing pre-molar, the shape of the teeth, and minor defects matched perfectly. This evidence was almost as good as a fingerprint match and the pathologist was now quite certain that the skull was that of the person in the portrait photograph. To reinforce his opinion he invited an eminent surgeon to view it and without hesitation he concurred with the evidence.

To cap it all, the detectives who had been trying to locate the dentist who had last treated Herr Niedermayer found him in the nearby town of Lisburn. He still retained the contemporaneous record of that final examination. He willingly came along to the mortuary and confirmed that the details in his notes matched perfectly the dentition in the skull.

The West German authorities were then officially notified that their missing Consul had now been found and a few days later two officers from the German federal police, the Bundeskriminalampt, flew into Belfast to prepare a report for their government. I spent several hours explaining to them the events to date and when they learned all that they possibly could they returned to their headquarters at Wiesbaden.

The pathologist and other scientific experts had completed their work on the remains and the coroner for Belfast gave authority for the body to be released to the Niedermayer family who wished to accord it a proper Christian burial. This took place in a quiet churchyard at Dunmurry near Belfast and was attended by many civic dignitaries. Some of my colleagues and I, who had become so involved in the case, felt compelled to attend also. We sat quietly at the rear of the church during the service and watched as the body was lowered into the ground for the last time. The Niedermayer family seemed to be bearing up well to the ordeal but Ingeborg looked increasingly frail. I am sure she was reflecting on the events in their lives which had led them to this tragic moment.

The CID had of course by now re-opened the murder incident room on the case, hoping to tap into the widespread press-coverage which the discovery of the body had been given and the resulting public interest. We hoped that perhaps people who held some vital information back in 1973 and who were then too frightened to come forward would now, with the passage of time, feel confident enough to make contact with us. Consequently, we launched appeals for help and within days information began to filter through from a number of different directions.

Gradually a picture of the events surrounding the abduction and killing began to come together, including the names of most of the gang who had carried out the crime. Seven years is a long time in the career of an active terrorist. Almost all of the suspects were well known members of the Provisional IRA but they had fallen to a variety of fates and were now scattered to the four winds. We also learned in that phase of the investigation that during his period of abduction Herr Niedermayer had been held in a small modern semi-detached house at Hillhead Crescent in the Andersonstown area of Belfast, only about one mile from his home. However, in relation to the events which befell Herr Niedermayer and led to his death we could find out little except that something had gone wrong with the operation, causing it to be prematurely terminated.

In every criminal investigation there comes a stage when one has to calculate the time to move. At the end of April 1980, some six weeks after the discovery of the body, we felt we had accumulated all the information that was possible. The next logical step was the arrest and interview of the prime suspects. Almost all of them who were still around lived at addresses in the Andersonstown area. At six o'clock on the morning of the operation I went to an army base in that area and briefed the police officers who were to make the necessary arrests and the soldiers who were to protect them from sniper attack. A forensic team was also on stand-by to examine the house at Hillhead Crescent, although there was little hope of finding any evidence after so many years. I should also say that the family who lived in it in 1973 had long since gone to another address. The people now in occupation were totally innocent and unaware of the dramatic events which we believed had occurred there.

Just as dawn was breaking at half past six a convoy of police and army vehicles quietly left the army base and fanned out to a number of different addresses. Altogether, the arrest operation netted only four suspects, two of whom I regarded as principals in the crime — fifty year old Eugene McManus, who in 1973 was adjutant of the Belfast Brigade of the Provisional IRA, and forty-two year old John Bradley who was traced as having held the rank of training officer with the first battalion of the Provisional IRA based at Andersonstown. The other two suspects were the wife of the household who had resided at the kidnap house in Hillhead Crescent and the owner of the car used by the kidnappers. Our enquiries to date led us to believe that these latter two were acting under a considerable amount of duress from the terrorists and this was borne out during the subsequent interviews.

The four prisoners were taken to Castlereagh Detention Centre where I thoroughly briefed the team of interviewers who had been allocated to me, mostly from the Belfast Regional and Headquarters Crime Squads. Within a short time the first 'breaks', as we referred to them, began to occur in the interviews with the female prisoner admitting that on Boxing day 1973, a number of men called at her home in Hillhead Crescent. She learned she would have to vacate their house for a few days. She complied and went to stay with her mother who also lived in the Andersonstown area. She did not get sanction to return to her home until 31 December, and when she did she found it generally untidy and heavy with the smell of stale cigarette smoke.

She had certainly become aware during that period that Herr

Niedermayer had been kidnapped and presumed her house had been used in the operation. In the days which followed the small front bedroom was completely redecorated and the door handles, bed and carpet were replaced. The neck tie which had been found with the remains of Herr Niedermayer, and which remained unidentified, was then shown to the woman. She said it looked familiar, thereby solving another aspect of the mystery. However, she did not recognise the woollen tights used to bind the lower legs of Herr Niedermayer. She told us that she was in total disagreement with the Provisional IRA and at that time had been acting under pressure from others.

The man whose car we believed had been hijacked to carry out the crime also began to tell the truth. He described how he had been in a drinking club in Andersonstown on the evening of 27 December 1973 when he was called outside to speak with men whom he presumed belonged to the Provisional IRA. They told him they wanted to borrow his Ford Cortina car and in the circumstances he was unable to put up any resistance. He gave them the keys and they drove off in it. The following day, when news of the Niedermayer kidnapping began to break, he realised his car had probably been used in the crime. The car was not returned to him, which would be the normal course of events, but instead he was forced to go searching for it and found it some days later abandoned in a side street in Andersonstown. He had long since sold the car but was able to remember its registration number. I was keen to locate it just to complete another part of the puzzle, even though it would not now reveal anything of evidential value.

McManus, who was no stranger to Castlereagh, proved a more difficult subject and he spent several hours denying any connection with the Provisional IRA. It hardly needs stating that anyone involved in the abduction and killing of Herr Niedermayer recognised it as a most serious crime. We gambled on the supposition that those who played a lesser part might wish to clarify their relatively minor role.

This approach eventually began to pay dividends with McManus and he conceded that at the time of the kidnapping he had indeed been the adjutant of the Belfast Brigade of the Provisional IRA.

McManus claimed that although he had held what appeared to be a responsible rank he was little more than a messenger for his commanding officer who required him to visit the battalion areas in Belfast each day and to report on the disposition of the volunteers available to carry out operations.

When it was put to him that he was therefore in a good position to know who had carried out the Niedermayer operation he denied that he was. He said his only knowledge of the crime came when his commanding officer and he were watching television some days after the event. A news item came on about the missing German and his commanding officer commented to him that Niedermayer had done a 'wobbler' and was now in a hole. McManus said he then recognised that the subject was sensitive and knew not to ask any more questions about it. The interviewers were not satisfied that McManus was telling the truth but during the whole of the first day's questioning he refused to budge from this position.

McManus obviously reflected on his situation overnight in his cell because his second day's questioning brought quite a different response. He admitted that he had been untruthful the previous day and stated that the Niedermayer 'job' had been sanctioned by the Provisional IRA at General Headquarters level in Dublin. McManus said he genuinely had been unaware of the plans to kidnap Herr Niedermayer and first heard about it on the news.

However, over that Christmas period in 1973 he was aware that a high ranking member of the Provisionals, attached to GHQ in Dublin, whom I shall only refer to as Mr A, and who was 'on the run' from the police and army, had come to Belfast to visit his children. Such a man would find it necessary to sleep at different addresses in order to avoid arrest and McManus had agreed to put him up for the night of 30 December, which was three days after the kidnapping.

McManus said he and Mr A were having a quiet drink together that evening when at around half past ten someone knocked on the front door. He answered it and the young man on the doorstep asked if Mr A was in the house. McManus said he remained non-committal initially but Mr A obviously recognised the voice and appeared in the hallway. Mr A and the caller conversed out of hearing of McManus and Mr A then grabbed his coat, saying he would be back later.

At around one o'clock the next morning, Mr A returned in a somewhat agitated state and confided in him that the Provisional IRA had kidnapped Niedermayer in exchange for the Price sisters but that things had gone wrong. Mr A went on to explain to him that Niedermayer had panicked and had to be subdued by the men guarding him. They had knocked him out and the caller at the house earlier on had been one of the guards who had come to notify him of this unexpected turn of events. Mr A said he had since examined Niedermayer and found him to be dead. According to McManus Mr A said 'What a fuck up' and was obviously worried about how he would explain it to the other members of GHQ. Mr A then bedded down on the settee for the night but had gone by the time McManus arose at eight o'clock.

McManus said he then went and spoke with his commanding officer who was apparently up-to-date with the events. The officer gave him instructions to pass a message on to the kidnappers that they were to have the house at Hillhead Crescent cleaned up. When the message was relayed word came back that they would need the sum of two hundred pounds to do the job properly as a room needed to be fully re-decorated and a bed replaced. McManus acquired the money, presumably from the battalion finance officer, and passed it on to the kidnappers. Some days later he received confirmation that the clean-up work had been completed. This tied in neatly with the information supplied to us during the interview by the woman who resided in the house at the time.

The whole Niedermayer affair, which would have been a masterstroke for the Provisional IRA had they succeeded in forcing the British government to move the Price sisters to a prison in Northern Ireland, had now turned into a major embarrassment. Orders were issued to the limited number of people who knew something of the crime that there was to be no discussion whatsoever about it from that point onwards.

McManus admitted that some weeks later his commanding officer instructed him to act as a guide to a German journalist who had come to Belfast to follow up the Niedermayer story. He was to ensure that the journalist spoke only with members of the organisation who knew nothing of the crime, thereby making it genuinely appear that the Provisional IRA had had no hand in it.

Overall, the account of events as given by McManus seemed reasonably credible. It certainly helped provide answers as to why negotiations between the Provisional IRA and 10 Downing Street had suddenly ceased and why they had not claimed responsibility for the kidnapping at the time.

However, much of the detail of what had taken place during the three days that Herr Niedermayer was held at Hillhead Crescent was still missing and I knew that Bradley held the answers. During his first morning's interview at Castlereagh he seemed quite nervous and stammered out unconvincing denials to the two detectives who were questioning him.

On the afternoon of that day, accompanied by a colleague, I spoke with Bradley, who was a short, burly, dark haired man. I could see that he was distinctly uncomfortable and that something was weighing heavily on his mind. I suggested to him on a number of occasions that he had been involved in the imprisonment of Niedermayer and his subsequent burial. Bradley just stared at me and I sensed he was sizing me up to see if I could be trusted to deal with him fairly. When he eventually broke his silence he invited us to get on with beating him up. I told him that such a statement was unworthy of an answer.

We then changed the subject and asked him about his family and background. He said he had not worked since 1970, but that he had four children and had once served with the RAF in Aden. McManus also had a background of service with the RAF.

The subject of Niedermayer was raised by us again and Bradley lowered his head into his hands for a few minutes. He then looked at us and said he was confused. We assured him we were not alleging that he was the prime mover in the crime but that in reality he had been used by much more sinister and evil men. At this Bradley began to wring his hands and it was apparent that his mind was in turmoil.

He then asked us where he should start and we simply told him to tell us his story from the beginning. After a short pause he said we must understand he had not been one of the men who had gone to Niedermayer's house to carry out the kidnapping but had been later brought in to guard him at the house in Hillhead Crescent. He arrived at the house during the late evening of the day of the kidnapping and joined three other men who were already there. The house was kept in almost total darkness, with only a dull table lamp burning in the front downstairs lounge. He had not fully understood the nature of the operation until he arrived at the house and the other men explained to him that they were holding a foreign Consul or diplomat upstairs whom they hoped to exchange for the Price sisters.

Bradley said he spent the first hour in the dimly-lit lounge and at the request of one of the other men he went upstairs to the small front bedroom where he saw Niedermayer lying on a mattress on the floor. The small window in this room which overlooked the street was covered with a venetian blind and the only light came from the bars of a small electric fire. One of the other three men was guarding Niedermayer and Bradley took over from him. According to Bradley, Niedermayer was calm at this stage and tried to talk to him but he had been given instructions not to respond to these attempts.

Looking back on this now, Niedermayer may have been trying to build relationships with the kidnappers so that it would make it more difficult for them to harm him. This approach is now known as 'Stockholm Syndrome' and was first recognised during a lengthy bank siege in that city several years earlier. It arose when a number of armed and dangerous criminals tried to rob a bank but became trapped when the police were alerted. They retreated to the strong rooms taking with them several members of staff as hostages. The siege wore on into weeks and it gradually became clear during negotiations between the police and those under siege that some of the staff, as they got to know their kidnappers, had begun to identify with them. Towards the end they were more on the side of the robbers than of the police. It also became clear from that situation that as time dragged on the kidnappers would have found it extremely difficult to harm the staff. From this, the psychology of a kidnap situation was looked at in a completely different light.

Bradley remained with Niedermayer for about an hour and a half and was then relieved by one of the other kidnappers. On some occasions, for no explicable reason, two men would guard Niedermayer and those not 'on duty' would relax in the downstairs lounge or snatch a few hours sleep in one of the larger bedrooms next to Niedermayer's. A woman brought fresh food to the house and this pattern continued uneventfully for two days, but in the outside world the kidnapping was grabbing the world's headlines.

According to Bradley, things started to go wrong on the third day. Niedermayer began to display the first signs of the enormous stress he was under when he became restless and irritable. Although he certainly had no idea of the precise location of where he was being held he knew that it was but a short car journey from his home. Obviously in such circumstances he would have expected to have been rescued rather quickly by the police or army. Looking back at the events this may seem to be an entirely reasonable expectation. However, one must remember that although only a mile from his home, Niedermayer was in a densely populated area where most of the residents were hostile to the security forces. To search every house or building in West Belfast would have required regiments of troops and large numbers of police. Furthermore, the resentment created would have caused widespread civil disorder.

As the third day progressed into the evening period Bradley was resting in one of the bedrooms when he heard a commotion on the landing outside. He jumped up to investigate and found the three other kidnappers trying to restrain Niedermayer. The victim apparently had asked to go to the toilet but when he got to the landing had made a dash for the stairs in a vain attempt to escape. All four kidnappers tried to drag him back into the small bedroom but Niedermayer clung onto the banisters. He was persuaded to let go and return to his room but remained highly agitated with thoughts of escape still obviously foremost in his mind.

Suddenly, Niedermayer made a grab for the small window covered with the venetian blind and began to scream for help. Once again the four kidnappers managed to drag him back. They implored him to be quiet but he continued to shout for help. The gang was now in a real predicament and realised it was a grave mistake having him in the middle of a built-up area.

The situation continued to deteriorate, with Niedermayer becoming increasingly irrational and hysterical. The four men dragged him down onto the mattress and tried to gag him, probably with the neck tie found with the body although Bradley, with the confusion of the situation, was unclear on this point. The victim was still flailing his arms and legs so they held him face down on the mattress and tied his legs with a pair of tights and his arms behind his back with a belt. However, he still managed to scream and struggle and his kidnappers were now becoming desperate. One of the men then produced an automatic pistol and crashed the butt of it on Niedermayer's head a number of times in an effort to knock him out. But this did not have an immediate effect. The four men then lay across Niedermayer and Bradley claimed he used him weight to restrain his bound legs while one of the others shoved his face down into the mattress. Gradually he went limp. A few minutes went by and one of the gang announced that he was now dead.

This unexpected and unwelcome turn of events left the gang confused as to what they should do next. One of them left the house to seek instructions and this was probably the man who called to speak urgently with Mr A at McManus's house. Eventually he arrived back at the house followed shortly afterwards by two other men, presumably Mr A and the local commanding officer.

The gang was given instructions to secretly dispose of the body and to clean the house. They decided to let the body remain where it was until the following night in order to give themselves time to find a safe method of getting rid of it. The following evening three of them went out in a car and drove to Colin Glen. They stopped at an old dump at the left side of the road and in the darkness explored a level area down among some trees. They had with them spades and a shovel and Bradley and one other man stayed to dig a grave while the third man went away to collect the body from the house in Hillhead Crescent.

Bradley stated that he and his accomplice dug a hole about three feet deep but then came upon an area of rock. The two remaining kidnappers returned with the body after an agreed period of two hours. Niedermayer was in the boot and they lifted him out, dragged him down a slope to the freshly dug grave, and placed him in it, face down. Before filling it in with the excavated soil the four said a prayer over it and Niedermayer was covered up. In order to conceal the freshly dug soil they found an old mattress in the nearby rubbish and pulled it over the top of the grave.

All four returned in the car to Hillhead Crescent where they tidied up the house by removing the mattress and other items and placing them in the car. Bradley said he was then told he could go home as he was finished with the operation. He walked the few miles to his own home. When asked by us how he felt at that point he said he was completely drained and was glad to get home. He pointed out that there never had been any intention to hurt Niedermayer but events, as they turned out, dictated otherwise.

When asked how he felt about the whole affair Bradley said he had been swept up in the troubles like so many others and felt the death of Niedermayer was a silly but terrible disaster. Each time it was mentioned on the news down through the years he made a point of leaving the room rather than listen to it but for the sake of Mrs Niedermayer he was glad that the body had now been found.

Although Bradley declined to name any of his accomplices I knew that essentially he was telling the truth. We had not given him any details of the crime but he had mentioned a number of quite significant matters which only someone involved in the incident could have known. For example, the binding of the arms and the tying together of the legs with the pair of tights, the possible gagging with the neck tie and the blows to the head from the butt of an automatic pistol all matched perfectly with the established scientific facts. Also, the location of the grave, the burial of the body face downwards and the clean-up and evacuation of the house at Hillhead Crescent four days after the commencement of the crime all tied in perfectly.

As the interviews continued with McManus, Bradley and the people who had owned the house and car back in 1973, the forensic science team was completing its inch-by-inch search of the small bedroom at Hillhead Crescent. Not surprisingly, after seven years, nothing of interest was found. I called at the house while the team was still working there and found it compelling to be standing in the room where those dramatic, and for a long time, mysterious events had occurred so many years earlier. In due course we traced the car used by the gang to a barn at a farmyard in Dungannon, County Tyrone, about fifty miles from Belfast. It had now been reduced to a shell but still helped quench my insatiable desire to know and see everything about the crime.

McManus and Bradley were both charged with the false imprisonment and murder of Herr Niedermayer, and with membership of the Provisional IRA. Both men appeared at Belfast Magistrates Court and were remanded in custody pending the preparation of papers for the Director of Public Prosecutions. These I submitted within about six weeks. The DPP directed that the murder charge should stand against Bradley alone and altered McManus's charges to those of withholding information about the crime, impeding the arrest of those involved, and membership of the Provisional IRA. The DPP agreed with my views that no charges be brought against the woman who lived at the kidnap house in Hillhead Crescent. He also declined to prosecute the owner of the hijacked car, acknowledging the fear which terrorists instil in people.

As the months went by a number of others involved in the crime, who had gone to ground when the body was discovered, were located and arrested. They declined to admit their complicity in the abduction and killing and consequently had to be released. Mr A was detained in Northern Ireland but the London Metropolitan Police were seeking his arrest on charges of conspiring to cause explosions within Great Britain. He was flown to England and at his trial on these charges he received a sentence of eighteen years imprisonment. In due course I accompanied a senior RUC detective to Brixton Prison to speak to him about the Niedermayer case. As expected he declined to speak and merely sat staring at us with venomous eyes.

The case against McManus and Bradley came to trial in February 1981. In the days leading up to it I was anxious to see what way it would run and whether or not they would contest the admissibility of their admissions which was the only possible defence open to them. A few days before the trial was due to commence I got the first indication when their defence counsel Mr Richard Ferguson QC, one of Northern Ireland's most eminent and respected barristers, asked for the court to be convened as he wished to make an application. The case was due to be heard in the court of Lord Justice Jones, a very senior member of the Northern Ireland judiciary who had once been a Kings Counsel and a Unionist member of Parliament. He had a fearsome reputation as a man with uncompromising views on right and wrong and was acknowledged as a judge who did not shrink from the duty of handing down stiff prison sentences in appropriate cases. Lest anyone should think that with his Unionist background he reserved this only for republican cases it should be noted that around this same period he sentenced some members of a loyalist terrorist gang to thirty-five years imprisonment for their involvement in the murders of members of a Roman Catholic showband who were ambushed on a lonely country road and gunned and blown to death.

During the application Mr Ferguson informed the court that he would not be available for all of the McManus and Bradley trial the following week as he was due to make a submission on a point of law to the House of Lords concerning another case. He asked Lord Justice Jones to move the Niedermayer case to a later date. Lord Justice Jones declined the application and ordered that the trial should commence the following Monday.

On that day McManus and Bradley returned to the dock of Belfast Crown Court but, acknowledging the fact that the gang had not set out to kill Herr Niedermayer, the Crown Court accepted a plea of guilty to manslaughter from Bradley. He also pleaded guilty to a number of ancillary offences and McManus pleaded guilty to withholding information and membership of the Provisional IRA. They received the severe dressing down expected from Lord Justice Jones and were respectively sentenced to twenty years and five years imprisonment.

The case was to claim yet one more victim when some years after the discovery of her husband's remains Ingeborg Niedermayer booked into a hotel in a seaside resort in southern Ireland. She went for a stroll along a deserted beach but suddenly turned in the direction of the sea and walked steadily into the crashing waves which rapidly engulfed her. Some hours later, her body was recovered.

6

INVESTIGATING OUR OWN

As soon as I had submitted the case papers to the DPP on the Niedermayer investigation, around May 1980, and nine months or so before the trial of McManus and Bradley, I was transferred from the Belfast Regional Crime Squad back to Headquarters Crime Squad, or A Squad as it had originally been known. I was sad to leave behind the many fine colleagues I had worked with in the Belfast Squad but I was excited and pleased at the prospect of getting back to my old friends. However, I would not be working solely with number five team but would have overall responsibility for three investigative units.

The work of Headquarters Crime Squad was perhaps more varied as they had a Province-wide remit. A few weeks after taking up my new post I was called into the office of the detective chief superintendent who was head of the operational CID. He asked me to take on an investigation which eventually led to widespread repercussions for the RUC and took a heavy toll on several fellow police officers. This was to be one of the most demanding cases of my whole career.

The crime he asked me to look at was the murder of forty-eight years old RUC Sergeant Patrick Joseph Campbell who had been gunned down at the entrance gates to Cushendall RUC station, County Antrim on the evening of Friday, 25 February 1977. At this early stage in the story I should explain that the reason the crime caused such ripples was that at the end of the investigation I charged Special Branch Detective Sergeant Charles McCormick and his terrorist informer, Anthony O'Doherty, with offences related to the murder.

It was believed that the motive for the killing was that Sergeant Campbell had uncovered evidence to connect McCormick and O'Doherty with a series of crimes such as bank robberies and they had felt the need to silence him as a desperate act of self-preservation. They carried it out in such a manner as to make it look like an ordinary terrorist killing of a policeman. At their trials McCormick was acquitted of the murder owing to lack of sufficient evidence but, on his plea of 'guilty', O'Doherty was sentenced to a term of imprisonment for withholding information about the murder and for possession of firearms.

The town of Cushendall where the murder took place is a small seaside resort, with a population of around one thousand, situated on the scenic eastern coast of County Antrim and about fifty miles from Belfast. It is famed for its rolling glens. The local people speak with a hint of a Scottish accent which is not surprising as Scotland lies only about twenty miles away across the North Channel. Indeed, on a clear day the Scottish coastline is plainly visible and it is even possible to pick out white-washed cottages on this distant landscape across the Channel.

The population of the area is mainly Roman Catholic. Many of the people live by fishing or hill sheep-farming while others travel for employment to some of the larger towns further inland. The people would therefore be regarded as nationalist in their political outlook with mild aspirations for a united Ireland, but much to their credit they have not pursued this by means of the bomb and bullet.

The police have always been well accepted in these Glens and small villages. This is due in no small part to the work of Sergeant Campbell, who was himself a Roman Catholic, in charge of the small party of constables based at Cushendall and in turn answerable to divisional headquarters at Ballymena some twenty miles away across a range of low forest-covered hills. He lived with his wife and children about five minutes walk from the station. His philosophy on policing was that he was there simply to serve the community. This he did superbly. His everyday work was therefore dedicated to resolving their problems, guiding those who were perhaps straying off the path of order and decency, and acting as confidante in times of need. It is no exaggeration to say that he was the most respected figure in the area in which he served and also among his colleagues. Although still a serving police officer he had some years earlier suffered a mild stroke and therefore did not enjoy the best of health.

As a consequence of the state of law and order which existed in the community of the Glens, there really was little demand for the services of the police. Cushendall station was open only for limited hours between nine and eleven o'clock in the mornings and seven to nine o'clock in the evenings. However, a permanent mobile patrol was available. Callers requiring the urgent services of the police, perhaps for a road traffic accident, could dial '999' and speak to the control room in Ballymena, which in turn would contact the local patrol car by radio and dispatch it to the scene. Also, persons calling at the station outside the limited opening hours could use a free-phone at the front gates and speak directly to staff in the Ballymena control room. If their need was urgent the mobile patrol car would return to the station to assist them.

Ironically, on the Friday that Sergeant Campbell met his death he was having a day off but at around half past eight in the evening he decided to call into the station. The reason for his doing this was never satisfactorily resolved but we did learn that he had received two mysterious phone calls at home, one of which may have been from someone making an arrangement to see him at the station. Or he may have simply decided to look in on the lone constable who was on desk duty and due to finish at nine o'clock. This would not have been unusual in a small, rural station. Prior to leaving home a member of the family noted that he was oddly irritable. His wife had noticed him becoming somewhat moody in recent weeks. This was a departure from his quietly confident amiable self. One of his closest colleagues too had noticed a change in him and he had recently begun to carry his official-issue pistol which was not in keeping with his normal attitude to policing.

The station is located on a steep, narrow roadway known as Barrack Hill off the main street in Cushendall, surrounded by detached houses and bungalows. If one continues up past the station the road eventually peters out into a narrow country by-way known as Knockans Lane which rises steadily into open, hilly countryside. Every police station in Northern Ireland is vulnerable to terrorist attack and Cushendall was no exception. Consequently it was protected by a high wall and security fence. Vehicular access was through two large solid metal gates.

On arrival at the station that evening Sergeant Campbell, who was in civilian clothes, exchanged a few pleasantries with the constable on duty and browsed through the routine correspondence which had arrived that day. At nine o'clock Sergeant Campbell and the constable began to close down the station by switching out the lights and locking the offices. The Constable had his car parked in the station yard and Sergeant Campbell obliged him by opening the two metal gates to allow him to drive out onto Barrack Hill. On his way through the gates the constable paused briefly with the sergeant and they bade each other good night. The constable then drove off in the direction of Ballymena. Sergeant Campbell had just closed and locked the gates from the outside when there was a loud crack and he fell, wounded in the head from a single high velocity rifle bullet. A number of local people heard the shot and ran to the station where they found Sergeant Campbell lying against the gatepost. He was still alive but was bleeding profusely from the wound which appeared to be to his right temple. The people made him as comfortable as possible and summoned another policeman and a doctor, both of whom lived locally. An ambulance was sent for but it had some distance to come from Ballymena. In the meantime the doctor arranged for Sergeant Campbell to be carried into the station where he rendered what assistance he could with the help of a nursing sister and a nun who also lived nearby. A short time later the constable who had left the station at nine o'clock arrived back. He had a police hand radio in his car and when he was but a few miles outside Cushendall, on his way to Ballymena, he heard transmissions about the serious incident at the gates to the station.

The ambulance duly arrived and Sergeant Campbell, who was still breathing, was admitted to the casualty unit of the Waveney

Hospital in Ballymena where, despite the efforts of a consultant surgeon, he died a few minutes later.

Meanwhile back at Cushendall the scene of the murder was sealed off to preserve it as intact as possible for examination. A forensic science ballistics expert was brought to the station and he found a bullet hole in the gate at about average head height. Some blood was found adhering to the hole and on the roadway just below it. A strike mark was identified on a rough cast wall in the station yard and there was evidence that the bullet head had fragmented on impact with the surface. No spent cartridge case could be found in any potential firing points, but when the forensic expert lined up the strike mark on the wall with the bullet hole in the gate he established that the gunman had been in the area of an entrance to a bungalow some short distance up and across the road from the police station. At the time of the shooting the gunman would have been in darkness but Sergeant Campbell's figure would have been clearly illuminated by the security lights of the station. The scene was photographed in detail and the forensic scientist had the station yard carefully swept in the hope that this would bring together some pieces of the fragmented bullet head, but when this debris was later carefully examined back at the laboratory nothing of significance was found.

The scene was kept intact until daylight. Once again experts carefully examined every inch of ground in the hope of finding the spent bullet case or parts of the bullet head, but without success.

The state pathologist for Northern Ireland, Professor Marshall, personally carried out the required post-mortem examination of Sergeant Campbell and the forensic science ballistics expert also assisted. They concluded that the deceased had died from massive head injuries caused by a high velocity bullet passing through the head from left to right and that the injury to his right temple noted by those who assisted him at the scene was actually the exit wound.

The CID set up a major incident room within Cushendall RUC station and began to investigate what seemed to be yet another senseless killing by one of the republican paramilitary groups who were active throughout other parts of County Antrim and elsewhere in the Province. No group claimed responsibility for the murder. At the time the detectives did not find this surprising as the killing caused unexpected shock-waves throughout the local community, who, like most other people in Northern Ireland had become used to reports of terrorist violence and were now somewhat anaesthetised to its effects.

His wife and family were obviously devastated by the loss of such a dedicated husband and father and some days later multitudes of people attended requiem mass in the local chapel after which Sergeant Campbell was buried in the graveyard outside.

The investigation team spoke to practically every inhabitant of Cushendall in the hope that some light could be shed on the murder but nothing was learned which could lead to the identification of the killers. A few known Provisional IRA sympathisers lived in the area. They were arrested and interviewed but their alibis checked out and they were released from custody. After a period of some weeks every possible avenue of enquiry had been explored and the investigation was wound down pending any new information which might come to light.

I was chosen to re-open the investigation because I had been involved with an intriguing enquiry in September 1977 during my last period of service with Headquarters Crime Squad, and this now seemed to have some relevance to the murder of Sergeant Campbell. The circumstances are quite complex and began when my number five unit assisted in the investigation into yet another crime involving a German businessman. The businessman was Herr Jurgen Gradel who was the manager of a local German-owned factory. He lived in a comfortable modern house in the suburbs of Ballymena and coincidentally he had succeeded to the post of Honorary West German Consul following the disappearance of Herr Niedermayer. In mid-September 1977 he was having a quiet evening at home with his wife when suddenly two armed and masked intruders appeared in his hallway. A scuffle ensued during which one of the intruders accidentally discharged a single shot from his sub-machine gun into the ceiling. This caused the raiders to panic and flee. A follow-up search by police located a car near the house. It contained various items which indicated that the incident had been an attempt to kidnap Herr Gradel. The raiders had obviously failed to reach the car but instead escaped across open fields. A search the following day uncovered two sub-machine guns hidden in a ditch. They were obviously to be collected when the 'heat' died down. It was later established that the crime had been committed by members of the Irish National Liberation Army (INLA) and that they had intended to hold Herr Gradel for a financial ransom.

In a follow-up operation the CID detained a number of INLA suspects and brought them to Castlereagh for interview. Among them was twenty-eight years old Anthony O'Doherty, a member of a well known republican family residing near the town of Portglenone in County Antrim. At this point in the investigation into the attempted kidnapping of Herr Gradel, I and other members of my unit learned that Anthony O'Doherty was an informant to Detective Sergeant Charles McCormick who was attached to the small unit of Special Branch based at Ballymena RUC station. The function of Special Branch is to penetrate subversive paramilitary organisations who pose a threat to the state and to learn of their current activities and future intentions. Detective Sergeant McCormick had managed to cultivate Anthony O'Doherty as an informant in the early 1970s. O'Doherty was then on the fringes of the official Irish Republican Army and later its splinter-group, the INLA. Information received from O'Doherty was reported by McCormick through official channels to RUC headquarters but in the interests of security he was never referred to by name as the source of information. He was allocated the code 'Agent 294'.

My unit was detailed to question O'Doherty at length, to establish if he had had a key role in the affair. But as the investigation progressed the identities of the principals became known to us. It was clear that they had since fled to the Republic of Ireland and that O'Doherty had not played a significant role.

Although this was the first occasion I had met O'Doherty his name was not new to me as it had been mentioned on occasions by one of my colleagues in my A Squad unit. This colleague is a most astute detective who had served in the local CID in Ballymena prior to the inception of the squad, of which he was a founder member. We had worked together on the investigation into the murder of Yvonne

Dunlop who was killed in the Ballymena bombings. Detective Sergeant Charles McCormick was present at the initial briefing concerning that atrocity. As the Yvonne Dunlop investigation progressed I met Detective Sergeant McCormick on a number of occasions and he always presented an affable, perhaps over-friendly, image.

At that time my close colleague confided in me that during his time with the CID in Ballymena he and a small number of other experienced policemen, including some special branch officers, suspected McCormick of involvement in crimes, particularly bank robberies in Cushendall, along with his informant O'Doherty. I was also told that there was some basis for these suspicions: nylon stocking masks had been discovered in a van which the Special Branch used for undercover work, and the van had been observed in suspicious circumstances. Altogether, it seemed that the real McCormick was somewhat different from the image of the friendly, efficient police officer he was now portraying to us. The officers who harboured these suspicions had voiced them to more senior ranks within the force. However, in the absence of cogent evidence these serious allegations were treated with a good deal of incredulity and McCormick was allowed to remain in his post.

Three robberies had occurred at the Northern Bank in Cushendall. The first of these was on the morning of Monday, 25 November 1974. A number of male members of staff were working behind the counter of the bank when suddenly a man wearing a nylon face mask and carrying a pistol appeared among the customers in the public area of the premises. The gunman pushed aside the customers. He then passed a white cloth bag into the counter well and ordered that it be filled with cash. The robber was interrupted by the entrance of a woman to the bank. He pushed her towards the other customers but she protested that her baby was in a pram outside. She was allowed to collect the child and join the others who were huddled together under the watchful eye of the robber. The staff had by now filled the bag with all of the available cash. This amounted to just over £3000. The robber grabbed it and quickly left by the front door, pulling off his mask as he did so.

About fifteen minutes later a masked gunman walked into a post office in the village of Knocknacarry, some three miles further along the coast from Cushendall. The elderly post mistress was ordered to hand over all her available cash, and the gunman left with £145. The timing of these two crimes, the description of the gunman and the rare occurrence of robberies in the Glens left little doubt that they had been carried out by the same man.

The scenes of both crimes were attended by detectives from the CID in Ballymena. At around half past four in the afternoon they found a green coloured Mini car abandoned at Craigagh Wood on the main road between Cushendall and Ballycastle, about two miles from Knocknacarry. They transmitted the registration number of the car to the control room at Ballymena. It was discovered that the Mini had been hijacked the previous evening at Lisnahunshin Road, about eight miles on the opposite side of Ballymena from Cushendall, by a lone masked gunman carrying a torch. The driver of the Mini, upon seeing a figure in the middle of this lonely country road waving a torch, presumed he had come upon a proper police or army vehicle checkpoint. A vehicle was already stopped at the 'checkpoint' but had driven off just as his passenger's door was opened and a masked figure, carrying a rifle, appeared and said, 'I want this car.' The driver surrendered it to the gunman who immediately drove off in it. He then thumbed a lift into Ballymena where he reported the hijacking to the police only to find that the driver of the car in front of him at the 'checkpoint', a woman, had also called at the station. An attempt had been made to hijack her car but the gunman gave up when he tried unsuccessfully to start her vehicle with the ignition key. Her car was actually an older model with a push button starter on the floor between the two front seats.

The two detectives continued with their enquiries into the robberies. By a quarter past six in the evening they had accomplished what they could at that stage and were travelling on the main road between Cushendall and Ballymena. As they passed through the village of Cargan, which lies about one third of the way from Cushendall, they saw the Ballymena Special Branch van going in the opposite direction towards the Glens.

The second robbery at the same bank took place about six months later at noon on 7 May 1975. On this occasion a man wearing sunglasses and carrying a handgun and what appeared to be a grenade appeared in the bank. He pushed a floral pillowcase into the counter well and ordered the staff to 'fill it up'. The staff on this occasion hesitated and tried to satisfy him by placing in the pillowcase only the bank notes which were visible. The gunman caught on to this and menacingly growled, 'There's more than that. What about the back?', an apparent reference to the contents of the walk-in strongroom. The staff were now very frightened. They assembled all the money in the bank and placed it in the pillowcase. The gunman grabbed it and went towards the door of the bank. There he met a woman customer on her way in. He grabbed her by the shoulder and ordered her to lie on the floor, shouting, 'If you move you'll be shot.' On this occasion the bank again lost just over £3000. The staff were uncertain as to whether this was the same man who had robbed them previously.

At around this time the local Church of Ireland clergyman was leaving his rectory at High Street, a steep hill leading up from the direction of the bank. He noticed the figure of a lone man carrying a pillowcase coming towards him. As they passed they exchanged pleasantries about the weather. The lone man got into a Ford Escort car parked on the hill and attempted to start it. It refused and the man got out of it and began to tinker under the bonnet. Meanwhile, the clergyman had by now been joined by his wife. They got into their own car and headed off towards Ballymena to conduct some private business.

The following morning the clergyman noticed the Escort car in the same position and decided to contact the police at Cushendall station about it. Sergeant Campbell responded to the call. He checked out the car against the current stolen car list and found that it had been taken the previous day from an isolated crossroads. It had been left by a young woman who parked it at that spot every day while a workers' bus took her the rest of the way to Gallaghers Tobacco Factory in Ballymena. There seemed little doubt that this had been the robber's getaway car but that he had abandoned it when it failed to start.

The bank was robbed yet again, this time on the early afternoon on 18 November 1975, thus establishing a pattern of crimes at intervals of approximately six months. On this occasion, however, two masked men entered the premises. One of them was armed with a sub-machine gun and he stood guard by the front door while the second one, armed with a handgun, approached the counter, pushed a plastic bag into the counter well and ordered the staff to 'fill it up'. Once again the staff, although by now thoroughly fed-up with these repeated raids, kept their cool and tried to deceive him into accepting only the cash that was visible in the counter area. But the gunman demanded that they also include the money from the strongroom. All of the available cash, which amounted to just over £2500, was then put into the plastic bag and passed to the gunman. The two raiders fled into the street but no one saw how they made their getaway. It was presumed they did so by car.

The police responded to the robbery by closely interviewing all the members of the bank staff and by carrying out a search of the surrounding roads in an effort to find an abandoned car which could have been used in the crime. They eventually found a Ford Cortina car parked in an unusual manner in a quiet laneway off Gaults Road some three miles from Cushendall. The front number plate had been pulled off but the rear plate was in position and a check with the control room revealed it had been stolen at half past six on the morning of the robbery from the car park of the giant Michelin tyre factory. It therefore seemed highly probable that this was the car used by the two robbers.

Now, in September 1977, O'Doherty was in Castlereagh Detention Centre. He had been to some degree absolved from full complicity in the crime against Herr Gradel. However, we decided to take advantage of his position and probe him about his relationship with McCormick, in an effort to clear up the suspicions about their alleged involvement in these crimes.

It had become abundantly clear during our interviews with O'Doherty over the previous days that he was a wily and cunning character who would be difficult to corner by questioning. We did however notice one weakness in his defences. He liked to be regarded as something of an adventurer and to regale us with tales of his exploits as a Special Branch informant. There was a definite twinkle in his roguish eyes as he tried to persuade us that in this dangerous role he constantly lived on a knife edge between life and death.

We played along with O'Doherty on this theme for several hours and after some initial verbal and mental fencing we gradually introduced the subject of the robberies at the bank in Cushendall. He grinned smugly at their mention and certainly did not dismiss them out of hand. We knew then that we were in business with him. As the minutes wore on it became increasingly clear that he was rather proud of how he had pulled off these crimes and was pleased that we credited him with such daring exploits.

However, he was not so proud that he was prepared to go to prison for them and steered well clear of anything which could be interpreted as a direct admission. Instead, he chose to speak in the third person by saying, for example, 'I know two persons who carried out a series of robberies at the Northern Bank in Cushendall. They were carried out because one of these persons was in deep financial trouble. This person received the bulk of the proceeds. He faced losing his job because he could have gone to prison for failing to keep up maintenance payments to his wife from whom he was separated. Also he had a large mortgage to meet. It was pure distress on his part. On occasions he sobbed about his financial troubles. I know that on occasions between £3000 and £4000 was taken in the robberies. I know also that in one of the crimes the main recipient of the proceeds took the local military intelligence officer away on a day's fishing, as he was the only person who could give authority for an army helicopter to carry out aerial searches in the area.'

This is but a small sample of what O'Doherty related to us. He left us in no doubt that he was speaking of McCormick and himself and that the suspicions held by my close colleague and other officers in Ballymena were based on a solid foundation. A major problem lay just below the surface.

O'Doherty had now been in police detention for seven days. This was the maximum period we could hold him and it was apparent that he was not prepared to go a stage further and make direct admissions to the robberies. As a result he was released from custody. We related what we had learned to our senior CID officers at RUC headquarters who asked us to prepare a full written report outlining the evidence and suspicions to that point. This was compiled without delay and went as far as the Chief Constable, Sir Kenneth Newman, who ordered that the matter be passed to the Police Complaints and Discipline Branch for investigation. A superintendent and a chief inspector were nominated to take on the case. They began by contacting O'Doherty and arranging to meet him. O'Doherty turned up on time but of course he had by now had an opportunity to speak with McCormick and tell him of our suspicions. Consequently, they had time to consolidate their positions. When questioned by the two officers from Complaints and Discipline, O'Doherty claimed that during his period of detention at Castlereagh we had pressurised him into making these false semi-confessions and that he now wished to retract them. The investigation file was then returned to RUC headquarters where it was set aside pending any new developments.

I personally took little further interest in the affair and in any event I was fully occupied with the other investigations I have referred to in this book. However, the officers in Ballymena who held the suspicions about McCormick, remained far from satisfied and still felt sure that they had a rotten apple in their midst. It also became something of an embarrassment to them as the rumours of McCormick's suspected involvement in the robberies were widespread within the station. Not only were McCormick's immediate Special Branch colleagues concerned about the robberies but some of them very shrewdly deduced that he may have had a hand in the murder of Sergeant Campbell.

Also, they had the advantage of studying and analysing all of the intelligence gathered from the local paramilitary groups, both republican and loyalist, and there was a distinct absence of information concerning the murder of Sergeant Campbell. This was highly unusual. The feelings of deep concern among these officers were now beginning to be felt at headquarters level. They reached such a pitch that by mid-1980 my detective chief superintendent was asking me to re-open the Sergeant Campbell murder investigation, with a view to allaying the concerns of the force. I shared the opinion of my senior CID officers that McCormick and O'Doherty committed the robberies at the bank, but I felt that it was too preposterous to contemplate them as the murderers of Sergeant Campbell.

It was with this attitude that I set off with my team to commence the investigation. As with every such enquiry I felt the need to read, see and touch everything concerned with it to gain the whole picture of the events. I wanted to be able to piece together those matters which seemed relevant and to set aside those issues which had no apparent connection with the case.

Consequently, during the first week of the enquiry we read all of the witness statements in the case, spoke to those people who seemed to hold the most important evidence concerning the timing of events, consulted Sergeant Campbell's closest colleagues in the station, and conferred with the forensic scientist who had examined the scene and attended the post-mortem examination. We studied the police photographs and maps prepared at the time and familiarised ourselves with the geography of the area around the station and the roads and by-ways of the surrounding countryside.

The first thing to strike us was that if any of the republican paramilitary groups wished to attack the police in Cushendall they could have mounted a more spectacular attack by luring the local patrol car into an ambush, probably killing several policemen by means of a concerted gun attack or by a large landmine. Sadly, some years after the murder of Sergeant Campbell such an event occurred when terrorists blew up the local patrol car, killing two officers on the outskirts of Cushendall.

Also, we felt it quite significant that Sergeant Campbell should have been shot seconds after he had closed the gates of the station, having just paused to say goodnight to the departing constable. Any of the terrorists engaged in such attacks would have found it an opportunity to kill two police officers instead of one. Or could it be the case that the gunman had just arrived at his firing position in the few seconds that Sergeant Campbell stood alone at the gates after the constable had driven off? Not impossible but highly unlikely.

Then there was the distinct absence of a spent cartridge case at the scene. This was a most unusual occurrence. We asked for details of all shooting attacks carried out by terrorists in the areas of County Antrim and County Londonderry during the preceding three years. This is the hinterland of Cushendall and was plagued with the scourge of terrorism, evidenced by the list of some one hundred and fifty shooting attacks which came back to us for analysis. On almost every occasion, with the exception of three attacks on Portglenone police station, and an attack on a part-time policeman at his home in the same general area, spent shells had been left at the scenes. It was apparent that whoever had shot Sergeant Campbell was keen that no ballistic evidence should be found. In addition, house-to-house enquiries at the time of the killing had failed to uncover evidence of a getaway car. This point was reinforced by local people who had heard the fatal rifle shot but had not heard the banging of car doors or the sound of a vehicle moving off afterwards.

Altogether, the events surrounding the murder were certainly out of the ordinary and I began to have distinct feelings of unease that whoever had fired the fatal shot had intended it for Sergeant Campbell and Sergeant Campbell only. However, I was determined to keep an open mind on the case and I sat down with my team of detectives to decide where we should go from there. We came to the conclusion that perhaps the views of McCormick's colleagues were not so preposterous after all and that the murder was linked to the bank robberies. Certainly Sergeant Campbell would have considered these crimes an affront to his policing of the Glens. If we were now reasonably certain the robberies had been carried out by McCormick and O'Doherty, then one could be sure that Sergeant Campbell, who was a clever and shrewd individual, would also be onto them.

Consequently, we decided that the best way forward was to take a very close look at the three bank robberies. Our knowledge of them until now had been fairly superficial. We also agreed that the key police officers in Ballymena harbouring the suspicions about McCormick should be thoroughly interviewed to see on what grounds they based their beliefs. Fortunately, there was little chance of McCormick catching on to our activities because some weeks after the murder of Sergeant Campbell he had been transferred to Belfast.

In relation to the first robbery at the bank followed immediately by the crime at Knocknacarry post office, we discreetly obtained the investigation files from Ballymena CID offices. We studied the evidence in detail, including the hijacking of the Mini car the previous evening and the finding of it abandoned at Craigagh Wood. The one thing that was missing was evidence that the Special Branch van had been sighted travelling through Cargan village at a quarter past six in the evening by the two detectives who were coming from Cushendall. We located these two officers and obtained witness statements from them so the details of the sighting were reduced into hard evidence. Also, we spoke to all of the Special Branch officers, with the exception of McCormick, who had access to the van. None of them had used it on that day, so it must have been McCormick who was driving it. In fact one of the officers recalled that McCormick had left the Special Branch office in Ballymena just before six o'clock in the evening, announcing that he was intending to do a call in quite the opposite direction from Cushendall.

The second robbery at the bank, which occurred on 7 May 1975, the one in which the lone raider carried a gun and a hand grenade, was also closely analysed. Some of the Special Branch officers had interesting information which they now willingly imparted to us. It transpired that on the day of that robbery Detective Inspector Jim Blair, now deceased, who was then in charge of the Special Branch in Ballymena, was having a day off and responsibility for the running of the office fell to McCormick. A detective constable was on duty also and he recalled being dispatched by McCormick to Portglenone police station on what turned out to be a wild goose chase.

A second detective constable, namely Eric Kettles, now unfortunately also deceased, had more revealing information. He had just joined Special Branch a few weeks earlier and was due to commence duty at two o'clock in the afternoon of that day. He was a very conscientious policeman and arrived at the station twenty minutes early so that he could bring himself up-to-date with occurrences over the previous twenty-four hours. As he walked across the station car park he met McCormick who was driving towards the exit in his own car. McCormick, who was alone, stopped, wound down his driver's window, and told Detective Constable Kettles that an incident had occurred in Cushendall, but that he was to go to the Special Branch office and remain there. If anyone contacted him about putting up an army helicopter he was on no account to do so without his, McCormick's, approval. McCormick was emphatic on this point so Kettles went to the Special Branch office where, as instructed, he remained. He soon learned that the incident McCormick appeared to be rushing off to was the bank robbery in Cushendall. Kettles felt it odd that McCormick should choose to attend the incident alone and not take him along, if not for additional security then to help build up his experience as he was comparatively new to the job. Even more interestingly, another Special Branch officer disclosed that sometime previously he had recovered a Mills hand grenade from a derelict house but when it was examined by the army bomb disposal officer it turned out to be a dummy practice grenade. This officer had secured it in the Special Branch office but some weeks before the robbery McCormick had asked to borrow it, saying he was carrying out investigations into the arrival of a consignment of similar grenades to the Province.

I was intrigued by a disclosure O'Doherty made to us at Castlereagh in September 1977. He claimed that during one of the robberies 'the main recipient of the proceeds took the local military intelligence officer away on a day's fishing as he was the only person who could give authority for an army helicopter to carry out searches in the area'. We discovered that the MIO who had been attached to Ballymena during this period had since left the Province and was back with his regiment in southern England. He was therefore easily located and when interviewed about this assertion we discovered to our satisfaction that he was a meticulous man who kept a detailed diary. He still had his diary for 1975 and when he checked it he found he had a record that on the day of this robbery McCormick had taken him fishing to a local river during late morning and early afternoon. This covered the period between the Special Branch officer being sent off to Portglenone and the arrival of Kettles into the station.

On the occasion of the third robbery, Detective Constable Kettles, who was by now deeply suspicious of McCormick, had a clear recollection. Detective Inspector Blair was absent on a police training course in England and Kettles arrived into the office at nine o'clock that morning. McCormick appeared at around half past ten, stayed for a few minutes, and left. But before doing so he told Kettles that he was going to a particular restaurant some five miles from Ballymena to have lunch with a Special Branch officer from the neighbouring division. Kettles was instructed to remain in the office. He had rather astutely anticipated that McCormick would take advantage at some stage of the absence of Detective Inspector Blair and he watched to see how things would develop. Kettles' theory now seemed to be falling into place. He defied McCormick's directions to stay in the office and instead got into his own car and drove to the restaurant. McCormick's car was not there. Kettles returned to the Special Branch office and was not surprised to learn that the bank had been robbed yet again.

When asked for his whereabouts on this date the military intelligence officer told us he had gone with other army officers to carry out a private transaction in County Tyrone some sixty miles from Ballymena. Before doing so he had sought directions from McCormick as to the best route to take.

Kettles also informed us that about one year after the last robbery at the bank in Cushendall, but at a time when robberies were occurring elsewhere, Detective Inspector Blair and he had carried out a surreptitious search of the Special Branch van which seemed to be the preserve of McCormick. They had found two nylon stocking face masks in a plastic bag which they left in place so as not to alert him to their suspicions.

In the light of all we had now learned in the investigation I was in no doubt that we were on the right tracks in suspecting O'Doherty and McCormick of complicity in the bank robberies. But what of the murder of Sergeant Campbell? Once again Detective Constable Kettles provided valuable information. It was clear he had been burdened for some time with the belief that the man he was forced to work with daily was in fact the killer of Sergeant Campbell. I was pleased that he seemed to regard my investigation team as intending to do a thorough job on the crimes and he disclosed to me all that he knew. He said he had been particularly close to Sergeant Campbell whom he regarded as his mentor. Three days after the last robbery he had met Sergeant Campbell in the car park of Ballymena police station. The sergeant took him aside. He appeared uneasy and kept moving from foot to foot. This was highly unusual for him and he certainly was not in his usual good humour. He asked Kettles if he could trust him not to pass on something which was worrying him. Kettles assured sergeant Campbell that he could speak to him in confidence. The sergeant then said he believed McCormick was involved in crimes in his area but that it was something he wished to work on alone for the time being, without involving a higher authority. Although I never had the pleasure of meeting Sergeant Campbell, from what I learned of him later this would be so typical of the man. He would wish to resolve his own policing problems. In the months which followed Kettles said he met Sergeant Campbell several times. The sergeant repeatedly warned him to be careful of McCormick, saying he was a dangerous man.

Kettles had a particularly vivid recollection of the evening of the murder of Sergeant Campbell. This was not surprising as he had lost a good friend. He was actually off duty at the time but had arranged to meet a CID colleague at nine o'clock in the station to go to a local club for a drink and a game of snooker. As Kettles entered the station he met a sergeant who told him that Sergeant Campbell was lying injured at the entrance gates to Cushendall police station. At first Kettles thought that perhaps Sergeant Campbell had had a recurrence of his stroke and had simply been taken ill but news then came through that he appeared to have been shot.

Kettles went immediately to the Special Branch office, hoping to find Detective Sergeant McCormick who was the Special Branch Duty officer that evening. He searched the station for him without success, then returned to the office and used one of the two telephones to telephone McCormick. There was no answer so Kettles placed the handset on his desk and let it ring for about ten minutes while he used the second telephone to make calls to others about the incident at Cushendall. Kettles then left the office, collected the CID colleague he was due to meet socially and both went to the Waveney Hospital to await the arrival of the injured man. About fifteen minutes later an ambulance with flashing blue lights carrying Sergeant Campbell drove into the casualty entrance. They saw him as he was carried into the casualty unit and it was apparent that he was in a very bad way.

Kettles and his colleague could achieve nothing by remaining at the hospital so they made their way to the scene at Cushendall and were joined a short time later by Detective Inspector Blair. The two Special Branch officers assisted their CID colleagues with the many immediate enquiries to be carried out following such an incident and did not leave Cushendall until four o'clock the following morning. Significantly, McCormick never appeared at the scene despite the fact that he was the duty officer. But his absence was not lost on Kettles or Blair.

Kettles went home and managed a few hours sleep but he was back in the Special Branch office by nine o'clock that same morning to ensure he was available in the event of the investigation team requiring any Special Branch checks to be carried out.

McCormick arrived half an hour later and Kettles told me he was shocked by his appearance. His eyes were wild and staring, his hair was untidy and his general bedraggled appearance gave the impression that he had slept in his clothes. McCormick was normally verbose but now he was unusually quiet and Kettles sensed that something was disturbing him.

McCormick then spoke in a distinctly subdued tone and asked Kettles if he had been to the scene of Sergeant Campbell's murder the previous evening. Kettles said he had and McCormick announced that he was going to take disciplinary action against the staff in the control room. He claimed that they had failed to contact him in his flat about the murder. He said he had spent the whole evening there. Kettles shrewdly said nothing about having telephoned the flat without getting a reply. He allowed things to rest there.

During the next few days Blair and Kettles attended the daily CID conferences at Cushendall police station. All members of the investigation team were brought up-to-date with the latest developments and work sheets were allocated. At no time did McCormick attend any of these conferences which Kettles mentally noted as being out of the ordinary.

On the day of Sergeant Campbell's funeral the Special Branch officers from Ballymena intended travelling to Cushendall as a group to pay their last respects by attending the requiem mass and burial. They first assembled in the Special Branch office. McCormick was also present but he intimated that he was not going to go to the funeral and instead would look after affairs in the office.

We also found out that on the evening of Sunday, 6 March 1977, some nine days after the killing of Sergeant Campbell, McCormick had gone with his girlfriend to visit people who lived in a detached modern bungalow in a quiet country area some few miles outside of Ballymena. They were aware that McCormick was being transferred to Belfast and had kindly decided to throw a small tea party for him to mark the occasion, although McCormick intended to continue residing in his flat in Ballymena and would travel the forty or so miles to work each day. McCormick had his own car parked at the back of the bungalow and at around eight o'clock in the evening the woman who resided there went to the back door to carry out a minor chore. Although it was dark McCormick's car was partly illuminated with the light from the kitchen and the woman noticed an object on the ground underneath it. The booby-trapping of policemen's cars by terrorists in Northern Ireland was an all too common feature and she immediately alerted McCormick. He seemed initially to treat the matter as a joke but was 'persuaded' to go and have a look under his car. The object was plainly visible to others who had by now joined McCormick. He declared that the object was indeed a bomb. He urged the others to check their cars which were parked nearby but nothing suspicious was found. McCormick ordered that the house be evacuated and the family and guests moved for safety to a neighbour's home some three hundred yards away.

McCormick, instead of telephoning for assistance, borrowed one of the other cars, drove to the home of Detective Inspector Blair and informed him of what had occurred. Detective Inspector Blair agreed to go with McCormick to the bungalow to confirm that it was a bomb before alerting the police and calling an army bomb disposal officer to the scene. On arrival he looked underneath McCormick's car and saw what appeared to be a crude bomb held by means of a nylon fishing line and hook which was embedded in the tyre of a front wheel. The bomb disposal officer was notified and when he later attempted to disrupt it by remote control it exploded, causing severe damage to McCormick's car and to the rear of the bungalow. A forensic examination of the scene later recovered components of the bomb and it was estimated that it had contained over a kilo of commercial explosive. Needless to say, Detective Inspector Blair and the other Special Branch staff, particularly Kettles, were extremely sceptical of the events surrounding this incident. They felt it might have been stage-managed by O'Doherty and McCormick to draw some public sympathy in McCormick's direction, and away from Sergeant Campbell.

When my investigation team had assembled all of this evidence in the form of signed witness statements we sat down as a group and carefully digested all that we had learned. I had always found it healthy in such situations to invite some members of the team to be the devil's advocate and to pick holes in any particular line of investigation. I made no exception on this occasion. We had a very lengthy discussion and analysis of the facts but at its conclusion we were at one in the view that a serious situation had been allowed to develop with O'Doherty and McCormick and that our worst fears that they were probably involved in the murder of Sergeant Campbell were well founded. I conveyed our findings to the senior CID officers at RUC headquarters who were understandably dismayed at the news but were fully supportive of the view that the investigation should continue with no stone left unturned.

There was now little doubt that our investigation would culminate in the arrest and interviews of O'Doherty and McCormick but on this occasion we would have to be certain of our facts if we were to have a chance of success. I returned to my investigation team and told them that we had the support of RUC headquarters to proceed with the enquiry. This pleased all of them.

We recognised that if our two suspects had been responsible for three bank robberies and a murder then goodness knows what else they had been up to. As a consequence we decided to look at every serious crime which had occurred in the general area where

McCormick had served since he struck up his relationship with O'Doherty. This was an enormous task bearing in mind that all of the paramilitary groups, both republican and loyalist, were active. But we set to it and soon found that many of the incidents could be easily attributed to the various paramilitary organisations by a number of means, e.g. successful prosecutions, reliable intelligence, claims of responsibility, forensic links etc.

Our study took several weeks and eventually we finalised a list of crimes which could have been committed by O'Doherty and McCormick or by O'Doherty acting with others. We had refined the number down to about sixty. This was still a fairly broad sweep and included several robberies, shooting attacks and explosions. A careful comparison of descriptions supplied by witnesses to these incidents, the method of carrying out the crimes, together with some forensic links left us reasonably certain that O'Doherty and McCormick had committed at least half of these.

I took the list along to Detective Inspector Blair and his Special Branch staff in Ballymena. He showed great integrity by disclosing that two of the crimes were in fact Special Branch operations. This no doubt sounds outrageous but before rushing to any judgements let me explain how they came about. In late 1973 O'Doherty was supplying reasonably reliable intelligence on the activities of local terrorists and a number of successful arms and explosives seizures had been made, thus preventing loss of life or serious injury to others. Unfortunately the terrorists began to suspect O'Doherty of having 'grassed' on them so they tried to lure him to the Republic of Ireland for investigation. This would no doubt have ended with a bullet in the head and his body being dumped on a grass verge along the border. He sensed the danger and was consequently forced closer to his Special Branch handlers. They advised him that the worst possible thing he could do was to prove his guilt to the terrorists by disappearing off the scene.

Instead, Detective Inspector Blair and McCormick told O'Doherty that he should raise the profile of his own terrorist activities in the hope that this would detract some suspicion from him. They agreed to assist him in staging a few incidents. Detective

Inspector Blair arranged for O'Doherty to fire a burst of shots over a mobile patrol of police officers which he would direct along Gortgole Road close to O'Doherty's home. On the evening of 14 November 1973 Detective Inspector Blair took a patrol of police officers along the road and, as arranged, O'Doherty discharged a burst of shots from a sub-machine gun over the roof of the landrover. The flashes of O'Doherty's gunfire could clearly be seen by the other police officers in the vehicle but of course they had no idea that they were bit players in a staged ambush. Detective Inspector Blair added to the subterfuge by leaping from the front seat of the landrover and returning a burst of twenty shots at the 'gunman' from a Sterling sub-machine gun but making sure they were aimed well above his head. In order to complete the act the CID, who were unaware of the real events, were called to the scene. They recovered a number of spent cartridge cases from O'Doherty's firing position and these were deposited at the forensic science laboratory.

Whatever benefits O'Doherty was to receive from his fellow terrorists by this 'ambush' the effects were soon lost when disaster struck a month later. During his relationship with Special Branch O'Doherty had met a number of officers from that department including Detective Constable Ivan Johnstone. Johnstone had resigned from the RUC some months earlier and had entered into a road haulage business which necessitated journeys back and forth across the border between the Republic of Ireland and Northern Ireland. A republican paramilitary group soon caught on to this and the unfortunate Johnstone was pulled from his lorry at gunpoint and taken away for interrogation. His body was found some days later in Northern Ireland, close to the border. He had been shot in the head and there were indications that prior to death he had been maltreated. In the weeks which followed, intelligence began to filter through to the police that during his period of detention Johnstone had been forced to disclose all he knew to the paramilitaries. This included confirmation that O'Doherty was an informant.

The situation for O'Doherty was now becoming desperate. The Special Branch were becoming increasingly concerned for his safety but decided in the meantime to continue with their current strategy.

They arranged for O'Doherty to stage another 'ambush', this time on an unsuspecting mobile patrol of soldiers from the locally raised Ulster Defence Regiment. The incident occurred just before midnight on 12 February 1974 as the patrol moved along the Gortgole Road in two landrovers. A sustained burst of automatic gunfire was heard coming from high ground to their right but the soldiers were quick to react and immediately returned fire. Once again the CID attended the scene and in daylight identified the 'gunman's' position from the twenty-two spent bullet cases he had left behind. These too were sent off to the forensic science laboratory.

Although such incidents may now seem outlandish they must be viewed in the context of the situation at that time. Northern Ireland was in a state of turmoil with ever-increasing violence and lives were being lost daily. In those far-off days a large amount of autonomy fell to RUC officers on the ground and, as is demonstrated by these two 'ambushes', they occasionally resorted to desperate measures for desperate times. The whole structure of the force has now been so radically altered that it would be impossible to carry out such operations without being called to account.

I appreciated the honesty of the Special Branch officers in declaring their knowledge of these two incidents and not attempting to lead me up the garden path as it were. However, I was concerned that the forensic reports on the two shootings confirmed that the weapon which had been used on both occasions had also been used at around the same time in an attack on the home of an off-duty member of the RUC who lived just outside Portglenone. This member is a personal friend of mine and we had both served together as uniformed constables in Tennent Street. At that time he did not have a car and, like me, resided in the sleeping quarters of the station. My home was to the north of the Province and I passed close to Portglenone when I wished to visit my parents. On many occasions I had given my friend a lift to his home and collected him afterwards. It was at this address that the attack took place.

At the time of the attack in early 1974 my friend had acquired his own car. In the early hours of a Sunday morning he returned from visiting his girlfriend, parked his car at the rear of the house and went inside. Suddenly, a burst of gunfire broke out and he took cover until it was over. He then sent for help and when the police arrived they discovered that his car and the back of the house had been raked with bullets. A total of fifteen spent cartridge cases were found at the corner of a shed about forty feet from the rear of the house. The forensic experts were now saying that these had been fired from the same weapon used in the two staged 'ambushes'. As confirmation of this evidence the weapon had also been identified as one of those recovered by the police in September 1977 during a search of the fields at the rear of Herr Gradel's house in Ballymena following the attempted kidnapping, a crime with which O'Doherty had tenuous connections. The weapon, a Sten sub-machine gun, had an interesting history. It had belonged to the British Army but had been stolen with several others during a daring IRA raid on the armoury of Gough Barracks in Armagh in 1954 just at the outbreak of a previous campaign.

When I revealed the information relating to the attack on my friend's house to Detective Inspector Blair and his staff they seemed genuinely unaware of the evidential connections which had been made. The only conclusion we could come to was that O'Doherty had staged the attack on his own initiative or perhaps with the help of McCormick.

Of particular interest to us on our list were three shooting attacks on Portglenone RUC station which occurred on 10 August 1974, 21 November 1974 and 25 November 1975. On each occasion the gunman had fired from open ground to the rear of the station. The officers who were in the station at the time of these attacks were reasonably certain that the gunman was not using an automatic weapon because there was a distinct pause between each shot. After one attack the station sergeant found two .303 bullet heads in the rear yard. These could only have been fired from a bolt action rifle. He later gave them to Detective Sergeant McCormick for onward delivery to the forensic science laboratory. After each of these attacks a search was made in daylight for the gunman's firing position but all that was found was an area of flattened grass. No spent shells were found. This was very odd, and bearing in mind that in order to fire a .303 rifle one has to manually activate the bolt between each shot and in doing so eject an empty shell. The only explanation was that the gunman was anxious not to leave any unnecessary ballistic evidence and was pocketing each shell as it was ejected. This is quite a feat in darkness and, as previously stated, these were the only shooting attacks where this was happening — except of course in the murder of Sergeant Campbell.

If we suspected O'Doherty of having committed these attacks on the station, and of carefully removing his empty cartridge cases, then this was a distinct departure from his actions during the two staged 'ambushes' and the attack on the home of my friend. On each of these occasions he had left ample ballistic evidence in the form of numerous spent shells. It was my view at the time that as a result of having received sanction from his Special Branch handlers to carry out the 'ambushes', and possibly from McCormick on the third attack, there were no compelling reasons to remove his spent cases. Also, it was almost impossible to collect the spent cases from a sustained burst of fire from a Sten sub-machine gun. This weapon rapidly spits out the cases in an indefinite pattern to a distance of over six feet away. Bearing in mind that fire was returned on two occasions one did not hang around in darkness trying to collect incriminating evidence.

By the end of July 1980 I believed we had learned all that we could about O'Doherty and McCormick without actually interviewing them. I also recognised that McCormick was an experienced police officer who had himself been engaged on many occasions in interviewing terrorist suspects at Castlereagh. He certainly knew the ropes and would be a hard nut to crack. Instead of arresting the two suspects simultaneously we opted to go for O'Doherty alone and to do so without alerting McCormick. This should not prove too difficult as we understood from the Special Branch in Ballymena that the relationship between the two suspects had not been so close since McCormick's transfer to Belfast.

O'Doherty was known to sleep at a number of different houses in the interests of his own security and we realised that it would be a major setback to the investigation if we went to an address to arrest him and found he was not there. This would alert him unnecessarily and I had no doubt he would run to McCormick and have an opportunity to fortify himself against our questioning.

Consequently, we all agreed that we should not risk a false start to this vital aspect of the enquiry and decided to try and take him by surprise by snatching him off the street. Once again the local Special Branch were able to assist. They were aware that the only positive routine he had was a visit to some of the bars in the centre of Ballymena every Saturday night.

At that time many of the provincial towns such as Ballymena were sealed off at night with security barriers to prevent the Provisional IRA from gaining access with large car bombs. We knew that O'Doherty's girlfriend picked him up in her car at the security barrier in Hill Street when the bars closed at eleven o'clock.

An operation involving all members of my investigation team was mounted for the evening of Saturday, 2 August 1980. I arranged for us to keep surveillance at the security barriers from two carefully positioned squad cars. We planned to let O'Doherty get into his girlfriend's car, at which point we would pounce and detain him. O'Doherty was a slippery customer and I certainly had no intention of letting him escape in this important phase of the investigation. It was planned that once he got into the car I would come in at right angles to it in one of the squad cars, so close that it would be impossible for him to open the front and rear doors on the driver's side. The other car was detailed to approach from the rear of his girlfriend's car. I also took with me a very athletic member of the squad whose sole function was to outpace O'Doherty should he manage to take to his heels.

O'Doherty's girlfriend turned up at the barrier just before eleven o'clock and she sat alone for about twenty minutes. We were becoming slightly anxious that perhaps he had fallen into other company and was going to depart from his usual routine. But our fears were unfounded when he appeared and got into the waiting car. I drove my car right up to the side of it and he and his girlfriend were blinded by the full beam of my headlights. As planned the second car came in from the rear. We got out of our squad cars and already O'Doherty was trying to make a break for it. But he was quickly surrounded and I led him to the back door of my car and placed him inside. Immediately he slid across the rear seat and tried to get out the other door but my athletic friend had got there before him. I then sat in beside O'Doherty, placed a pair of handcuffs on him and we set off for Castlereagh.

On the journey to Castlereagh I kept the conversation with O'Doherty to a minimum but he intimated that he could see we meant business and that he knew he had run his course. It was after midnight when we arrived in Belfast and as O'Doherty seemed to have consumed a considerable amount of alcohol I lodged him with the uniformed staff and left him for the night. When someone is arrested it is normal for details to be circulated within the force in the event of anyone else having an interest for some other crime. However, on this occasion I arranged for O'Doherty's details to be withheld to minimise the risk of alerting McCormick.

The following morning my investigation team assembled at nine o'clock. It was agreed that the interviewers should concentrate on the robberies, shootings and explosions O'Doherty was believed to have been involved in and that for the moment we would steer well clear of the murder of Sergeant Campbell.

As the interviews progressed O'Doherty began to make the first of his confessions. He was quick to bring in the fact that senior Special Branch officers had sanctioned the two 'ambushes' at Gortgole Road. He was somewhat deflated when he realised we were aware of this. I felt it an opportune time to mention the shooting attack on my friend's car and house in Portglenone when the same weapon had been used. O'Doherty admitted that he had carried out this attack. He claimed he had been urged to do so by McCormick who had waited in a quiet side road during the incident and had driven him away from the scene after the shooting. When asked what the motive was O'Doherty claimed it was merely to impress the other terrorists active in the area so that they would more readily accept him. O'Doherty's admission that he had been driven away from the scene was borne out to some extent by the quite independent evidence of a police dog handler who had been called to the incident that night. His animal tracked from the area of spent shells across fields for a distance of three hundred yards to a side road where fresh tyre tracks were found in a quiet lay-by.

When it was put to O'Doherty that it therefore seemed a likely proposition that he had carried out the shooting attacks on Portglenone police station he conceded that he had. He said he had been using a .303 rifle and that McCormick had supplied him with a bandolier of ammunition. On the first occasion McCormick had dropped him off with the rifle in a side road some distance from the station and told him not to rush. McCormick wanted time to get to Ballymena police station so that he could return to Portglenone with other police and help 'investigate' the shooting. O'Doherty made his way across fields until he was about eighty yards from the rear of the station. Here he discharged about six shots and lifted his spent cases. When the station was attacked the second time they adopted the same procedure.

On the third occasion the chain of events was also basically similar but O'Doherty claimed McCormick had not only dropped him off in his car but had driven him away from the scene afterwards. He also said that prior to carrying out this attack McCormick advised him that he had two minutes to get to his firing point, three minutes to carry out the attack and two minutes to get back to the car; and that for the seven minutes McCormick would go for a drive.

The investigative strategy we had adopted seemed to be working out so far and I was keen to get on to the subject of the robberies at the bank in Cushendall. O'Doherty did not disappoint us. He admitted involvement in all three crimes and strongly implicated McCormick. He outlined how, prior to the first robbery, McCormick had taken him to the Glens area a number of times so that he could familiarise himself with the locality of the bank and the surrounding roads. On one of these forays they had concealed the handgun close to Cushendall. On the night before the actual robbery McCormick had driven him to Lisnahunshin where he set up the 'checkpoint' and hijacked the Mini car. He also agreed that after robbing the bank he went to Knocknacarry post office where he took the money from the post mistress. O'Doherty said he then abandoned the car and lay low in the Glens until McCormick picked him up in the Special Branch van after dark. This tied in neatly with the van being seen travelling through Cargan village on its way to the Glens. According to

O'Doherty they both spent that night in McCormick's flat and his part of the proceeds were gradually doled out to him over the following months. O'Doherty claimed that McCormick had timed him to do this first robbery on a day when the entire party of police at Cushendall would be at Belfast Crown Court attending a trial, in other words when the coast would be clear. This was checked out and it was found to be perfectly correct. Sergeant Campbell and his small unit of police had indeed been away at Crown Court, an event so rare as to be more than a coincidence.

On the second time that he robbed the bank O'Doherty said he had adopted the same basic procedure as on the first occasion except that instead of wearing a mask he put on a wig and sunglasses. He and McCormick agreed on a different pick-up point. However, their plans went somewhat awry when the stolen car he had parked on the hill outside the clergyman's house refused to start. As a result he made off on foot, concealed the money and other incriminating evidence, walked across the mountains, and eventually made it back to Ballymena. The following day McCormick and he returned to the Glens and recovered the money and other items. O'Doherty was quite unconcerned at having to walk over the mountains. McCormick had assured him no helicopters could be put up as the military intelligence officer was enjoying a day's fishing, a point on which we already had firm evidence.

In respect of the third robbery at the bank, O'Doherty said he and McCormick had been the two raiders who had carried out the crime. He explained that the reason they returned to Cushendall again was that a few days before the crime the pair of them had carried out a robbery at a furniture store outside Portglenone known as Century Twenty One. This crime had yielded a lot less than expected so they were forced back towards the more reliable source of cash at Cushendall. This admission to the robbery at the furniture store was quite striking for us as it was one of the crimes we had on our list.

O'Doherty said he was reluctant to rob the bank again by himself and eventually persuaded McCormick to join him. According to O'Doherty, McCormick said he was due on duty on the day they had chosen to rob the bank but that he would make an excuse to get out of the office. This piece of information coming from O'Doherty seemed to fit neatly into Kettles' recollection of McCormick proclaiming he was going to a particular restaurant to meet a colleague and the absence of his car when Kettles later went there.

During this interview O'Doherty went on to describe how they stole the car from the car park of the Michelin tyre factory. He claimed McCormick followed him in his own car to a forest above Cushendall. McCormick parked his car, they changed into combat jackets, and put on hats with stocking masks rolled under them. They both got into the stolen car, with McCormick driving and pulled up outside the bank. They entered and he went to the counter as usual, demanding the cash. After taking the cash they retreated to the getaway car and drove off, but in his haste McCormick almost lost control of it on a bend. The car was abandoned at a pre-arranged spot and they made their way across fields to McCormick's car, taking an indirect route back to Ballymena.

As we were on the subject of robbing banks we decided to put another one from our list to O'Doherty. This robbery had occurred just three weeks before his last visit to the bank in Cushendall. It took place at the Northern Bank in the small village of Armoy, about ten miles from Ballymena but in the opposite direction from Cushendall. The bank is a small branch office and serves the needs of the local farmers and traders. At about eleven o'clock on the morning of 14 April 1975 the manager was attending to a number of customers when a man, described as having a full head of hair, approached the counter, and said, 'Put 'em up'. The manager was not in a very compliant mood. He immediately put his foot on the panic alarm which went off causing the gunman to flee empty handed. O'Doherty left behind a pillow case. When interviewed later by the police the manager said he thought the raider had been wearing a wig.

A subsequent search of the surrounding area by police located a Ford Cortina car parked in a quiet road about half a mile from Armoy. It was not on the stolen list but a check with the registered owner revealed that he had parked it at a crossroads outside Armoy during the early morning and then got a lift into work. He was not due back to where he had parked his car until half past five in the evening and would then obviously have reported it stolen. Significantly, when the police attempted to move the stolen car they could not as it was out of petrol.

O'Doherty readily admitted he had carried out this crime and once again implicated McCormick. According to O'Doherty they had driven in McCormick's car to where the Ford Cortina was parked. They pulled up alongside it and he had little trouble entering it and getting it started. He drove in it to Armoy, parked the car, walked into the bank, tried to rob it but ran for it when the manager set off the alarm. He returned to the stolen car and sped out of the village but after a few hundred yards it ran out of petrol. He once again returned to the fields but made it to a pre-arranged pick-up point where McCormick collected him at half past seven. I am sure it has not escaped the notice of the reader that O'Doherty and things mechanical were not compatible. He humorously admitted to us that he was the 'world's worst driver' which is a distinct disadvantage if one chooses bank robbery as a career.

Significantly, and quite unknown to O'Doherty and his accomplice, they had been seen stealing the Ford Cortina car by a witness who lived in a house overlooking the scene. This witness was hesitant in reporting the matter to the police as she felt the car may have simply been taken away for repair by arrangement. She got quite a good look at the two men, and although unable to identify them facially, she said that the one who drove away the stolen car had black curly hair, which O'Doherty has, and the second man had neck-length straight ginger hair, which McCormick has.

O'Doherty was by now talking reasonably freely in Castlereagh. From time to time he would deny involvement in particular crimes only to then admit to them when some other piece of compelling evidence was revealed to him. Such was the case in the attempted robbery at Killygarn post office and grocery store, situated in an isolated country area about five miles from Portglenone. It occurred on the late afternoon of Friday, 19 November 1976, when the owner and his wife were alone on the premises. Suddenly, a lone masked gunman appeared through the front door and demanded that the safe be opened. The owner was not for parting with his hard-earned cash so easily. He took a flying leap at the raider and pulled him to the ground. The two men wrestled around the floor, knocking over boxes of fruit. The owner only gave up the fight when his wife urged him to desist as the raider seemed to be getting to the point of desperation where he would use the gun. As the raider fled from the premises the owner thought he would give him something else to remember him by and flung a wooden orange box after him.

The police were called to the scene and brought with them a tracker dog which followed a scent across a field for about five hundred yards when it suddenly ended at a side road, perhaps an indication that the gunman had been picked up in a vehicle.

It was later on that same day that Blair and Kettles carried out the discreet search of the Special Branch van and found the nylon stocking face masks with slits cut for the eyes and mouth. O'Doherty eventually admitted to this crime and in doing so implicated McCormick by saying he had dropped him off and collected him at the side road. He claimed that when he told McCormick of the events at the post office he brushed it off saying, 'You can't win them all.'

O'Doherty went on to admit having carried out two robberies at Glenravel post office which is situated in the main street of Cargan village. The first of these took place on 23 November 1976, only four days after the fiasco at Killygarn post office. A lone masked gunman arrived into the post office at around five o'clock and ordered the female assistants to place the money into a white pillow case with a floral design. The staff did as they were ordered and dropped £240 into the pillow case. The post office was robbed again in a similar manner some six weeks later on 4 January 1977 and O'Doherty claimed McCormick had driven him to and from these crimes.

One of the crimes we had on our list which we believed O'Doherty could help us with was an attempted robbery at a large public house known as the Countryman Inn, situated on the edge of a housing estate in Ballymena town. At around closing time on 12 December 1977 two men had tried to rob the manager of the day's takings but were unsuccessful as he had locked the money in the safe and did not carry it with him. There was reasonably reliable intelligence as to who had committed this crime and it certainly did not involve McCormick. O'Doherty was not quite in the clear but told us that he knew who had carried it out. He had jibed the two culprits, who were also believed to be connected to the attempted kidnapping of Herr Gradel, about having made a mess of the robbery by not knowing that the takings were kept in the safe of the bar. According to O'Doherty the two men were upset about his remarks about their stupidity and vowed to eventually get the money from the Countryman Inn.

On the late evening of 23 December 1976, just two days before Christmas when business in the bars was brisk, the manager of the Countryman Inn received a telephone call from a male who said, 'You foiled an attempted robbery by two of our volunteers. Consequently, yourself and your wife have been condemned to be shot. The only way of getting a reprieve is to follow our instructions. Take all the money out of the safe, put it in a carrier bag and drive to a spot a quarter of a mile outside Cargan village where you will see a double road sign. Leave the money there and do not tell the police.' The manager was understandably frightened by the threats and more so when the caller let it be known that he had details of his car by accurately describing the make, colour and registration number. As a result he decided to comply with the demands and took the day's takings to the lonely place specified by the caller.

O'Doherty said that on the night of this crime he had been drinking in the bar. At closing time he saw that the manager appeared agitated. He asked him what was wrong but the manager simply said that something terrible had happened. The next day O'Doherty heard the true events. He then knew that his two associates had carried it out and their wounded pride had been healed.

However, the same basic ploy was used some six weeks later, 7 February 1977, on the unfortunate manager of the Northern Bank in Cushendall whose resistance was probably worn down by all the robberies which had taken place. Just after four o'clock in the afternoon, when the bank had closed to the public and the staff were balancing the books, he received a call from a male who said, 'You have had a couple of raids and due to the help you have given the police, two of the raiders are now on the run. Because of this you have been added to our death list. There is only one way to get off it and that is by taking all the notes from the bank and driving about four and a half miles towards Ballymena where you will see a red marker. Leave the money there and do not tell the police.' The manager was given fifteen minutes to comply but he protested that this was not enough time as his car was at home and not at the bank. The caller acknowledged this by saying, 'I know that your car, your green BMW, is at your house, but it only takes you four minutes to get it. The time is now six minutes past four and you have until four twenty-six to do as you are told — don't try and waste time.'

The details of this call were almost identical to those received by the manager of the Countryman Inn. It was sufficiently threatening to make the bank manager do as he had been instructed. Consequently, he piled over £18,000 into two plastic carrier bags, drove to the isolated spot near a forest, and left the money.

When quizzed by us on this crime O'Doherty admitted complicity and said the others involved were the same two who had blackmailed the bar manager. He said one of the team went to a public telephone box in Cushendall from where he made the threatening call. He and the other participants concealed themselves in the wood and watched as the bank manager deposited the two bags of money. When he had driven off they broke cover, collected the bags of cash and made their way through the trees to a pre-arranged spot where the man who made the telephone call was due to pick them up. O'Doherty said he knew the cash was destined for the coffers of the INLA so he and his accomplice pocketed £1,000 each before being collected in the car.

The next crime on our list was the murder of Sergeant Campbell but we adhered firmly to our strategy and did not mention it to O'Doherty at that stage. We moved onto the incident where the bomb had been found under McCormick's car. O'Doherty conceded that he had planted it and claimed he had done so at the instigation and with the help of McCormick. When asked what possible motive they could have for doing such a thing O'Doherty said that McCormick wanted to 'make himself out a hero in the eyes of the people in Ballymena and wanted them to think of him as a big-time operator'.

O'Doherty continued by saying that McCormick and he had made up the bomb in the back of the Special Branch van a couple of days before he actually planted it. McCormick had supplied the explosives, which were sticks of gelignite, and early on the day of the actual planting of the bomb, they had driven to a spot near the house where the tea party was to be held, and concealed the device among whin bushes. O'Doherty claimed that his final instructions from McCormick were to make his way to where the bomb was concealed that evening, walk across the fields to the bungalow and put the bomb under the car in such a position that it could easily be seen. He did as he was told and found McCormick's brown coloured Toyota Celica car parked at the back door of the bungalow. The bomb was then planted in a conspicuous position which is borne out by the evidence of the lady of the house who detected it in the light thrown from the open kitchen door.

As a result of our now detailed knowledge of how O'Doherty operated we had good reason to suspect him of carrying out a gun and bomb attack at the home of a reserve police constable who ran a farm about three miles from Portglenone. The incident occurred at about half past nine on the evening of 21 March 1977 when the reserve constable, who was at home with his wife and children, heard a number of shots being discharged a short distance from his house. He was quick to react and ran to the back door where he discharged two rounds from his shot gun. The reserve constable was uncertain if he was being attacked from the front or the rear so he then made his way to the front window at the landing near the top of the stairs. He fired two more rounds from his shotgun and more gunfire was directed towards him, but he could see the flashes from the attacker's weapon on a hillside opposite. The reserve constable produced his police-issue personal protection pistol and loosed off some shots towards the gunman. The firing then ceased. The police from Portglenone soon arrived at the scene. They detected a number of bullet strike marks at the front of the house and collected some bullet head fragments which were later identified as having been fired from a .303 rifle. The gunman's firing position was also identified by an area of flattened grass but significantly the terrorist had removed his spent cartridge cases. This initially led us to believe O'Doherty had been involved.

However, we had another reason to suspect O'Doherty and this was because of an occurrence the following day at the same farm. A friend of the reserve constable walked into a tripwire made from nylon fishing line and set off a small bomb which hurled him several feet into a ditch. He sustained a leg injury from shrapnel but was not seriously hurt and was discharged from hospital the next day.

An expert examination of the scene was carried out and it was discovered that the nylon tripwire had been stretched across a path between a scrap car and an old tractor cab. It was estimated that half a pound of commercial explosives had been used. Several components of the bomb were found, thus enabling the forensic experts to deduce how it had been constructed. Each bomb maker has his own little idiosyncrasies and the scientists were able to say that whoever had constructed the bomb under McCormick's car two weeks previously had also made the device which had now gone off at the farm.

O'Doherty readily admitted this crime to us and said McCormick had also been involved with him. He explained that they had some materials left over after having made the bomb for McCormick's car. They decided to use it in order to create another incident against a policeman. This might make the bombing of McCormick's car look more genuine. According to O'Doherty, McCormick and he made up the bomb and before the attack McCormick drove him to have a look at the farm. They parked the car some way off and made their way in darkness to the farm buildings, staying well away from the dwelling house. They selected the spot for the bomb and agreed that on the day of the attack it should be planted first and followed by the shooting attack. On this reconnaissance run they hid the bomb near the farm. The following night O'Doherty made his way on foot with the .303 rifle to the farm, planted the bomb and carried out the shooting attack, all by himself. He also made his escape on foot by running back to his home about three miles away.

Around this time McCormick was transferred to other Special Branch duties in Belfast and lost the intimate knowledge of the movements of the police in the Ballymena area. This also seemed to mark a watershed in his relationship with O'Doherty and we did not suspect McCormick of any further criminal activity from that point onwards.

O'Doherty too seemed to reduce his level of activity for a while and he maintained a somewhat loose connection with Detective Inspector Blair. The next time he came under significant police notice was when he was interviewed by us in September 1977 following the incident at the home of Herr Gradel. It was obvious to us that he was now attached to the INLA. We believe he had assisted them in several incidents. It no doubt seems odd that a man who had once been branded an informant by the Provisional IRA should now be accepted by the INLA. However, there were reasons, the principal one being that O'Doherty had blood connections with the command structure of that organisation. Also, several years had passed since his cover was blown and events like that can become clouded in the mists of time as paramilitaries who were prominent then go off the scene for a variety of reasons such as death or imprisonment.

When questioned by us in Castlereagh about this phase O'Doherty decided to 'clear his slate'. He began by admitting having teamed up with a man named William Lee and another terrorist who was later shot dead by the security forces. Together, they carried out an attempted blackmailing of a bank manager in Draperstown in County Londonderry and a robbery at an isolated restaurant in the Glens. In this latter crime O'Doherty had used one of two shotguns stolen during a burglary. During his time in Castlereagh, we took him, firmly handcuffed, to where they were now concealed in a forest and we recovered them. The barrels had been sawn-off in the manner preferred by most robbers.

O'Doherty, Lee and the now deceased terrorist also committed a most dastardly crime when they made up a booby-trap bomb in an empty five-litre paint can. They left it on the outskirts of Ballymena together with some car tools and phoned the police anonymously, reporting that there were items of stolen property at that location. A patrol of uniformed police responded to the call and when they saw the items called for the CID. A detective constable went along and after some initial examination decided to take the items back to the station. One of the officers lifted the large paint can and as he did so it exploded, causing him grievous injuries. The detective constable was also quite badly injured in the blast but both men made a good recovery in due course. In addition to O'Doherty admitting to his part we also detained his accomplice, Lee, some weeks later. He too made a full confession to these crimes.

O'Doherty had now been in Castlereagh for four days and my colleagues and I had spent most of that time writing down his confessions in detail. I was anxious to get on to the subject of the murder of Sergeant Campbell but there were a number of other petty robberies we suspected him of committing in earlier years and decided to deal with these now. The first one was a robbery at Ringsend post office, County Londonderry, way back in 1973. O'Doherty readily agreed that he had carried it out. He admitted robbing the owner of a mobile butcher's van close to his home in early 1974. He also admitted robbing a farmer in 1975 in the mistaken belief that the man carried a large amount of cash. At no time did he implicate McCormick in these crimes nor did we suspect McCormick of involvement in them.

When I put my pen down after recording what he wanted to say about these robberies O'Doherty visibly relaxed. However, my co-interviewers and I were far from relaxed. The moment we had waited for so long had at last arrived. I gathered my thoughts carefully and then announced to O'Doherty there was one more incident he had not yet touched upon. As I spoke I watched his facial expression intently and saw a look of anxiety coming over his eyes. He sat bolt upright and asked what we were referring to. I decided to gain maximum impact from what was now a tense situation and told him bluntly that we believed he had been involved in the murder of Sergeant Campbell at Cushendall. At such crucial moments it is vitally important for an interviewer to have his facts correct as suspects quickly regain their confidence when a mistaken or false assertion is made. In the preceding four days O'Doherty had related such a catalogue of crimes, the circumstances of which only reinforced my suspicions that he and McCormick had carried out the killing. But I still could not be sure which of them had fired the fatal shot. It was as a result of this uncertainty that I decided to keep my options open. I alleged to O'Doherty that I believed he had been 'involved' in the murder, but I felt confident enough of my position to add that McCormick had been a participant in the crime as well. O'Doherty was visibly shaken by this dramatic allegation and blurted out, 'Most definitely not'.

He then added that he did not even know Sergeant Campbell. But we countered by saying it was not necessary to know a person in order to kill him. We pressed home the allegation by saying we had carried out an intensive investigation into the murder and had found that the circumstances in which it had been carried out were somewhat unusual; certain aspects of it set it apart from other terrorist killings. O'Doherty seemed puzzled by this. I explained to him that a study of other crimes committed by him and McCormick had revealed certain habits which were peculiar to them both. Some of these habits were showing through in the murder of Sergeant Campbell, or in other words, they had 'left their calling card'. O'Doherty asked me to tell him what these were but I preferred to play my cards close to my chest for the moment and refused.

O'Doherty seemed to be losing his confidence and I decided to give him no quarter. I rose from my seat, leaned across to O'Doherty, and told him in no uncertain terms that he had been involved in the murder of a man who was a highly respected member of the community. O'Doherty stammered out that he had heard a certain well-known member of the Provisional IRA had carried out the killing. I replied that he was merely trying to shift the blame, that the gunman he had just named would not let a suspected informant get anywhere near him to discover whether or not he had killed anyone.

O'Doherty was becoming increasingly distressed and asked us did we honestly think he had it in him to kill someone like Sergeant Campbell. We told him it was a matter for him to clarify but we were certainly alleging that he had had a hand in the murder. He rose from his seat and with tears welling in his eyes asked me to look him straight in the face and accuse him of pulling the trigger of the gun which had killed Sergeant Campbell. I was unbelievably thankful that we had stuck to the allegation that he had been 'involved' in the crime and reminded O'Doherty of what we were saying. He urged me several more times to accuse him of pulling the trigger. I knew that he would find solace if I did, so I stuck to my position. From that point onwards I firmly believed he had not been the gunman but that he had certainly been at the crime.

O'Doherty was by now very emotional. He slumped down into his chair and asked for a cigarette which we gave him. We quietly asked him to tell us the truth of what had happened and he said he had not shot Sergeant Campbell but that McCormick had. I told him to tell us the whole story from beginning to end. He said McCormick and he had carried out the robberies at the banks and post offices just as he had earlier described. He went on to explain that sometime after the last of these crimes McCormick approached him and said, 'That bollocks Campbell is on to us.' O'Doherty said he could not see quite what McCormick was driving at and asked him to explain. McCormick told him that Campbell had spotted them after one of their crimes. From this he presumed that Sergeant Campbell had perhaps seen one of their pick-ups after a robbery, but McCormick never really clarified this to him at any stage.

In any event, McCormick only seemed to voice his concerns about Sergeant Campbell a few weeks before the actual killing. McCormick had told him that as a result of what Campbell knew his career would be in danger and he was not going to let that happen. O'Doherty said he queried McCormick on this and asked him if he meant that Sergeant Campbell's knowledge would lead to him being transferred by the police authorities out of Ballymena. McCormick replied that it was more serious than that and could lead to both of them standing in the dock. McCormick said they would have to get rid of Campbell but initially O'Doherty did not take this as a serious proposition.

He continued to meet McCormick regularly after the first mention of Sergeant Campbell knowing about their activities. McCormick kept on and on about it and O'Doherty suggested that perhaps they could threaten Sergeant Campbell into silence. McCormick turned on O'Doherty following this suggestion and asked him if he expected him to walk into Cushendall police station, shove a gun down Campbell's throat and tell him to shut his mouth.

McCormick then asked him if he would be prepared to go with him to Cushendall to silence Sergeant Campbell and he said he would.

O'Doherty related how on the day of the actual murder he met McCormick by arrangement on a quiet country road on the outskirts of Ballymena just as darkness was falling. They did not drive directly to Cushendall but first of all went to a small village some miles on the opposite side of Ballymena from Cushendall. McCormick went into a house he had once lodged in while he, O'Doherty, remained in the car. On the journey to this village McCormick asked him what he thought of the 'gear' in the back of the car. O'Doherty looked into the rear of the car and saw a rifle with a telescopic sight on it. It had a walnut butt and the metal parks were black. When asked what type of rifle it was McCormick allegedly said it was a treble two (.222) and was as good as an Armalite rifle, which fires a .223 bullet. According to O'Doherty, McCormick was also armed with a loaded .38 revolver which looked brand new and it too was furnished with a walnut handgrip.

McCormick completed his call in the village and returned to the car. They then drove towards Cushendall, taking an indirect route. McCormick asked him to do the shooting, saying he would find it easier than robbing a bank and he would have him back in Ballymena in no time. O'Doherty refused. They drove into the village of Cushendall and after a couple of right turns stopped at a gateway on a quiet road some distance above the town. McCormick and he got out of the car. McCormick opened the boot lid and pulled out the wires connected to the rear number plate illumination light. He put on a balaclava hood, collected the rifle and revolver from the back seat of the car and headed off by himself down a laneway in the direction of Cushendall. O'Doherty hung about McCormick's car for about half an hour and then, in the stillness of the night, heard what he thought were two shots, or one shot and its echo. About fifteen minutes later McCormick arrived back at the car out of breath. He said to O'Doherty, 'That is either the end of the trouble or the beginning of it', a statement which, with the benefit of hindsight, was remarkably prophetic.

McCormick placed the weapon in the boot. He told O'Doherty to get into the car and recline the front passenger seat so that he would be out of sight, thus giving the impression that there was only one person in the vehicle. They drove back to Ballymena. On the way McCormick warned him that he, O'Doherty, was a hot potato with the CID and could expect to be detained and questioned. He warned him to keep his mouth shut.

On arrival back in Ballymena McCormick dropped him off and O'Doherty made straight for a bar to have a drink. As the evening wore on news began to filter through that Sergeant Campbell had been shot dead in Cushendall and the next day the newspapers extensively covered the killing. A couple of days later he met McCormick and broached the subject of the murder to him. McCormick refused to talk about it and said the matter was closed.

When we asked how they could have known that Sergeant Campbell would be at the police station on the night he had been killed O'Doherty said that McCormick had told him that there would only be two policemen at the station. One of them would be Sergeant Campbell who would be around to lock up even though it was his day off.

I told O'Doherty that one point was troubling me, and that was his claim that he had waited at the car while McCormick carried out the killing. I pointed out to him that in all of the incidents in which he had implicated McCormick it was always he, O'Doherty, who had carried out the crime while McCormick waited for him in the car or the van. Now, when it came to a murder, there had been a reversal of roles and he had waited at the car. O'Doherty said the explanation was simple and it was that he just could not find it in himself to kill someone. However, I kept an open mind on this and hoped that some means could be found to substantiate this one way or the other.

At the conclusion of this interview we put O'Doherty back in his cell and I related details of what he had said to my senior CID authorities. My immediate colleagues who had worked on the case with me were also told of the developments and although quietly satisfied that our enquiries were now coming to fruition there was a distinct absence of jubilation at the prospect of a policeman having killed a fellow officer.

The assistant chief constable in command of the CID came to Castlereagh from his office at RUC headquarters, bringing with him several other senior CID officers. The divisional commander-in-charge of policing in Ballymena was also summoned and a conference was set up at which all aspects of the case were discussed. I was given the floor and permitted to outline what we had so far learned. After several hours of debate all present were convinced that we were on the right tracks. The ACC directed that McCormick be arrested the following day and brought to Castlereagh just like any other suspected terrorist.

A detective superintendent was given the responsibility of arresting him. It was agreed that, using elements of my investigation team, we would detain McCormick the following day when he turned in for duty in North Belfast where he was now serving. On that day we assembled in the detective superintendent's office at nine o'clock in the morning and after a number of seemingly innocuous telephone calls we found out that McCormick was attending a meeting with CID officers in Newtownabbey police station. We proceeded there in two police cars and to the amazement of those in conference with McCormick the detective superintendent arrested him under the Prevention of Terrorism Act. McCormick came quietly and I sat beside him on the journey to Castlereagh. The conversation was distinctly muted and only broken when McCormick said, 'What do you want me for? Sure I never took anyone's life anyhow,' which I thought was a strangely odd response to his arrest. On arrival at the detention centre he was processed in the normal manner and two of the senior CID officers who had attended the conference began to question him.

On the afternoon of that same day we removed O'Doherty from Castlereagh and took him to Cushendall so that he could indicate the precise spot where he alleged he had stood by the parked car and waited while McCormick carried out the killing. He found it easily enough on the Middlepark Road and almost opposite it was the lane he claimed McCormick had used. We left O'Doherty firmly handcuffed to one of two detectives while I walked the lane with another colleague. We found that we were on Knockans Lane which is about one mile long but remarkably brought us out at the top of Barrack Hill in Cushendall and a short distance up from the police station. When we got back to the CID car I brought O'Doherty over the events of the killing. He repeated these in detail, including the fact that he had heard two shots being fired or else one shot and an echo. From that a germ of an idea began to form in my mind as to how we could prove he had indeed waited at the car.

We returned O'Doherty to Castlereagh and I met some of the senior officers who were interviewing McCormick. As expected he was strongly denying involvement in any of the crimes mentioned by O'Doherty, including the murder of Sergeant Campbell. Over the next few days he was made aware in detail of the evidence from Detective Constable Kettles, particularly the fact that he could not be found on the night of the killing, his absence from the scene of the murder, his non-appearance at the police station that same evening and his non-attendance at the funeral. He was also told of the sighting of the Special Branch van in Cargan village following one of the bank robberies, the finding of the masks in the van, the day's fishing with the military intelligence officer, and Kettles' observations on the car park of the restaurant. McCormick was evasive in his answers and was careful not to tie himself down to specifics.

On the second day of his detention, all the interviewers agreed that it might prove useful if O'Doherty would confront him face to face and repeat the allegations, particularly in respect of the murder. I put this proposition to O'Doherty and he agreed to it but said that he felt nervous about it. I told him all that was required of him was to answer questions from me and that I would be noting down the questions, his answers, and any comments made by McCormick. I then took O'Doherty along to the interview room where McCormick was being questioned and opened the door. The two senior officers who were present were of course expecting us and as we entered McCormick rose from his chair and glared menacingly at O'Doherty. I asked O'Doherty to now repeat what had happened on the night Sergeant Campbell was murdered and he quietly said, 'Me and Charlie did it.' When asked how they travelled to and from the crime he replied, 'In Charlie's car'. I asked him to state what happened at the murder and he answered, 'I stayed at the car and Charlie shot him, then he drove back and dropped me off.' McCormick retorted, 'Tony, why are you saying this about me?' and O'Doherty said, 'Because it's the truth, Charlie.' O'Doherty continued, 'I have had enough. I want it all cleared up. I have told the truth about it all, Charlie, and I'm for the court.' McCormick, in a somewhat desperate tone said, 'Why are you telling lies about me, Tony? I was good to you.' To which O'Doherty replied, 'It's the truth, Charlie, you were good to me but I've had enough. I've told the truth.' McCormick then became visibly agitated and accused O'Doherty of being drugged. It was apparent that nothing further was to be gained so I took O'Doherty back to his cell. His period of lawful detention was now drawing to a close and soon we would have to place him before a court.

All the indications so far from McCormick were that he was going to ride out the storm by denying everything and hoping to be released from police custody at the end of the seven days we were entitled to hold him. This was not a happy prospect for us but one possible way round it was to see if O'Doherty would be prepared to give evidence against him. We all accepted that this would be an extremely difficult route to take. Even the most inept defence barrister would have little difficulty in discrediting him, given his criminal record and the crimes he had now admitted to us. However, nothing ventured, nothing gained, so we sought O'Doherty's attitude to this and he was agreeable. O'Doherty was then charged with a number of the crimes he had admitted, including withholding information on the murder of Sergeant Campbell. He appeared before Belfast Magistrates Court and was remanded to the protection wing of Belfast prison.

A few days later McCormick, despite his denials, appeared at the same court charged with the murder of Sergeant Campbell. This understandably caused a sensational news story at the time. On that day a truly ironic event occurred when Sir John Hermon, the Chief Constable, arrived into RUC headquarters. He had of course been kept abreast of events but as he passed through the entrance foyer he paused at the book of remembrance to all the policemen who have died in Northern Ireland as a result of the troubles. A page is dedicated to each murdered officer and the name and circumstances of the death are outlined in scrolled writing. The book is unfortunately somewhat bulky with the details of the several hundred officers who have been killed and each day a page is turned. On this particular day the page dedicated to Sergeant Campbell was on display. When the Chief Constable was told that McCormick would be charged with the murder the coincidence was not lost on him and he asked that McCormick be made aware of this fact.

If the case against McCormick was to have any chance of success it was important that O'Doherty's evidence be supported in every possible way and my investigation team set out to do this. I had assisted in the search of McCormick's flat following his arrest and we had found the two bullet heads which the station sergeant at Portglenone had handed to McCormick after one of the shooting attacks. He had failed to submit these to the forensic science laboratory and it could be construed that he had deliberately concealed them. It was little matters like this which would assist the case.

Also, every policeman who is attached to the Special Branch or the CID is required by Home Office regulations to keep a journal of his day-to-day activities. We found a number of McCormick's journals covering the period under investigation. On several of the occasions that O'Doherty claimed McCormick and he had been together leading up to or during their alleged crimes McCormick had made a note of being 'on duty with Agent 294'.

Of particular interest to me was the assertion by O'Doherty that a few weeks prior to the killing, McCormick had begun to voice his dislike of Sergeant Campbell and claimed he was onto their activities and would eventually put them both in the dock. This seemed to coincide with the onset of Sergeant Campbell's moodiness as observed by his family and also the carrying of a gun which was noted by his colleagues. I personally felt that McCormick and Sergeant Campbell must have had a verbal confrontation at some stage around then about the crimes being perpetrated in the Glens. The only evidence of the two men having met came from McCormick's journal in an entry dated 6 February 1977, some two and a half weeks before the murder. Among other matters noted by McCormick was, 'Discussed safe houses with RUC in Cushendall'. We traced all members of the Cushendall policing party who were on duty that day and none had spoken to McCormick. By a process of elimination then it had to be Sergeant Campbell and I suspect there may have been a bitter exchange of words that day.

I was still intrigued by O'Doherty's claim that he stayed with McCormick's car on Middlepark Road on the night of the murder and heard two shots or one shot plus its echo. The idea which had formed in my mind of proving this was to reconstruct the crime at the same time of day and in similar weather conditions and to find out just what could be heard at Middlepark Road. I discussed this in depth with the forensic scientist who had examined the original scene and he agreed to assist. A few days later we set the experiment in motion and began by covering the yard of Cushendall police station with sheets of clear plastic material. I then positioned a detective one third of the distance between the police station and Middlepark Road and another two thirds of the way. A colleague and I went all the way to the spot where O'Doherty alleged he had stood at the time of the murder. On receipt of a pre-arranged radio message from us, and after all the appropriate safety precautions had been taken, the forensic scientist discharged a .222 rifle into the gate of the station from where he had deduced the murderer had been. The detective who was one third of the way along the lane heard only a single shot, the officer two thirds of the way also heard one shot, but my colleague and I heard the shot followed a second later by its echo. Although O'Doherty was wily and cunning there was no way he could have invented that claim. I then became satisfied that he had told us the truth and that he had not been the gunman.

The forensic scientist was also anxious to establish how a bullet head from a .222 would perform after penetrating the gate and impacting with the hard-cast wall; hence the covering of plastic sheeting in the yard. At the conclusion of the experiment the forensic scientist swept the plastic but only recovered minute particles of the bullet head, the greater part having totally disintegrated.

We also managed in 1980 to locate the Toyota Celica car owned by McCormick in 1977. This was the one which O'Doherty said they used on the night of the murder. McCormick had traded it to car dealers in late 1979 but they had sold it in early 1980. On receipt of the vehicle, the new owner had his brother look over it for defects. Among those detected was the disconnection of the wires leading to the rear number plate illumination light. The wires were re-connected and the light immediately began to function. This seemed again to bear out what O'Doherty was saying.

The case against O'Doherty and McCormick, not forgetting William Lee, was a complex one and my report concerning their alleged involvement in crimes stretched to four hundred and fifty pages, supported by several volumes of witness statements and documentary exhibits. The DPP directed no less than forty-six charges against O'Doherty and twenty-seven against Lee. He held back on a decision against McCormick until it became clear what way O'Doherty intended to approach his own case. Obviously, if he pleaded 'not guilty' at his trial then there was no way he could be called to give evidence against McCormick. On the other hand if he pleaded 'guilty' then the way was open for him to make a witness deposition against McCormick and we could proceed from that point.

The matter was soon resolved when on 29 October 1981 O'Doherty and Lee appeared at Belfast Crown Court before Lord Justice Gibson. It took the court clerk a long time to arraign the two accused on the numerous counts but they each pleaded guilty and were sentenced to terms of eighteen years and twelve years imprisonment respectively.

In view of the fact that O'Doherty had accepted his guilt and was now a sentenced prisoner with no advantages to be had in giving evidence against an alleged accomplice, the DPP finally decided to proceed against McCormick. As part of the judicial process he had to go through a committal for trial stage at which all the evidence would be served upon him and a magistrate would decide if there was sufficient on which to go forward to a Crown Court trial. Normally all of the evidence is served in the form of written witness statements but the defence have the right to ask that a particular witness be called to make a deposition. This takes the form of the witness relating what he has to say in front of a magistrate in open court and the evidence is typed, read over to him and signed. In McCormick's case the defence elected to have the committal proceedings by this means as it obviously meant they had an opportunity to size up the witness before the major trial took place. The committal proceedings in relation to McCormick began on 7 December 1981 and O'Doherty was in the witness box for two full days.

McCormick's trial commenced on 23 February 1982 at Belfast Crown Court before Lord Justice Murray sitting alone and without a jury. As anticipated McCormick pleaded 'not guilty' to all charges. He was neatly dressed in a green blazer, white shirt, tie and dark trousers as he sat in the dock between two prison officers. It was immediately apparent that he had aged considerably since his arrest. Throughout the formal part of the trial he kept his head bowed and appeared to write an occasional note in a pad he had with him.

O'Doherty was eventually called to the witness box to give his evidence. He spent four days giving his direct evidence and being cross-examined, most of which was dedicated to discrediting him. Altogether, the trial lasted three weeks and the judge reserved his ruling until 2 April 1982.

On that day the court was crowded with the press and onlookers. McCormick appeared quiet and calm as he kept his head bowed in the direction of his note pad. The judge duly appeared and began to read his ruling on the case. He said that in British law the evidence of an accomplice has to be regarded with great care and where possible should not be accepted without sufficient corroboration. The judge continued that in view of O'Doherty's character he could not accept his evidence without sufficient corroboration and found this only in the case of the robbery of the Northern Bank at Cushendall on 25 November 1974. Accordingly he found McCormick guilty on that charge and sentenced him to twenty years imprisonment. I glanced over to McCormick in the dock as the verdict was announced and watched as he wiped a tear from his eyes.

However, McCormick immediately lodged a notice of appeal against this conviction which was not heard until January 1984 before the Lord Chief Justice for Northern Ireland, Lord Lowry, who ruled that the trial judge had wrongly accepted aspects of the evidence against McCormick as corroboration of O'Doherty's testimony. Accordingly McCormick was set free and he left the court after having spent just over three years in prison. O'Doherty continued to serve out his sentence but the Secretary of State for Northern Ireland exercised his prerogative of mercy and gave him some extra years remission in recognition of the help he had given the police.

Although McCormick and O'Doherty eventually walked free the case was to claim yet more victims when within a few short years Detective Constable Kettles died, a comparatively young man. I hope I do not cause additional distress to the family by suggesting that the case caused him so much strain that it played a part in his premature death.

Detective Inspector Blair eventually left the police and took up a civilian career but his life too came to an abrupt end when some years later he hanged himself from a beam in the garage of his home in Ballymena. In his case too I believe the affair caused him a great deal of anguish and may well have played a part in his death.

McCormick was released from prison twenty-seven years after he first joined the RUC. It was obvious he could never resume duty again as frankly no one would be prepared to work with him. He was quietly pensioned off by the Police Authority for Northern Ireland.

O'Doherty, despite his early release, found it difficult to change his old ways and in the mid 1990s he was convicted of another robbery and was sentenced to a lengthy term of imprisonment. No doubt the Campbell family in Cushendall continue grieving for a lost husband and father.

7

MURDER IN THE SHANKILL

During the McCormick trial at Belfast Crown Court I was summoned one afternoon to take a telephone call from the assistant chief constable in-charge of the CID who, in a congratulatory tone of voice, told me that on 5 April 1982 I was to be promoted to detective chief inspector. He asked me if I would like to take up the post of head of the CID in the Tennent Street and Oldpark areas, to replace the current incumbent who was also being promoted in recognition of his work in solving sectarian murders. I was of course honoured to be asked to return to take charge of the CID at a station, where, some twelve years earlier, I had walked through the front door as a probationary uniformed constable fresh from initial training.

On the day of my actual transfer I arrived into the station car park with a great deal of apprehension at the responsibility which now fell to me. But this soon vanished when I entered the main CID offices, where I was warmly received by some of the longer serving members of the department who had been there during my days as a constable. I knew their capabilities and what they had experienced down through those traumatic years. I realised that if I was to make a success of my new post it would be essential to gain their support, so right from the start I tried to treat all members of the department with the respect their onerous work deserved. Most of them, over the following months, reciprocated and a contented but highly productive department continued to develop.

Of particular interest to me was the murder squad for the division. This comprised some of the most experienced detectives in the station headed by a detective inspector. The walls of their offices were lined with row-upon-row of file boxes, each of which contained the evidence relating to a particular killing. For ease of reference the victim's name and date of death were boldly printed on the boxes and for me, understandably, they were symbolic of headstones in a graveyard. Often I watched with interest the visual impact this had on visiting police officers who entered that room for the first time. It was indeed a stark reminder of the deep malady in the divided society of Northern Ireland. Quite remarkably, about half of these killings had been solved. This bore testimony to the skill and hard work of the detectives in the division.

Although each of these file boxes was representative of some human tragedy, of particular poignancy were those relating to the savage murders carried out by the infamous Shankill Butchers gang, most of whom had been brought to book a few years earlier by some of the detectives still attached to the murder squad.

The members of this murder gang mostly belonged to the loyalist paramilitary group The Ulster Volunteer Force, but they had, to a large extent, broken away from the main body of this organisation and were in fact something of a splinter group led by a ruthless young man named Lenny Murphy. Although the gang are also known to have shot dead a number of people, their principal method of killing was to cruise, late at night, those quiet neutral districts which separated some of the tribal areas of north Belfast, on the lookout for Roman Catholics walking these streets. The gang would pull up alongside their intended victim, leap from the vehicle, and fell their prey with a heavy blow to the head from something like a wheelbrace or a hatchet. The unfortunate victims would be hauled into the vehicle which would speed off into the loyalist heartland of the Shankill Road. During the short journey the victim would be taunted about his religion and severely beaten. On some occasions the abductors would sadistically make a number of small cuts on the victim's neck or face with a razor-sharp butcher's knife to let them know what their fate was shortly going to be. On arrival at a suitable backstreet alley or a patch of waste ground the victim would be dragged from the vehicle. One of the gang, usually Murphy, would then cut his throat right back to the spine, almost separating the head from the body.

At the outbreak of the troubles in 1969, Murphy was seventeen years of age. During his school years he had earned the reputation of being something of a thug and a thief, having already been convicted of petty theft. There is no doubt that with the onset of the sectarian violence in Northern Ireland, Murphy found his niche in life by becoming a member of the UVF. He is believed to have first killed in mid-July 1972 when a Roman Catholic man, named Francis Arthurs, was dragged from a taxi in north Belfast and taken to a UVF drinking den where he was tortured by a number of men before being stabbed to death by Murphy. Arthurs' body was found lying in a side street the following day. The year 1972 went down as having produced the highest level of sectarian killings in Northern Ireland. One can be sure that this was not the only such murder Murphy had a hand in during that period.

However, Murphy did not confine his activities to killing Roman Catholics and in September 1972 he shot dead a Protestant man in east Belfast. His victim was Edward Pavis who had recently been released from prison after having served a sentence for acting as an illegal arms dealer. During Pavis's trial it emerged that he was prepared to trade weapons with anyone and there was evidence that he had supplied a shotgun to a Roman Catholic who wanted it for sporting rather than for sectarian reasons. At that time Murphy was still accepting orders from the command structure of the UVF. They ordered him and a youth named Mervyn Connor to eliminate Pavis. The pair travelled to Pavis's house in a stolen motor cycle. On arrival Murphy engaged his victim in conversation for a short period before treacherously pulling a handgun from his jacket and shooting him in the head.

There were a number of witnesses to the killing and the subsequent police investigation led them to arrest Murphy and Connor. They were placed on a formal identification parade but as each witness was brought into the room Murphy cunningly stepped out of the line-up, proclaiming that he was the suspect. This tended to negate the identification evidence. However, Murphy and Connor were duly charged with the murder and remanded in custody to Crumlin Road prison pending their trial.

The police were in no doubt that Connor was out of his depth by becoming involved in the murder and knew he was acting very much under the influence of the more sinister Murphy. The CID were obviously anxious to obtain a conviction which would put Murphy away for a long time so they discreetly approached Connor in prison and he accepted an invitation to give evidence against his accomplice. The approach was not discreet enough. Murphy soon got wind of this and in the weeks which followed he acquired a small quantity of cyanide. He waited patiently for an opportunity to get to Connor in his cell and when he did he forced him to consume the poison which killed him almost instantly. A wall of silence met the investigating detectives and they were unable to produce enough evidence to charge Murphy with the killing of Connor. Murphy was not content to let matters rest there and during his period of remand he made two unsuccessful escape attempts. In June 1973 he appeared at Belfast Crown Court on the Pavis murder charge but his defence counsel kept hacking away at the evidence of identification and he was acquitted. Ironically, the two escape bids now worked against him. He was convicted of attempting to escape from lawful custody and sentenced to three years imprisonment.

He was released from prison in the middle of July 1975, having earned some remission. But before long he was back into his old ways. In October of that same year he took part in the mass murder of four innocent Roman Catholics who worked in a Wholesale Wine and Spirit Merchants at Millfield, just on the edge of the Shankill district close to Belfast city centre. Murphy and three others drove into the yard of the premises in a hijacked van and began by attempting to rob two female members of staff in the office. This was only a cover for the real motive behind the crime. Two women were told to kneel down and they were both shot in the head. Two young men who worked in the warehouse loading goods for delivery were also gunned down and killed. The police investigation into this massacre was swift and two of the killers were eventually brought to justice, but Murphy's silence under interrogation ensured that he walked free yet again.

Murphy was by now getting into his stride with sectarian killings. In November 1975 he and several other members of the UVF drove late at night down into Library Street close to Belfast City centre and not far from where he had taken part in the killings at the Wine and Spirit Merchants. They saw the lone figure of a male wending his way along the street. Murphy got out of the car and knocked him to the ground with a blow from a wheelbrace. The dazed man was bundled into the car and driven into the Shankill area where Murphy and his accomplices dragged him up an alleyway and cut his throat until his head was almost completely severed. He turned out to be a Roman Catholic named Francis Crossan who had been drinking in a club in Ardoyne. When abducted he was making his way on foot to his home in west Belfast.

Within days of this brutal killing Murphy was in action again when he was asked to enhance the reputation of the UVF among the working-class people of the Shankill by investigating the robbery of an elderly woman in her home. The identities of these petty criminals soon became known to him and among them was a young man named 'Stewartie' Robinson. I had first encountered Robinson in 1971 when I was a uniformed beat constable in north Belfast. He at that time was known as a notorious car thief who frequently gave the police the slip by his wild and high speed style of driving stolen cars. I recall vividly going to the scene of a car accident on the Ballysillan Road during that period and being met on arrival by the sight of a gold coloured Ford Cortina GT, completely cut in half. The rear seats and back end of the car were separated cleanly from the front section. This had been caused by a sideways impact with a concrete lamp standard. A check on the registration number with the Belfast control room revealed it was a stolen car. We later learned that Robinson had been driving the car at the time accompanied by at least one other person and that they had run from the crashed car unscathed.

On another occasion, in the early hours of one morning I was on the beat in the middle Shankill when I heard the sound of a car in the distance travelling at high speed. As it drew closer, but still out of sight, it sounded like a high performance car. The driver was obviously enjoying himself by making rapid changes up and down the gears. Instinctively I knew it was Robinson. When it appeared over the brow of a hill I could see it was a small Lotus sports car. I somewhat foolishly tried to stop it by stepping onto the road and flashing my red torch but he drove straight at me, forcing me to jump for my life. My colleague was so incensed that he drew his revolver and was about to fire shots at the car, but I restrained him. Robinson was by now a real problem in the area and the divisional commander even went so far as to request the RUC traffic branch to allocate a fast car with a skilled driver to patrol the main roads and side streets in the hope that he could out-chase him. A police Triumph TR6 remained with the division for a number of weeks but Robinson lowered his profile and the operation came to nothing.

Some weeks later my opportunity to equal the score with Robinson came when a local criminal, whom I had arrested for an offence sometime previously, telephoned me at the station to say that Robinson and another car thief were on their way to strip a stolen car of its wheels where it had been abandoned in Elizabeth Street on the edge of the lower Falls Road. This area was normally only patrolled with strong army support. I went to the local army base, explained my requirements to the duty officer, and he offered me the services of one of his patrols who were using an armoured personnel carrier. I went with the soldiers in the APC. Their normal patrol pattern was to cruise slowly around the maze of side streets looking for paramilitary suspects on the move. We entered Elizabeth Street and sure enough there was the stolen car as described. Robinson and his accomplice were not to be seen but after half-an-hour's patient patrolling he and his accomplice turned up in another car and began to jack up the stolen vehicle. The driver nosed our APC into the street and maintained his slow cruising speed until we drew level with the two men. They never for one moment suspected that an army mobile patrol would take an interest in them. Just at the right moment two soldiers, who had been well briefed by me, burst from the rear doors of the APC and at gunpoint ordered Robinson and his friend to stand still. I quickly followed, grabbed Robinson and led him into the back of the APC, while the soldiers did the same with the second man. Robinson was in an obvious state of shock and in case he was contemplating trying to fool us as to his identity I said to him, 'How are things, Stewartie?' He said little on the way to Tennent Street police station where I handed him over to the CID. During the course of interview by the detectives he admitted stealing no less than one hundred and sixteen cars and he received a heavy term of imprisonment at his trial.

Now, in 1975, Robinson was obviously still engaged in crime. Murphy ordered his unit to 'Arrest him' and his two alleged accomplices in connection with the robbery of the old woman. They were soon rounded up and Murphy and his cohorts began their interrogation. The odds were definitely stacked against the 'prisoners' and within a short time they made their 'confessions' allegedly at the point of a gun. Murphy 'sentenced' them to be kneecapped, or, in other words to be shot in the legs, the usual form of punishment meted out by all of the paramilitary groups in Northern Ireland. As Robinson was about to be kneecapped by one of Murphy's henchmen he made a break for it and was callously shot in the back. He died almost immediately while the punishment of the other two proceeded.

Robinson was not without friends in some of the other gangs of loyalist paramilitaries and they easily discovered who had been involved in the punishment shootings. They took quick revenge by hunting down his killer and shooting him dead. Murphy was incensed at this impudent threat to his authority and he extended the cycle of violence by ordering his unit to bring the men who had carried out this revenge attack to him. The only one they could locate was Noel Shaw, a man whom I had known from my uniformed days on the Shankill. He was a suspected loyalist paramilitary whom we had frequently stopped and frisked. As soon as Shaw was captured Murphy assembled his entire unit, which numbered around twenty, in their usual drinking club and Shaw was hauled in front of them. He received quite a severe beating with almost everyone joining in but Murphy quickly took control of the situation and ordered that Shaw be tied to a chair and placed on view on a small stage. Murphy produced a handgun and after pronouncing Shaw as the killer of a member of his unit he shot him five times. Shaw died instantly. Murphy had re-asserted his authority and he coolly ordered that the blood-stained stage be cleaned up and Shaw's body disposed of. A taxi was hijacked and someone produced a large wicker laundry basket.

Shaw's body was squeezed into it, carried to the taxi and driven off and abandoned half a mile away. When it was discovered by the police and delivered to the mortuary the pathologist concluded that before death, Shaw had indeed received a severe beating.

The advent of 1976 saw no let-up in Murphy's activities and in early January of that year he went on the prowl of the streets and roads of north Belfast indiscriminately seeking out another Roman Catholic victim for assassination. On this occasion he was driven in a taxi owned by one of his gang. They toured the Cliftonville Road and streets leading off it for a considerable period without success and were about to give up for the night when they spotted a man and a woman who were in fact making their way home from a late-night party. Murphy ordered his driver to pull in at the kerb just in front of the couple and he then alighted from the taxi, giving the impression that he was a normal fare being dropped off. As he drew closer to the couple he suddenly produced a handgun and fired a number of shots into the body of the man. This victim was a Roman Catholic named Ted McQuaid and he died on his way to hospital.

Within days Murphy set out to satisfy his blood-lust again when late at night he and two others returned to Millfield where they saw the diminutive figure of a middle-aged man ambling along. As the car pulled alongside him, Murphy, who by now was well-practised, appeared through the rear passenger door and with a single blow from a wheelbrace easily knocked the small man to the ground. He was quickly bundled into the back of the car and the ritual beating began. Murphy ordered that they be driven to the Glencairn housing estate at the upper end of the Shankill area. On the way he teased the unfortunate victim by drawing a razor sharp knife across his throat but not sufficiently deep to have caused death. Murphy was waiting to savour those final strokes of the blade and at a suitable patch of waste ground the victim was dragged from the taxi and the butchery began. Murphy drew the blade back and forth across the throat of the man until he reached the spine and could go no further. The victim was later identified as fifty-five years old Thomas Quinn, a harmless individual who worked during the day as a municipal road sweeper. He lived alone and in the evenings sought solace and comfort by drinking in various bars. The post-mortem examination revealed that just prior to his death he had consumed a considerable quantity of alcohol.

At the time of the murders of McQuaid and Quinn, Murphy was in the process of planning a more spectacular crime which he hoped would result in the deaths of several Roman Catholics. He had received intelligence that just before eight o'clock each work day morning a building merchant's lorry, with several workers on board, stopped at a newspaper shop in Cambrai Street which is in the upper Shankill Road and forms a convenient link road between north and west Belfast. Murphy's information was that the workers on the lorry were all Roman Catholics. On the morning of 9 February 1976, Murphy stole a car and with three other members of his unit went to Cambrai Street where they patiently waited for the lorry to turn up at the newspaper shop. It arrived on schedule and there was a total of seven men on board. The prospect of a mass-killing no doubt pleased Murphy. He was armed with a Thompson sub-machine gun of the type often seen in the hands of gangsters in American movies. Another of his team had an M1 Carbine which at one time was the standard-issue weapon used by American infantrymen. Murphy and his fellow gunman got out of their stolen car and approached the lorry, opening fire as they did so. Two of the workers were killed outright and two others were severely wounded but they survived to tell the tale. The ironic aspect of this tragedy is that Murphy's intelligence was wrong. All of the workers were Protestants. But I am sure this mistake caused him little anguish.

Just over two weeks later Murphy and his henchmen returned to the quiet streets close to Belfast city centre where they had previously seized Crossan and Quinn. They spotted a man, later identified as Francis Rice, who was making his way on foot from a city centre bar to the Roman Catholic New Lodge area. He was far from being drunk but still he was no match for Murphy who approached him from behind and downed him with the now familiar wheelbrace. The usual routine was followed. Rice was hauled into the car and driven to the area of the middle Shankill where he was left in an alleyway with his throat cut right back to the spine.

At this stage the police response was intense, but these killings still only represented a small proportion of the total murders occurring in north Belfast as all of the other paramilitary groups, both loyalist and republican, were very active. Nevertheless, all available resources were deployed in the streets where the victims had been snatched. Some officers even volunteered to disguise themselves and act as bait in an attempt to draw the killers to them. However, luck was soon to turn against Murphy when on 2 March 1976 he returned to the Cliftonville Road to indiscriminately seek out yet another victim. At that time because of the cut-throat killings, fear stalked the streets of north Belfast and not many people ventured out on foot after dark.

One night Murphy and his accomplices toured the streets for a short period without managing to find a lone pedestrian. But just as they were about to give up for the night they saw a car with two young women on board. They were returning home from a dance they had attended in a provincial town some forty miles away. The killer gang overtook and drew alongside the women's car and Murphy opened fire on the occupants with a handgun. One of the women was hit a number of times but managed to keep control of her car as Murphy and his gang sped off in the direction of the Ballysillan Road, hoping to make it back to the Shankill. Unknown to them the army had set up a vehicle checkpoint on the route. Murphy and his gang managed to crash through it by mounting the footpath. The soldiers were quick to respond and two of them each fired a shot at the car which was now disappearing out of sight towards the Antrim Road. Both rounds hit the vehicle causing no injuries. Murphy and his gang soon abandoned and set fire to it. Then Murphy concealed the handgun used in the attack on the two women in a nearby hedge.

At daylight a full search was made of the area where the car had been burned out and a soldier came across the gun which Murphy had hidden. It was quickly delivered to the CID at Tennent Street and forensic comparisons proved it had been the weapon used to attack the women in the car. A calculated decision was taken to keep observations on the area where the gun had been found and at a quarter past eight the following morning Murphy turned up at the spot, driving a lorry. He alighted from the cab and began to rummage in the hedge. After a short while he climbed back into the vehicle and drove off but was stopped by the police a short distance away.

Murphy was arrested and taken to Tennent Street police station and his clothes were seized for forensic examination. They revealed heavy traces of firearm residues. When he was questioned by detectives about his movements he became evasive and non-committal. There was, however, sufficient evidence to charge him with the possession of the firearm. He appeared at Belfast Magistrates Court the following day and was remanded to Crumlin Road prison.

The arrest and detention of Murphy was sufficient to disrupt the smooth running of his gang and the cut-throat killings ceased with the suddenness of a light switch being turned off. This served to confirm the CID suspicions that Murphy was the principal killer in these atrocities. He was re-interviewed in prison in an effort to gain a confession but without success.

As the months wore on and Murphy stayed on remand his gang began to recover from the loss of their leader and the wheels of their killing machine began to move again. Because of his domineering and arrogant personality, his unit had been allowed a large degree of autonomy within the structure of the UVF but now, in his absence, the leadership felt confident enough to bring them back into line. In June 1976 they were ordered to join up with another unit and attack a Catholic-owned bar in the Smithfield area of Belfast in retaliation for the Provisional IRA bombing of a Protestant-owned bar elsewhere in the city which had left two dead. The target the UVF chose was the Chlorane bar, which had a mixed clientele. A number of hooded gunmen entered the premises on a quiet Saturday evening and sprayed the customers with a variety of weapons leaving a final death toll of five, some of whom were Protestants.

Then, in early August 1976, apparently on their own initiative, two of Murphy's most trusted men, who had accompanied him on several of the cut-throat killings, drove in a borrowed taxi to their old hunting territory of the Cliftonville Road. They saw a lone figure of a male and pulled in just behind him. One of the killers was armed on this occasion with a hatchet and he began to rain blows down on the unfortunate man's head. As he fell to the ground his assailant kept up the attack and then got back into the taxi and drove off. The injured man was fifty years old Cornelius Neeson who was employed as a bingo-caller and was making his way home after his evening's work. The injuries to his head were horrendous. When found by a passing motorist he was removed to hospital but not surprisingly died a few hours later.

In the autumn of 1976 Murphy came to trial on the charges arising out of the finding of the handgun following the attack on the two women on the Cliftonville Road. He initially pleaded 'not guilty' but after some legal wrangling he changed his plea to 'guilty' to possession of the gun and was sentenced to twelve years imprisonment.

Although Murphy's imprisonment kept him out of circulation he still maintained a large degree of influence over his unit and was able to issue policy directions through the weekly prison visits he received from his closest friends. It had not escaped Murphy's attention that with his arrest in March 1976 the cut-throat killings had come to an abrupt halt and he was somewhat concerned that the CID would re-double their efforts to connect him with these murders. The prospect of this happening did nothing for his morale. He knew that if he were connected to the cut-throat killings the key to his cell would be thrown away for a very long time.

Consequently, he instructed his gang to resume the killings at once in the hope this would throw the murder squad off his scent. His men remained faithful to him and almost immediately began to prowl the streets again. In the early hours of Saturday, 30 October 1976, they found their next victim in Millfield which forms the main road link between the lower Shankill and the lower Falls. One of the gang used his own car and with three others parked it in a side street off Millfield. They got out of the vehicle and hung around the shadows. After a short wait they saw a young couple walking from the direction of the Falls Road. They were seventeen years old Stephen McCann and his girlfriend, both of whom had spent a pleasant day in Belfast city centre rounded off with a party in the university area. They were making their way to their homes in north Belfast when about half way along Millfield the killer gang emerged and dragged Stephen McCann to the waiting car. He was little more than a child and did not prove to be a difficult victim to handle. His girlfriend managed to escape and eventually made her way to a police station. Stephen was now receiving a savage beating in the rear of the car. He was taken to the Glencairn housing estate where he was pulled onto waste ground, shot in the head, and his throat brutally cut open.

Murphy's gang had now most certainly become de-humanised and with the number and nature of the killings they had been involved in were devoid of all feeling. As sure as war steadily brutalises those involved in conflict, naked sectarian terrorism follows the same pattern.

The fact that they regarded human life as cheap was demonstrated in the following months when they became involved in two separate pub brawls killing two men, both of whom were Protestants. The first was battered to death with a large concrete block on waste ground. The second man received a severe beating before being stunned with blows from a heavy spanner after which his throat was cut and his body dumped on waste ground close to a Catholic area in an effort to shift police suspicions in that direction.

However, they had to remember Murphy's orders from prison to keep up the cut-throat killings and in early February 1977 some members of the gang went back to their favourite haunts for such crimes. They picked up a fifty-two year old Catholic man named Joseph Morrisey walking along Upper Donegall Street. He had been drinking in central Belfast for most of the day and was walking through the darkened streets on his way to his home on the Antrim Road. The murder gang pulled up alongside him and one of them crashed a hatchet down on his head after which he was bundled into a vehicle. It drove off in the direction of the Shankill. On the way Morrisey received a severe beating, and like some of the other victims, was teased and taunted. One of the gang wielded a razor-sharp knife and during the beating cruelly drew it back and forth across Morrisey's face just deep enough to draw blood. He was taken to the Glencairn housing estate and in the area of a small car park was pulled out of the car and his throat was cut in the usual manner. However, another dimension was added to this savagery when the knifeman tried to sever the head completely from the body by delivering a number of blows to the throat with the hatchet.

Some weeks later the murder gang ventured out again only on this occasion they went to Spamount Street in the hard-line republican New Lodge area. Here they spotted the lone figure of forty years old Francis Cassidy who had earlier consumed a considerable amount of alcohol. Two of the gang alighted from the car and set upon Cassidy with their fists and pushed him into the waiting car. He was taken to the Highfield housing estate, shot in the head and his throat cut.

Murphy was no doubt gloating in his prison cell as the news of each of these killings reached him but little did he or his gang know that the tide was soon to turn in favour of the police. The events which led to this situation began in mid-May 1977 when a twenty year old Catholic man was picked up on the Cliftonville Road by four men posing as detectives. They ordered him to get into their car parked nearby and he readily complied. He was driven to a derelict building on the main Shankill Road where he received a severe beating. On this occasion the gang changed their modus operandi and tried to strangle the man with a bootlace. When sufficient pressure had been applied the victim fell unconscious and did not wake up until he was in an alleyway in Esmond Street in the upper Shankill. In addition to the attempted strangulation both of the victim's wrists had been severely slashed and it was apparent that he had been left for dead.

He looked much worse than his condition really was and within a few days was released from hospital. He was closely interviewed by detectives who took him on a tour of the Shankill Road in an effort to identify his abductors among the many men who hung around the street corners. The detectives could hardly believe their luck when he pointed out two men as being part of the team who had captured him.

The CID exploited this opening to the full and over the following months the investigation snowballed. Eleven men confessed to a total of nineteen murders. When they eventually reached the dock of Belfast Crown Court they were given very lengthy prison sentences with two of the gang being told by the judge that they were never to be released except in the event of terminal illness.

Much of the detail of what I have written about these murders, particularly the cruel treatment of the victims between initial abduction and death, is derived from the confessions of those convicted. Time and time again they implicated Murphy but when the major breakthrough in these crimes came he was still in prison and the only way he could be charged was if he made admissions to the murders. He also knew that this was the situation so he remained silent and contemplated his day of release which was due on 17 July 1982, just over three months from the time I took up my new post as head of the CID in Tennent Street station.

Experience of detective work has taught me that sadists such as Murphy do not change their ways and the reputation he had now achieved brought him a perverse status which he could never have achieved in any other sphere of life. Such men relish the power this gives them and they have all of the fringe benefits which come with their positions such as a plentiful supply of money, usually gained from racketeering and robbery, foreign holidays and a dedicated following of admirers.

Murphy was released from prison on the date prescribed and we braced ourselves for a new wave of violence which would no doubt follow if he was to re-assert himself. There were already a number of paramilitary murder teams, both republican and loyalist, active within the Division. Sectarian killings on both sides were still a common feature although most were more clinical than Murphy's old methods and victims were simply gunned down.

On the evening of Saturday, 18 July 1982 I was having a quiet evening at home when my phone rang. It was someone from the murder squad offices and he informed me that a body had been found in Alliance Parade not far from the republican enclave of Ardoyne. I immediately made my way there and was briefed by some of the detectives at the scene who told me that a witness had seen a black London-style taxi enter Alliance Parade and stop in a darkened area of waste ground. The occupants had pulled what appeared at first to be a carpet from the taxi but when it had driven off the witness had taken a closer look and discovered it was the body of a man.

I was brought to the body which was lying face upwards and

together with a forensic medical officer carried out a preliminary examination. The body was cold to the touch and the doctor discovered a number of quite severe injuries to the head which still oozed blood. Owing to the extensive nature of the injuries he could not say if the man had been shot and only a post-mortem examination by a pathologist would reveal the actual cause of death.

When our examination had been completed and the scene carefully photographed, the body was placed in the mortuary van and delivered to the city morgue where the pathologist's examination revealed that the victim had been battered to death and in fact had not been shot.

There was no identification on the body but his physical appearance was distinctive insofar as he was over six feet tall, was extremely thin and had a large bushy beard. We checked these details against our list of missing persons but he did not fit any of the descriptions so we issued details to the press who gave it wide media coverage. Within a short time a member of the staff from the Salvation Army hostel in central Belfast made contact to say that the description fitted one of their residents, thirty-three years old Norman Maxwell, who had not been seen for a few days. As a result we arranged for the body to be viewed and it was confirmed that it was that of Maxwell.

As part of our initial investigation into his death we began to build up a profile of his background and activities. We established that he was a man who suffered from a mental illness and had spent periods in the local Purdysburn Psychiatric hospital. When not in hospital he resided in the Salvation Army hostel and, when he could afford it, spent his time visiting various drinking clubs in Belfast.

The crime was later solved to a degree when we learned that on the day Murphy was released from prison, some of his friends had decided to throw a drinking party in the Loyalist club which was located in the lower Shankill and frequented by many members of the UVF. The party drifted on into the evening and by a most unfortunate coincidence Norman Maxwell had chosen that time to visit the club for a quiet drink. With his bushy beard and tall lean figure he stood out from the rest of the crowd and Murphy enquired who he was. No one quite knew so Murphy had him brought to the hallway of the club to be questioned. Owing to his mental condition Maxwell was a poor communicator and I am sure he did not realise the dangerous situation he was in. According to a man later arrested for withholding information about the murder, Maxwell became agitated and Murphy and others took him to the large enclosed yard of the club where they set to him and gave him a severe beating resulting in his death. It is believed the body was concealed in the yard of the club overnight and the following evening was loaded into the taxi and driven some three miles away to Alliance Parade where it was dumped in an effort to frustrate the subsequent police investigation.

For me this crime reinforces the sheer depravity of Murphy who, on the very day he was released from prison, an occasion when most criminals would savour their freedom with a few drinks and renew old acquaintances, he felt the need to satisfy his blood-lust by beating a defenceless mentally ill man to death.

As the weeks went by the murder squad at Tennent Street station continued with their efforts to put Murphy behind bars again and from an unexpected quarter we received some preliminary evidence which, if allowed to develop with time, and a lot of effort, would have connected him to one of the earlier cut-throat killings.

Meanwhile, Murphy was enjoying life to the full and had acquired a distinctive mustard Rover 2000 car which at that time was an up-market model and somehow seemed out of place in the working class district of the Shankill. He dressed in a flashy but casual manner in a leather jacket, open-neck shirt, jeans and white shoes. He struck up a friendship with Jackie 'Nigger' Irvine, another established member of the UVF, and all sightings of them were carefully logged in the murder squad offices. He also found a new girlfriend, Hilary Thompson, and they lived together at 92 Forthriver Park in the Glancairn housing estate.

However, we were disturbed to note that he seemed to now have a following of younger members of the UVF. All the indications were that he was putting together a new unit which would inevitably lead to the deaths of more people. We decided that we should disrupt this by arresting them under the Prevention of Terrorism Act and taking them to Castlereagh Detention Centre where they could be held for up to seven days without criminal charges being brought. I was also anxious to meet Murphy face-to-face to get the full measure of him. On the day of the arrests I went to Castlereagh to brief the interviewers and as I entered the administration block where each new prisoner is processed by having a custody record opened and fingerprints taken I met Murphy in the corridor. I recognised him immediately from our photographs of him. He was stripped to the waist and it was clear that he was something of an exhibitionist and arrogantly wanted to be the centre of attention. I countered this in the best way possible by totally ignoring him and he disappeared along the corridor in the direction of the cell blocks with his uniformed escort.

During the following seven days Murphy was interviewed intensively. Initially he tried to maintain his attitude of self-importance but my staff, with a few carefully chosen phrases, divested him of this. When I first spoke to him in the interview room he was in a rather subdued frame of mind as he sat facing me with his arms folded. He was quite prepared to engage in small talk but when we accused him of involvement in a specific crime he merely replied, 'Nothing to say.'

I also made a point of interviewing all of his younger associates then in custody. I tried to point out that the course they had embarked upon with Murphy would only bring them misery. But they refused to communicate with us and it was clear that they had been well briefed and were full of youthful arrogance. At their end of the seven-day period of detention, Murphy and his gang left Castlereagh without being charged with any crime. But at least we had let them know we were aware they had banded together. I had a sense of foreboding that turbulent days lay ahead for us in dealing with them.

We had not long to wait and within a short time I found myself standing at the scene of the murder of a young Protestant man named Brian Smith who came from Bangor in County Down, about fifteen miles from Belfast. He was the front seat passenger in a car travelling along Crimea Street in the heart of the Shankill late one Sunday evening. The car drove along Crimea Street and turned left into a side street. Immediately a burst of shots were heard and Smith was gunned to death in the car. The man who was asleep in the back seat was seriously wounded by a stray round. When the driver was interviewed he claimed he and his two passengers had been drinking in the Loyalist club and when they had left it were followed by a motorcycle which overtook them just off Crimea Street and the pillion passenger had fired the fatal shots.

Our continuing enquiries into the crime revealed that Smith, who was a car dealer, was the man from whom Murphy had purchased his Rover 2000 car. On taking initial possession of the car Murphy had put a down payment with the promise of the balance later. Of course Murphy had no intention of paying up and Smith had begun to pressurise him. Murphy was becoming fed-up with the persistence of Smith and invited him to come to Belfast on that fateful Sunday when the matter would be settled by arranging for him to be murdered.

A few weeks later, one of my detective inspectors and I took a look at Murphy's home at 92 Forthriver Park. We had been doing this frequently and were always interested in any cars parked at the house. On this occasion we saw Murphy's Rover car in its usual spot and alongside it a car we had not seen on previous occasions. We decided to go to Murphy's house and find out exactly who was visiting him. We took the most convenient route which led us to the back door. It was opened by Murphy's girlfriend and we invited ourselves in as far as the kitchen.

Murphy soon appeared from the lounge and was by now back to his old arrogant and self-confident form. We engaged him in small talk but he was becoming distinctly uncomfortable with our presence which I tried to develop by staying firmly put. Eventually the lounge door opened and a familiar male voice shouted, 'We have to go now, Lenny'. Murphy became intensely angry and answered, 'You stupid bastards — if that had been me I would have stayed quiet in the lounge all night — you might as well come out now.' At that point the man who had been driving the car with Smith on the night he was shot dead, and another man, appeared in the kitchen.

Murphy was quite undeterred by the interest the police were now showing in him and his next opportunity to stain his hands with blood came on Friday, 22 October 1982. The sequence of events began when the Provisional IRA kidnapped a middle-aged part-time member of the Ulster Defence Regiment named Thomas Cochrane as he made his way to work at his day-time job in a factory in County Armagh. The PIRA issued a statement saying that they were holding Mr Cochrane for interrogation. In reality this meant torture followed by a bullet in the head. The crime made news headlines and the thought of what Mr Cochrane, if still alive, would be enduring, raised community tensions considerably. In north Belfast, which was far from the scene of the crime, one could almost feel it in the air.

On the evening of that date Murphy and his relatively new unit were drinking in the Loyalist club. At closing time they had decided to kidnap one, possibly two, Roman Catholics, whom they planned to hold as ransom for the release of Mr Cochrane. Murphy ordered two of his men to hijack a black taxi of the type which ply continually up and down the bus routes of the Shankill and Falls Roads.

A taxi was hijacked as ordered and Murphy was collected at the Loyalist club. A number of men were later prosecuted for this crime. I recorded an admission from a William Cowan who drove the taxi during the crucial part of this incident and who was later sentenced to life imprisonment, hence my ability to fill in the details. According to Cowan, Murphy ordered the hijacked taxi to be driven to Brookmount Street off the Shankill Road where his mother and father lived and where Murphy himself once resided in a different house prior to going into prison in 1976.

On arrival in the street Murphy disappeared for a short time and when he came back he was wearing a combat jacket and was armed with a Walther pistol. Murphy sat in the front passenger seat; Thomas Stewart in the rear. Cowan drove them down the Shankill Road on Murphy's instructions and turned right along Millfield and then onto the Falls Road. After a few hundred yards they saw the lone figure of a man standing at a bus stop. According to Cowan the man was swaying and seemed to be drunk so they pulled in alongside him. Murphy spoke through the front passenger window and asked the man if he wanted a lift to which he replied, 'Aye — thanks'. Murphy then got out of the taxi, opened the rear passenger door and invited the man to step inside which he willingly began to do. When the man was almost in, Murphy gave him a final push, climbed in after him, and closed the door. Cowan did a U-turn on the Falls Road and retraced his route back to the Shankill.

By now the unfortunate man was beginning to realise what was happening and started to struggle. Murphy and Stewart commenced the ritual beating and Murphy crashed the Walther pistol down on his head five or six times. When they reached the Shankill Road Murphy directed Cowan to return to Brookmount Street and stop at the entrance to the alleyway which runs behind the houses. He did as instructed and on arrival Murphy told Stewart to pull the now unconscious victim along the alleyway to the rear of his old, and by now almost derelict house, while he ran round and entered by the front, walked through to the small yard and opened the back door. Stewart began to pull the man along the alleyway, was joined shortly by Cowan and between them they carried him into the kitchen of Murphy's old house.

Stewart was left to guard the victim while Murphy now drove back in the taxi to the Loyalist club to find more help. It seems that at that stage he intended to keep his victim alive, at least until Thomas Cochrane turned up, but he obviously needed more men to take turns at guarding him. The Loyalist club was closed for the night but Murphy spotted two UVF members, one of whom was named Noel Large, later convicted of murder. Murphy instructed Large to get into the taxi. They returned to Brookmount Street and Murphy stopped the taxi. He then went to his mother's house nearby, taking Cowan and Large with him. According to Cowan, Mrs Murphy was still up and about and when the three of them appeared into the house she asked what was going on. Cowan said that in the light of the house he could see that Murphy's hands and clothes were bloodstained. Murphy took all his clothes off and changed into fresh ones.

Cowan noticed that his own hands were bloodstained from carrying the kidnapped man and he washed them under the taps in the kitchen sink. He saw that the spring in the magazine of Murphy's Walther pistol was protruding and seemed to have got broken when used to batter the unfortunate victim into unconsciousness.

Cowan's clothes were also stained with blood. He walked to his own house several streets away and changed but returned almost immediately to Brookmount Street where he rapped on the door of Murphy's old house. Murphy answered it and announced to Cowan that the man they had kidnapped was now dead. When asked what happened Murphy said that after the victim had been carried into the kitchen Stewart lost control of himself and finished the man off.

The gang decided to now begin to destroy the evidence of the crime and Cowan, accompanied by Large and Stewart, got into the hijacked taxi. Stewart brought with him a garden spade, the shaft of which was broken. It later turned out to have been the weapon which finally killed the victim and had been used with such ferocity that it broke in two. Cowan drove the taxi to the Glencairn housing estate, about one mile away, and he was followed by Murphy in another car. Cowan pulled into a quiet car park and Murphy set the taxi on fire by pouring petrol over it and setting it alight. Meanwhile, the dead body of their victim continued to lie in the vacant house in Brookmount Street.

The members of the gang went their separate ways. As they were doing so the family of a forty-eight year old Roman Catholic named Joseph Donegan, who lived in West Belfast, were becoming increasingly concerned at his failure to return from an evening's drinking in one of the clubs in the Lower Falls area. When the clubs emptied at closing time Mr Donegan normally took a bus or taxi home but it was well past midnight and there was no sign of him. The family eventually contacted the police about the matter and in due course they went public with appeals for help and giving the missing man's name.

There was still no sign of Thomas Cochrane, kidnapped by the Provisional IRA, and Murphy realised that in their frenzied assaults on their victim they had failed to get his name. Without it he and his unit could hardly go public and bargain for the release of Mr Cochrane with any credibility. As the news bulletins now covered the story of the missing Joseph Donegan, Murphy decided to recover what he could from the shambles of his operation and on the Saturday began to anonymously telephone local newspapers and politicians stating that, 'A dead Cochrane is a dead Donegan'.

Also, on that Saturday, Cowan returned to the Shankill Road after snatching a few hours sleep. He began to search out other members of the murder gang and shortly after nine o'clock in the morning, found Stewart sitting in a car in Crimea Street with another man. Cowan approached them and the following is an extract from his written confession, 'I was surprised to see that Stewart was still covered in blood. I could see blood on his hair, face, hands, jeans and T-shirt. I asked him was he mad running about like that and he just laughed. He then jokingly asked what was wrong with me being up so early and could I not sleep?' I am sure criminal psychologists could offer an explanation for this bizarre behaviour but for me it was simply the case of a killer being proud of his work. Blood was worn like a badge of distinction to impress his friends.

As the weekend wore on into Sunday there was still no sign of Mr Cochrane, and Murphy and his gang decided that that evening they would have to dispose of the body of Joseph Donegan. Their plan was to put it into the boot of a stolen car in the evening and dump it far from Brookmount Street. This would throw the police off their tracks. Cowan agreed to drive the car with the body in it. He reversed the car as far as the entrance to the alleyway and opened the boot lid. The other members of the gang shuffled along the alleyway with Mr Donegan's body but suddenly two members of the public appeared in the street. Cowan panicked at this, closed the boot lid and drove off. The men carrying the body dropped it in the alleyway, made off on foot and the operation was abandoned. As daylight broke on the Monday morning a number of men on their way to work saw the body lying in the alleyway and summoned the police who soon arrived and cordoned off the area. A full forensic team was brought to the scene. They had little difficulty tracing the movements of the body from where it was found back to the kitchen of Murphy's old house where heavy bloodstaining and a number of human teeth were found. During the post-mortem examination of Mr Donegan it was found that he had been savagely beaten to death. Contrary to some reports his teeth had not been extracted as part of a torture process but had been knocked out by blows delivered with great ferocity possibly from the spade.

Within a short time a battery of pressmen turned up at the scene and a small crowd of onlookers began to gather. Incredibly, Murphy also brazenly drove into the street in his Rover 2000 car. He was immediately arrested and taken to Castlereagh Detention Centre for interview. He was held for the full seven-day period. While agreeing that he had once lived in the house where the murder had taken place he said that he now had no control over it and of course emphatically denied any knowledge of the murder. Once again he had to be released from custody. Stewart too was interviewed at length but denied everything and had to be released. In October 1996 he was shot dead by the UVF in Belfast as he had by then aligned himself with the LVF in Portadown, against their orders.

About a week after the killing of Joseph Donegan the body of Thomas Cochrane was found near the border of south Armagh. He had been shot in the head and there were signs that he too had been maltreated prior to his death. Quite touchingly the true nature of the decent people of Northern Ireland shone through when the Donegan and Cochrane families contacted each other to exchange sympathies and offer condolences.

At around this period in the history of the troubles, unknown to us, we were about to embark upon a new phase which became known as the 'supergrass era'. This was to have a profound effect on all of the paramilitary organisations. Essentially it revolved around the capture of certain key figures who, mainly out of self interest, confessed to their own crimes and offered to give evidence against their colleagues in the hope of obtaining immunity from prosecution for themselves or at least an early release from prison. The system had serious implications for those who previously thought themselves untouchable but it also irrevocably affected my personal life and that of my family as I will explain in more detail in the next chapter.

However, in the period immediately following the murder of Joseph Donegan it brought me into contact with Murphy yet again. The events began in a quiet County Down village, about twenty miles from Belfast, when a gang of men tried to rob the local post office and in doing so stabbed the postmistress to death. A number of the culprits were captured including a man named Joe Bennett who was a prominent member of the UVF. He confessed to a large number of crimes and it became clear to those detectives dealing with him that if used as a witness he could lock up a lot of suspects in Belfast. The facts were placed before the Director of Public Prosecutions for Northern Ireland and he granted Bennett immunity from prosecution. Bennett was being dealt with by detectives in another police division on the opposite side of Belfast so I had little knowledge of these negotiations until one day I was summoned by the officer in charge of the CID in Belfast. He brought me up-to-date with developments in relation to Bennett and handed me a number of witness statements taken from him which implicated in crime several prominent members of the UVF who resided in my Division. I was instructed to have the men arrested on the basis of this evidence and to charge them accordingly. Unfortunately, this did not include Murphy as Bennett, who had previous convictions, was in prison during the period Murphy was on the loose and, *vice versa*, Murphy was in prison when Bennett was at his most active.

However, one of the men implicated by Bennett was Jackie 'Nigger' Irvine, the man previously referred to as having teamed up with Murphy shortly after his release from prison in July 1982. Within a few days my detectives had rounded up eight of the men named by Bennett, including Irvine. I personally charged them, put them before Belfast Magistrates Court and they were remanded in custody.

On 10 October 1982 Irvine made an application for bail at Belfast Crown Court and on that morning I went along to brief the barrister representing the prosecution. When I had done so in an ante-room I entered the large foyer of the court, which in early morning was crowded with barristers, solicitors and witnesses. Not surprisingly Murphy had also turned up to hear Irvine's bail application. When I first spotted him he was standing right in the middle of the foyer. Many of the other people present, including members of the legal profession, nudged each other as word spread that the infamous Shankill Butcher was there to be seen by all. It was obvious that Murphy was revelling in the attention. The bail court was due to commence at ten o'clock and a few minutes prior to that all interested parties, including Murphy, filed in and took their seats.

When the judge made his entrance everyone stood up in the usual mark of respect but Murphy chose this moment to dart from the courtroom. It transpired that the judge was the one who had sat on the trials of the eleven men convicted a few years earlier of the cut-throat killings and Murphy obviously felt very uncomfortable in his presence. Irvine's bail application was one of many listed that morning and when it was heard the judge ordered that he should remain in custody. As I left the courtroom and passed through the foyer Murphy was still holding centre-stage. I again ignored him and returned to my office.

A few hours later my telephone rang and when I answered it the station telephonist asked me if I would accept a call from Lenny Murphy. I said I would and when Murphy came on the line he sounded anxious and told me he had just received a threatening phone-call in his home at 92 Forthriver Park. When asked to describe the details he said that when he answered the phone a male caller simply said, 'We are coming to get you, Leonard,' and hung up. It hardly needs stating that I was amazed by the sheer audacity of Murphy. After all the carnage he had caused he had the nerve to contact the police following the receipt of a threatening phone call. My response to him was appropriately brief.

However, I must concede that within a week the threatening phone call to Murphy suddenly became relevant. The events surrounding this took place on the early evening of 16 November 1982 as Murphy drove his Rover car through the Glencairn housing estate on his way to his home at 92 Forthriver Park. As he entered the car parking area near the back of the house, a blue coloured Morris Marina van pulled in behind him. Suddenly the rear doors of the van burst open. Two gunmen stepped out and walked quickly to the driver's door of Murphy's car where he was still seated. The leading gunman fired three bursts each of seven shots from a Berretta sub-machine gun into Murphy, while the second gunman fired from a .38 special revolver. Murphy died instantly.

The two gunmen stepped back into the van and drove off. They went as far as a quiet road known as Harmony Lane which gives easy access to the housing estate from the main Crumlin Road. The killers stopped the van in the middle of the laneway in such a position that it would block any pursuing vehicle and set it on fire to destroy the evidence. They then got into a waiting Morris Marina car and drove to a side street off the Ligoniel Road some half-a-mile away where no doubt a 'clean' car took them a stage further.

Our investigations into the crime revealed that the van used by the assassins had been purchased for a few hundred pounds in east Belfast a few days previously. The Morris Marina car turned out to be a car stolen from Andersonstown. It had been 'ringed' with false number plates. In other words it bore the registration number of a car of similar make and colour which was not stolen so that if seen and put through the computer at police or army checkpoints no suspicions would be aroused.

In the days which followed the death of Murphy there was much speculation as to who had carried it out. The Provisional IRA eventually claimed responsibility but some people doubted the veracity of this and found it hard to believe that republicans could mount an effective surveillance operation on Murphy in a loyalist area which would be extremely hostile territory for them. Some believed the actual killing was carried out by loyalists in order to get rid of him as his barbarity was an embarrassment to them. The truth lies somewhere in between insofar as there was collusion between loyalist and republican paramilitaries in carrying out the killing. During the course of our investigations we had reason to believe that the hard intelligence on Murphy's car, his regular movements and home address was gathered by loyalists. The information they gleaned included his telephone number at 92 Forthriver Park. I believe that the threatening phone call he received six days prior to his death was part of the PIRA's process of checking out the intelligence which had been handed to them. No doubt they also visited Forthriver Park on occasions to confirm where he parked his car. The wheel of misery continued to turn even after Murphy's death when some years later the loyalist who is believed to have gathered the intelligence for the PIRA was shot dead in a bar in east Belfast and the actual PIRA killers of Murphy went to prison on other charges.

A few days later Murphy's funeral took place from his parents' house in Brookmount Street. Several of my detectives were placed at strategic points along the route of the funeral to observe who was attending. We were unable to get close to the family home as the street was jammed with hundreds of onlookers and blocked off with several of the Shankill Road black taxis. An army helicopter hovered overhead and when Murphy's coffin appeared from the house six masked members of the UVF stepped forward and fired a volley of shots. The Shankill Road was lined with thousands of people as I watched the cortege emerge from Brookmount Street. The flag of the UVF was draped over the coffin and a large number of pressmen were also in attendance. As they tried to photograph the events a number of women ran forward, opened umbrellas, and blocked the view from the cameras. The large number of people attending the funeral was a depressing sight as it demonstrated the degree of support Murphy enjoyed among the people of the Shankill but I would temper this by saying, or perhaps hoping, that many were there out of curiosity and to witness the spectacle of the event.

8

THE SUPERGRASS PHASE

Historians looking back on the civil unrest in Northern Ireland since 1969 will be able to identify a number of readily distinguishable phases. For example, 1969 and the early 1970s are remembered for the widespread street disorder; 1971 to 1973 was a period of internment; the late 1970s are recalled as the time the treatment of suspects at Castlereagh Detention Centre caused controversy; 1981 as the year of the PIRA hunger strikes and so on. Of course, the constant thread running through all these years is the unremitting violence and the steadily mounting death toll.

The next distinct phase was that of the 'supergrass' and this ran approximately from 1982 to 1985. It caused massive disruption in all of the paramilitary organisations and was clearly marked by a corresponding reduction in violence, acknowledged today only by the few of my former colleagues who were left to deal with these cases.

The system revolved mainly around disaffected members of the paramilitary organisations, or those who were captured during or following the commission of some serious crime, deciding to clear 'their own slate' of everything they had been involved in and giving evidence against their accomplices. This, on many occasions, resulted in mass follow-up arrests by the police. Hence the 'supergrass' sobriquet. There is no doubt that most of these 'supergrasses' acted out of self-interest, hoping to gain total immunity from prosecution for their own crimes or, alternatively, a reduced prison sentence. On only one occasion did a former paramilitary surrender himself as the result of a troubled conscience. He implicated himself and several others in a number of serious crimes and was duly sent to prison, but his assistance to the police was rewarded with an early release.

If one accepted that 'supergrasses', or 'converted terrorists' as they were euphemistically labelled by the police, acted out of self-interest, then their evidence had to be regarded with great care. There was the ever-present danger that they might be tempted to embellish their testimony, perhaps even falsely implicate others, to gain greater favour. Accomplice evidence was nothing new and a number of safeguards had been built-in to the British legal system to avoid innocent persons being sent to prison as a result of some corrupt piece of testimony. The law decreed, for example, that an accomplice could be adjudged a wholly credible witness or, if he or she fell below this exceptional standard, then the evidence should not be accepted without some form of corroboration. Therefore, each case was assessed by a court on its merits and, as in the case of O'Doherty who gave evidence against Detective Sergeant McCormick, the judge might decide that the accomplice's evidence should not be relied upon unless supported by this corroborative evidence.

The first of the 'supergrasses' to fall into the hands of the police during this period, and who in a sense sparked-off the others who were to follow, was Christopher Black, a PIRA member operating in North Belfast. He was arrested by police in early 1982 following the hijacking of a vehicle in Ardoyne. When taken to Castlereagh Detention Centre for interview, he confessed to a catalogue of serious crimes and named all his alleged accomplices. The facts of Black's case were placed before the Director of Public Prosecutions who granted him immunity from prosecution. The police swept up over thirty of his alleged accomplices and charged them with many criminal offences. I had no part in his case but enjoyed the fruits of it when I went to Tennent Street police station in April 1982 as the head of the CID. PIRA activity in the Division had dropped to an all-time low. Most of the suspected members of that organisation in Ardoyne and New Lodge were either in prison on the word of Black, or else had fled the jurisdiction to escape arrest. It was some eighteen months before the trial began at Belfast Crown Court and was heard by Lord Justice Kelly. He found Black to be a credible witness and convicted most of those in the dock, handing out a variety of sentences depending on the nature of their crimes.

Later in 1982, Black was followed by the emergence of a major loyalist 'supergrass', Joe Bennett, mentioned in the previous chapter, who had been detained for offences relating to the murder of a County Down postmistress. He too was granted immunity from prosecution. His evidence later demolished what we believe to be the command structure of the UVF in Belfast when Mr Justice Murray found them 'guilty' of most of the offences alleged.

The unpredictable and therefore highly dangerous republican paramilitary group, the Irish National Liberation Army (INLA), also produced a significant 'supergrass', Harry Kirkpatrick, whose evidence removed over twenty suspected activists off the streets of Belfast. However, Kirkpatrick differed from Black and Bennett insofar as he personally committed five murders. In no way could he be considered for immunity from prosecution. Instead he was charged with the murders and placed on remand in a secure and isolated annex of Crumlin Road prison, Belfast.

The system was now quickly gathering momentum and for a while it seemed that almost weekly somewhere in Northern Ireland some terrorist was offering his services as a witness. One can imagine the consternation and disarray this caused within the paramilitary groups. No effort was spared by them in trying to discredit the system. All forms of opposition to it were mounted, which was a good indication that the right people were indeed being brought to book.

Leaving aside my charging of some of the persons implicated by Bennett, my first real involvement with the system came in January 1983 when a young UVF activist named William 'Budgie' Allen was arrested on suspicion of having committed a robbery and was taken to Castlereagh Detention Centre for interview. The detectives who spoke to him got the impression that with his pleasant and mannerly demeanour he was a cut above the average. Soon he began to unfold details of his participation in numerous crimes ranging from robbery to attempted murder. He had grown up in an extreme loyalist area and, like so many other young men, had become caught-up in the violence. He now found the prospect of a lengthy prison term somewhat daunting. He offered to give evidence against his alleged accomplices but as CID officers we had to be careful not to offer him anything which smacked of a deal. We made it clear we would be charging him and that the decisions on future proceedings against him would rest with the DPP. Also, I was personally not in favour of 'supergrasses' being granted immunity from prosecution. I felt they were more credit-worthy if dealt with before the Crown Court when they could as it were, cleanse themselves, by pleading 'guilty' to their own crimes. This was the course adopted with Allen and he too was remanded in custody to the secure annex of Crumlin Road prison. Incidentally I should make it clear that Allen did not acquire his nickname 'Budgie' as a result of having sung to us but was labelled this by his erstwhile friends because of his similarity in appearance to a TV character of that name.

In the months which followed we put together a comprehensive file on the crimes admitted to by Allen and submitted the case papers to the Director of Public Prosecutions who agreed with our recommendations that he should stand trial for all of the crimes he had committed. The DPP saw no impediment to the police proceeding with the arrest and charging of all the alleged accomplices Allen had named. This amounted to well over fifty suspects. We made the first of our dawn raids on their homes in early July 1982 and netted only about twelve. This was not surprising as Allen's detention on remand in the secure annex of the prison was a clear signal that he was being considered for use as a 'supergrass'. Many of his former associates had now gone to ground at alternative addresses. However, we persisted with searches at various locations over the following weeks. Uniformed officers on patrol were given details of those now wanted for questioning and some were arrested on the streets or at vehicle checkpoints. The end result was that we located a total of forty-seven suspects, all of whom were interviewed at length at Castlereagh Detention Centre. Nine of these made admissions to the crimes alleged by Allen. As part of the procedure of processing these prisoners it was necessary for Allen to confront each of them face-to-face to confirm that this was indeed the correct person he had implicated in his confessions. This took the form of Allen being produced from prison and taken round the various interview rooms by me. I would take him as far as the threshold of each room and the interviewee would be seated at a table opposite the two detectives who were questioning him. I would then relate the details of the allegations made by Allen against this particular prisoner and formally ask him if this was the person to whom he had referred. He would confirm or otherwise that it was. These confrontations brought a variety of responses from the interviewees with a few resorting to physical aggression, but most made vociferous denials or simply remained silent. On one notable occasion the prisoner was magnanimous enough to tell Allen he bore no hard feelings against him and could understand why he had now turned against the UVF.

One of the most significant people to be implicated by Allen was William 'Wingnut' Cowan, who, as mentioned in the chapter relating to the Shankill Butchers, confessed to his part in the sectarian murder of Joseph Donegan. He also went on to admit having killed two other Roman Catholics namely Steven Murphy, a teenager, who was shot dead in his home in Oldpark Avenue, close to Ardoyne and Trevor Close, a milkman, who was gunned down as he delivered milk to a shop on the Cliftonville Road.

It is perhaps something of an understatement to say that my high-profile involvement in these investigations made me unpopular within the ranks of these paramilitary organisations. Whenever possible, I endeavoured to lead my detective staff from the front by personally charging the suspects with the crimes alleged against them and putting them before the remand court. As a consequence my name soon became synonymous with the 'supergrass' system and the mass arrests which flowed from it. I was not therefore surprised when intelligence began to filter through that I was being targeted for assassination. Much to my regret the senior police authorities felt compelled, in the interests of my own safety, to move me from north Belfast and place me as divisional head of the CID in the more normal policing environment of east Belfast.

However, I was by now too deeply immersed in the 'supergrass' investigations to simply be cut off from them, particularly as I would be required to give evidence at Crown Court trial stage on many matters such as having recorded 'Wingnut' Cowan's confession to the three murders. Also, to further complicate the matter, two more UVF 'supergrasses' came to the fore at around the same period and they too were remanded in custody to the secure annex of Crumlin Road Prison. One of these was a man named James Crockard who had been arrested after an attempted robbery. When interviewed in depth by detectives he revealed his involvement in several other serious crimes including two sectarian murders committed on behalf of the UVF. The other was John Gibson, a UVF assassin, who confessed to a multitude of serious crimes including four murders. Neither Crockard nor Gibson were recruited by me, if that is the correct term, but were being dealt with by two other senior detectives. Together, Crockard and Gibson implicated no less than ninety other persons in their lengthy catalogue of crimes and in conjunction with Allen's evidence brought the total of suspects who could be charged to almost one hundred and forty. The evidence in relation to the crimes allegedly committed by these suspects had to be presented to the DPP to a very exacting standard and if one were to take a typical crime, say the bombing of a bar, then we had to prove all aspects of it by assembling the written eye-witness accounts, the forensic evidence including the continuity of the handling of all of the physical evidence, the report of the army bomb disposal officer, statements from the injured and the evidence of their medical condition together with the written accounts of what the persons alleged to have committed these crimes said during lengthy interviews with detectives.

This was an enormous task so my transfer to east Belfast was placed in temporary abeyance. I was given the role of co-ordinating the preparation of all of these prosecution files with a staff of six suitably experienced police officers with supporting typists. We set up office in York Road RUC station and began to put the evidence together. Many of the one hundred and forty persons now accused were in custody so their legal representatives began to apply pressure to have the prosecution files submitted to the DPP as quickly as possible. On occasions their clients were appearing on weekly remands and frequently I attended the courts to be cross-examined by defence solicitors and to give presiding magistrates a progress report on each of the cases. As one can imagine this also served to further raise my profile among the paramilitaries and one could be forgiven for thinking from the outside that I was orchestrating the whole system on behalf of the police.

Further intelligence then came through that the paramilitaries were intensifying their efforts to get to me and had now probably obtained my home address. I accepted the risks of being an RUC detective and did what I could down though the years to cushion the effects of this on my devoted wife, but we now also had two children whose safety had to be considered. The advice from RUC headquarters was that I should move to a different address as soon as possible. I vividly recall breaking the news to my wife just as we finished our meal one evening, but we tried to put the matter in perspective by remembering all those dead police officers and other victims of the violence who had not had the benefit of a prior warning. Still, it was a wrench to be pulled away from a home we had spent several years putting together.

On 9 April 1984 William 'Budgie' Allen appeared at Belfast Crown Court to be tried on the crimes he had admitted to. The proceedings caused considerable interest among the relatives and friends of the persons charged on his evidence. They were very much aware that pleading 'guilty' was a prerequisite to him being used as a witness. The court duly convened and the clerk arraigned Allen by reading out the charges against him from the bill of indictment. He pleaded 'guilty' and Lord Justice McDermott sentenced him to fourteen years imprisonment. Until then Allen's confessions were in the form of written statements taken after caution. I now faced the job of re-interviewing him and taking down what he had to say as witness statements. This took eight days to complete and in the certain knowledge that defence counsel would later try to discredit this process by claiming I was simply schooling Allen on what to say I carried it out in the most scrupulous manner possible. I submitted the statements to the DPP who directed that the charges against the forty-seven accused should now proceed.

At around the same period James Cockard also appeared at Belfast Crown Court where he too pleaded 'guilty' to a whole series of crimes including two sectarian murders and was sentenced to life imprisonment. He was returned to the secure annex of the prison and the process began of converting what he had said under caution into written witness statements. On receipt of these the DPP ordered proceedings to continue against those already charged on his evidence, which totalled thirty-three.

The next logical step in the judicial process was to have these persons returned for trial and this necessitated each of the accused being served with the official legal documents, mainly written statements, which contained all of the evidence it was intended to use at their trial. As part of the process of having them committed for trial the accused were required to appear before a magistrate when they were entitled to raise legal arguments or call defence witnesses in an effort to persuade the magistrate that there was insufficient evidence on which to proceed to a full Crown Court trial. The accused also had the right to request that some of the prosecution witnesses be called to give verbal evidence during these proceedings. In such cases what is said by each witness under oath is typed by the court clerk and presented as a deposition to be signed. In the Allen and Crockard cases the persons charged on their evidence chose to accept the vast bulk of the formal written evidence against them but requested that their accusers be called to make a deposition. This was a useful legal ploy as it gave the defence lawyers an opportunity to size-up the 'supergrass' as a witness and cross-examine him. It also gave the accused a chance to try and persuade the witness not to continue to give evidence, if necessary by physical and verbal intimidation.

The documents served on the accused are known as the committal papers and each set ran into literally hundreds of pages. Bearing in mind the fact that the number of persons charged on the evidence of Allen and Crockard numbered ninety, it was quite a daunting task to get these ready and serve them on the accused. The normal station photo-copying facilities were unable to cope with this amount of work so we had to enlist the help of the RUC printing unit. Their staff helpfully came in at a weekend to operate their more sophisticated copying machines. On completion we loaded the papers into a police van and the prison authorities allowed us access to the prison yard. With the aid of a hand truck we wheeled the sets of documents into an interview room. Each of the prisoners was then produced and I formally served the documents on them. Most remained sullen and simply snatched the papers from my hands before turning on their heels. Others verbally abused me, while a few poked light-hearted jibes.

The Crockard committal proceedings were listed to commence on Monday, 25 June 1984. The legal authorities had decided that, because of the large number of accused, the normal magistrates courtrooms would be too small, so they utilised one of the larger Crown Court rooms which are located opposite Crumlin Road prison.

On that morning the huge foyer of the courthouse was crowded with people and there was no doubt that many of these were relatives and friends of the accused. They gradually began to filter into the actual courtroom and soon the public seating area, which holds about two hundred, was filled to capacity. Accompanied by a colleague I took a seat in an area designated for police witnesses and quietly watched as prison staff began to bring the prisoners up into the dock via the steps leading from the tunnel which connects the courthouse with the prison. Their handcuffs were removed but the dock area was too small to hold them all so the overflow was placed in two seating areas immediately adjoining the dock where they were closely supervised by prison officers. Those on bail were also beginning to appear and they were placed in the seats normally reserved for jurors in Crown Court trials. The atmosphere was boisterous with several of those in custody exchanging greetings with relatives and friends in the gallery, but there was also a definite tenseness in the air. The accused and their relatives hurled a barrage of abuse at me but I held my ground and remained impassive to their threats and insults. Crockard, of course, was not in the court at this stage but was in the custody of prison staff in an ante-room.

The magistrate appeared from his room and took up his seat on the bench. The formal proceedings then commenced with the clerk reading out no less than ninety-two charges, several of which were related to murders. This obviously took a considerable period of time to do and just before lunch the Crown prosecutor called Crockard to the witness box. There was a deathly silence in the courtroom as word was relayed to the room where he was being held. With a jangle of handcuffs he appeared and was led to the witness box. He was met with a tumultuous uproar from the public gallery and the dock but the magistrate responded by calling for order. It took a considerable period of time for the crowd to settle. Eventually the prosecutor began to elicit the evidence from Crockard and the clerk commenced to type it. However, those in the dock soon began to harangue Crockard with all possible insults imaginable, including that of being a sex offender. The magistrate continually asked for silence but the accused, particularly those in custody, never let up for one moment. Every so often, despite being legally represented, a few of the more articulate of the accused would interrupt by making 'submissions' to the magistrate, most of which were spurious. In addition, the accused began to make requests to go to the toilet. Those on bail were permitted to leave the courtroom unescorted and they did so by continually tramping noisily back and forth, while those in custody were led up and down the stairs of the dock.

However, Crockard was a robust and street-wise character and it soon became clear that he was not going to be easily dissuaded from giving evidence. The typewriter clattered on. As he described each crime he had been involved in and named his alleged accomplices the Crown prosecutor would also formally ask him to identify these persons. Crockard would turn towards the accused and indicate the persons he was referring to. When lunchtime came the court rose and Crockard was placed back in handcuffs and led from the courtroom with a further outburst from the dock and gallery. It took a total of three days for Crockard's deposition to be recorded and throughout the entire proceedings the disorder continued. At the conclusion the clerk was required to read the lengthy deposition to Crockard and he signed each page. When he was finally removed from the courtroom the usual threats issued forth from the dock but the magistrate decided that all of the accused had a case to answer. They were returned for trial which would not ensue for several months.

However, little did I know that these events would pale to insignificance when Allen's committal proceedings commenced in the same court, before a different magistrate, some weeks later on 6 August 1984. I arrived that morning into the foyer of the courtroom to again find it crammed solid with people. The buzz of conversation was intense. There was a distinct absence of bewigged barristers and solicitors as the Crown Courts were in summer recess. It was immediately apparent that the mass turn-out of people was for the committal hearing. Accompanied by a colleague I wound my way through the crowd with armfuls of documents but right away the verbal abuse began. I kept moving and went to the prosecutor's office where we ironed out some last-minute routine problems after which we made our way to the courtroom.

As in the Crockard hearing the accused in custody were emerging into the dock from the tunnel. The prison staff began to remove their handcuffs and place them in the seating areas. Those on bail were directed towards the jury box. The public gallery steadily filled until it could simply hold no more. The accused and their relatives and friends were in a distinctly rumbustious mood. All manner of cat-calls, insults and threats were hurled at me but the practice run I had had in the Crockard hearing came in useful. I calmly scanned the great sea of faces to demonstrate that I was not going to be intimidated.

The magistrate appeared from a door adjacent to the bench, the clerk called for silence, and everyone stood up in the required mark of respect. The clerk then took a roll call of the accused and all had answered to their bail including one middle-aged woman who was charged with handling the proceeds of a post office robbery. Meanwhile, Allen was under guard in the same ante-room once occupied by Crockard. The legal process now required that all of the charges be read out. These amounted to an incredible two hundred and twenty seven, several of which related to murders. This took up all of the morning sitting and the accused and their friends remained orderly as there was nothing to be gained from interrupting the clerk. At around one o'clock the court adjourned for the lunch break and as it was intended to call Allen to the witness box immediately after lunch I retired with the prosecutor to his office.

Just before two o'clock we returned to the courtroom using a corridor reserved mainly for members of the legal profession and police. The gallery was again filling up and the accused were taking their seats. The hostility towards me began instantly with the usual barrage of verbal abuse. Although few people will ever have this unpleasant experience I can assure you it creates a distinctly uncomfortable feeling to know that facing you are some two hundred and fifty people, anyone of whom would gladly lodge a hatchet in your back.

The magistrate reappeared just after two o'clock and once again all rose to their feet and a hush fell over the courtroom. The prosecutor asked that Allen be brought to the witness box and as he did one could almost cut the air with a knife. A minute later Allen appeared through a side door, escorted by prison staff. There was an immediate uproar. All two hundred and fifty people, as if with one voice, let go of their anger and frustration. It really was an incredible sight and sound and it took the magistrate several minutes to have order restored.

The prosecutor began to lead Allen through his evidence and the clerk commenced to type. After the first few sentences those in the dock started urging Allen to leave the witness box and join them instead, as if that were his rightful place, among old friends. He ignored them and continued with his evidence but as he described the first of his crimes and pointed out in the dock those he alleged were involved with him the tension began to rise. One of the accused suddenly sprang to his feet and hurled photographs of his wife and children towards Allen, shouting that he was depriving them of a husband and father. The magistrate took a strong line. He repeatedly warned the accused and the spectators to be quiet, but to no avail.

After the first hour of Allen's evidence, when it became clear that he was not going to be easily deterred, the first of what I believe were a number of carefully staged ploys began when the only female accused appeared to faint and had to be carried from the court by two uniformed policewomen. Those in the dock used this incident to appeal to Allen to give up but he remained resolute and when some semblance of order was restored he continued with his evidence. However, this respite was short-lived and complete disorder soon broke out. Allen had to be speedily removed for his own safety. The magistrate endeavoured to make himself heard above the howls of the mob and adjourned the court to the following day. He left the bench and I joined the prosecutor in the well of the court, assisting him in gathering up his law books and court papers. At that point the accused and the spectators rose to their feet and turned their attention towards me by screaming in a tumultuous uproar. It was an incredible scene and as I turned towards them I understood clearly for the first time how the victim of a lynch-mob felt just before being seized. Fortunately, there was a thin line of uniformed police officers separating me from them and I walked slowly from the court in a controlled manner, with the sounds of the mob still ringing in my ears.

At half past ten the following morning the court resumed and as we waited for the magistrate to appear the usual verbal haranguing towards me began. Allen was duly brought to the witness box and continued with his evidence. I pondered on what schemes the accused had planned for the day but was not long in finding out when two of those in the dock started to interrupt the proceedings by making 'legal' submissions. As they did so it soon became clear that they had been carefully chosen. Both were convicted prisoners serving custodial sentences for other crimes and had therefore nothing to lose. In addition, they were not legally represented and the magistrate had to give them some freedom to defend themselves which they exploited to the full. Despite all of this Allen made considerable progress with his deposition and as he recounted each of the crimes he had been involved in, pointed out his alleged accomplices. The accused tried a new trick to counter these identifications by concealing themselves behind other prisoners or hiding at the rear of the benches where they were seated. Amazingly, and much to their surprise, Allen courageously left the witness box during such occasions and approached the dock, saying that the men he had just referred to in his deposition were those concealing themselves behind so-and-so. The accused could so easily have physically made contact with him during these forays, despite the presence of uniformed police and prison officers, but they seemed stunned by his audacity and he returned to the witness box each time unscathed.

The third day of the hearing followed a basically similar pattern and Allen was making good progress with his deposition in spite of the unrelenting pressure from the dock and public gallery.

On the morning of the fourth day, which was a Thursday, the accused changed their tactics and began to assault the prison officers and policemen who were escorting them through the tunnel to the courthouse. The officers gave as good as they got and after a considerable delay the prisoners were eventually brought up into the dock area. When the magistrate appeared a junior barrister representing most of the accused informed the court that as a result of the fracas in the tunnel one of the accused was now suffering from high blood pressure and requested that the proceedings be adjourned to allow him to recover. The magistrate conceded to the application and as he was rising to leave the court, two of the prisoners, including the one supposed to be suffering from the high blood pressure, created a further scene by producing two pairs of handcuffs they had managed to steal from the prison officers and police during the confusion of the row in the tunnel. Obviously, if the case was not going to be adjourned that day some of the prisoners would have used the handcuffs as a weapon, probably to flail at Allen if he approached the dock. Now that the court was not going to sit they knew they would be bodily searched on return to the prison, so they seized that moment to gain maximum impact. Their supporters then filed out of the public gallery, blocked the traffic on the Crumlin Road and produced placards condemning the 'supergrass' system.

The court did not resume until the following Monday and Allen made good progress with his evidence despite the constant agitation from the accused and their supporters. Tuesday was little different only on this occasion Allen's mother-in-law suddenly stood up in the public gallery and shouted at him to cease his evidence. She was led from the courtroom by police officers. I have no doubt she had been put under considerable pressure to come to the hearing and create that scene. At around twelve noon on the Wednesday Allen had completed his evidence and his typed deposition was just over sixty pages long. The law required that it now be read over to him in the presence of the accused and each page signed. This was obviously going to take a considerable period of time to do and an application was made to adjourn the hearing for fifteen minutes to allow the accused to go to the toilets.

However, I sensed that this request by the accused was the start of some new scheme, particularly as all their previous efforts to intimidate Allen had failed. Their only remaining chance of avoiding being returned for trial was to prevent him signing the deposition.

When the fifteen minutes recess was coming to an end the public gallery was heaving with people and they were boisterously exchanging words with their friends in the dock. Several items were thrown towards the prisoners. These consisted mainly of packets of cigarettes and confectionery.

Allen was brought to the witness box and the clerk of the court began to read aloud the deposition. At the conclusion of the first page he handed it to Allen to sign and that was the signal, no doubt pre-planned by the accused and their friends, for the start of what can only be described as a full-scale riot. The people in the public gallery began to assault the uniformed police officers and the prisoners started to clamber over the dock in an attempt to escape. The prison officers and police with responsibility for their custody had to draw batons and a fierce hand-to-hand battle ensued. Several officers sustained quite serious facial injuries. The scene was one of utter chaos and probably unprecedented in a British court of law. Once Allen had been removed to safety the next priority was to get those in custody back into the tunnel and after some very ugly scenes this was achieved. The uniformed police in the gallery were also making progress in clearing it but the mob spilled into the foyer and had to be forcibly ejected from the court buildings altogether.

When the situation was brought under control and the courtroom cleared the magistrate returned to the bench and formally adjourned the hearing until the following morning. He ordered that the public be totally excluded henceforth. However, as previously stated, to comply with procedure, the deposition had to be read over to Allen and signed in the presence of the accused so the following morning they returned to the dock. Despite the continuing verbal abuse the deposition was read and signed, and the accused were returned for trial to Belfast Crown Court.

I made my way back to my office in York Road police station where, in my absence, my team had been working hard on putting the papers together on the Gibson case. When the DPP received the papers, he directed no less than one hundred and forty charges against Gibson, including four murders. Gibson appeared at Belfast Crown Court on 9 November 1984 and pleaded 'guilty'. It took all of that day for the crown counsel to outline the facts of the case to the judge. The case was adjourned to 14 November when Gibson was sentenced to life imprisonment.

He was still intent on giving evidence against his former alleged accomplices. As a large number of people had already been charged on his word, it was essential that what he had to say be now recorded in the form of written witness statements, as soon as possible. So I quietly arranged for Gibson to be produced to Castlereagh Detention Centre and spent a full six weeks taking down in writing the details of all of his crimes.

During that period he was allowed to have occasional visits from his wife and towards the end of that lengthy debriefing I began to detect a change in his attitude. He seemed to be going off the idea of giving evidence, although when questioned in-depth on this he maintained that he wished to continue. As a consequence I submitted the witness statements to the DPP. However, my intuition was right and in March 1985 he announced that he no longer wished to be regarded as a 'supergrass'. He was moved from the secure annex of Crumlin Road prison to a normal wing of the Maze prison outside Belfast. All of the persons charged on his evidence were immediately released from prison with the exception of those few who had made admissions to their crimes. Despite the disruption he had caused within the ranks of the UVF he quickly integrated into normal prison life. This was not surprising because the leadership shrewdly deduced that if he was physically harmed in any way it would make it more difficult to persuade other 'supergrasses' in future to return to the fold.

Meanwhile, the trial began of the thirty-three persons charged on the word of Crockard and ran for three weeks before a high court judge sitting alone. Crockard already had an atrocious criminal record. The defence lawyers exploited this to the full and had little difficulty in discrediting him. The judge decided that it would be too dangerous to convict on his evidence without substantial corroboration and the trial collapsed, allowing the accused to walk free.

The Allen trial was now coming on stream but the DPP wisely decided that they could not risk a repeat of the debacle of the committal proceedings so they decided to hold the case in three separate stages. The first phase would be that of William 'Wingnut' Cowan who had admitted to the three murders. His case would be heard in conjunction with that of Robert Grainger who had confessed to associated offences. Allen would not be called to give evidence at their hearing because some of their offences, such as the three murders, were committed outside his knowledge, and the case would go forward on their admissions alone. When this was concluded they proposed to hive off twenty-five of the remainder and put them on trial. Depending on how this was accepted they would move to a final phase.

On the morning of 26 February 1985 the trial of Cowan and Grainger began. Both pleaded 'not guilty' to a long list of charges. Their principal defence was that their confessions were inadmissible on the grounds that they had been duped by the police into making them during interview. The case ran for about three weeks and the trial judge ruled that Cowan's statements were admissible in evidence. He was found 'guilty' and sentenced to life imprisonment. Grainger asked to be re-arraigned and he pleaded 'guilty' to his charges. He was sent to prison for fourteen years.

The trial of the twenty-five then commenced at Belfast Crown Court on 20 March 1985 before Lord Justice Higgins. Once again the public gallery was filled to capacity and the accused were steadily brought into the dock. Those on bail were also called forward. The atmosphere was distinctly more orderly, and I had no doubt they were under strict instructions from the eight or so queen's counsellors and corresponding number of junior barristers who were defending them to behave themselves at this crucial stage. When the proceedings began one of the defence counsel asked for the case to be adjourned as some of the accused wanted to be represented by additional barristers who could not then make themselves available as they were engaged in other cases. The judge over-ruled this and stated that there were sufficient able defence counsel available in Northern Ireland to allow a fair trial to proceed at that time. The accused were arraigned, each of them tendered 'not guilty' pleas to all of the charges, and the proceedings continued.

The case progressed at a steady pace for a few days mainly by calling the various witnesses to prove the crimes alleged against the accused. These witnesses were the victims of shootings, bombings and robberies. From time-to-time further applications were made to the judge to adjourn the case in order to allow the additional defence counsel to be available, but he took a firm stand on the matter and refused. Then, about a week after the commencement of the trial the accused decided to make a protest at the intransigence of the judge by dismissing all of their defence counsel. About sixteen barristers filed out of the court laden with the law books which are the basic tools of their trade. The judge was unmoved by this and the hearing continued by calling the remaining witnesses to prove the crimes. But the vital stage of bringing Allen to the witness box was still some way off. The absence of defence counsel now gave the accused the freedom to address the bench. On several occasions their main spokesman endeavoured to persuade the judge that the European Court of Human Rights had ruled that accused persons were entitled to defence counsel of their own choosing. The judge patiently listened to these submissions from the dock but still refused to accede to their request for an adjournment.

At the end of March 1985 the trial went into a two-week Easter recess and when it resumed the accused announced to the judge that they now wished to re-engage their counsel. This caused some difficulty as many of those barristers had since taken on other work. So it was not until the end of April that they became available again and the trial re-commenced.

Allen was eventually called to the witness box on 1 May and the accused and their supporters remained orderly. They were obviously under strict instructions not to re-create the fiasco of the committal proceedings. It took a total of three days for Allen to give his direct evidence and as he described each crime he had been engaged in he formally identified each of his alleged accomplices. However, almost from the outset of his appearance in the witness box I sensed that the trial judge was hostile towards him. I felt right away that his evidence was not going to be accepted. When Crown counsel had finished with Allen it was then the turn of the defence. Altogether, Allen spent seven days under cross-examination and no effort was spared in rooting through every aspect of his personal life to discredit him. However, he bore up well and maintained his good natured and mannerly demeanour throughout.

On several occasions well known public figures appeared in the courtroom to witness the 'supergrass' system in operation. We were visited by no less a person than Mrs Geraldine Ferraro, an American who was then a potential presidential candidate. Also, Mr Tony Benn, the well known Labour MP sat in for a short time and Mr Patrick Mayhew MP, later to become Attorney General and Secretary of State for Northern Ireland, appeared. Their visits were a good indicator of how much controversy the system was provoking.

The trial rolled on through May and June 1985 and on 5 July the judge ruled that he was not prepared to accept the accomplice evidence of Allen. There were roars of jubilation in the dock and public gallery as twenty of the accused were set free. The remaining five were convicted on their own confession evidence and were given a variety of sentences, the most serious being life imprisonment on a man who had carried out a sectarian murder.

There were still twenty people charged mainly on the word of Allen and if his evidence had been accepted their cases would have been heard in the third phase of the trials. The Crown of course could no longer go forward with Allen as a witness so their charges were hastily withdrawn, again the only exception being four who had confessed to their crimes. Their cases were disposed of in September 1985 mainly on pleas of 'guilty' and only one received a custodial sentence. With the exception of one more murder case, covered in the following chapter, that was my last involvement with accomplice evidence. Despite the court's non-acceptance of Allen's evidence his assistance to the police was acknowledged by the Secretary of State who awarded him extra remission from prison. He was released after having served five of his fourteen years sentence.

Although the cases involving Crockard, Allen and Gibson had eventually led to mass acquittals or the withdrawal of charges, other such trials, for example those involving Black, Bennett and Kirkpatrick, had succeeded and several paramilitaries were now languishing in prison as a result. They had of course lodged appeals against their convictions and each was heard in due course by Lord Lowry, the Lord Chief Justice for Northern Ireland. He quashed each of the convictions and again we witnessed the mass release of suspected terrorists onto the streets. It was clear he was not in favour of the acceptance of accomplice evidence despite the most careful deliberations of some of his most senior judges who had originally convicted in these cases. I have often pondered as to why he chose this course. It may well be that he felt the whole process was a dilution of the high standard of the Northern Ireland legal system which he had steered through many difficult years. Or perhaps he saw his judges being placed in the invidious position of trying to resolve a paramilitary and political problem which more rightly rested with the government of the day.

Almost immediately some of the persons released in these cases returned to their old ways. The INLA, for example, embarked upon a bitter internal feud and several of those who had stood in the dock on the word of Kirkpatrick were shot dead. Some of the loyalists were also killed during inter-communal strife and many returned to prison on other charges including murder. The paramilitaries had not forgotten my role in the process and soon I was forced to move home again under threat. However, I do have the satisfaction of knowing that the level of violence fell during the 'supergrass' era and there are undoubtedly people whose lives were spared as the result of it.

9

SAFE HOUSES IN THE SUBURBS

It will be recalled from the previous chapter that, owing to the threat to my personal safety resulting from my deep involvement in the 'supergrass' system, I was ordered by my senior police authorities at RUC headquarters to vacate my seat as head of the CID in Tennent Street and take up a similar post in the quieter east side of Belfast. However, for several months I could only nominally hold this new position as I was temporarily diverted to York Road RUC station to co-ordinate the preparation of the large 'supergrass' files. During this interim period the CID in east Belfast was run by the four very able detective inspectors attached to the Division and only occasionally did I call into the divisional headquarters at Strandtown station to deal with various routine matters such as correspondence. I looked forward to the day when I would have the opportunity to settle into my new role uninterrupted.

I did, however, have to forget about the work in York Road for a period in March 1984 and go to Strandtown to head the investigation into the brutal murder of thirty-five years old Assistant Prison Governor William McConnell. He was shot dead by the Provisional IRA in front of his wife and three year old daughter as he left his home in the residential Hawthornden Drive area of east Belfast to go to his work at HM Prison, the Maze. This prison was about fifteen miles from Belfast and housed most of the convicted republican and loyalist paramilitaries.

The events which led to this crime began some months previously on a Sunday afternoon in September 1983 when thirty-eight republican prisoners made a daring break-out from the Maze prison, or H-Blocks as they are more commonly referred to owing to the structural shape of the buildings. During the break-out, one uniformed prison officer was killed. William McConnell was the most senior member of staff on duty that day. He was therefore responsible for having order restored within the prison while police and army reinforcements were called in to search the roads and open countryside for the escapees. During the following days nearly half had been recaptured and almost all were eventually arrested.

As a result of the mass escape the government ordered an enquiry to be carried out by Sir James Hennessey, HM inspector of prisons. He reported his findings in late January 1984. He apportioned much of the blame on the staff at the Maze, a verdict not totally accepted by the Prison Governors Association of which William McConnell acted as spokesman. They responded publicly by claiming that the constraints, presumably financial, placed upon them by the government, prevented the effective running of the prison. On one occasion William McConnell gave a television interview on the issue. But although he took the security precaution of appearing in silhouette form, his name appeared on a caption accompanying the broadcast. He gave the interview at his home in 5 Hawthornden Drive and, in addition to the television crews, it was attended by several other pressmen. Little did William McConnell know that as the result of the position he held within the prison he had already been added to the Provisional IRA's list of persons for assassination. His television appearance sufficiently provoked them to make him a priority target.

The area where William McConnell lived is on the suburbs of Belfast and is located at the upper end of the busy Belmont Road, close to open countryside yet only about four miles from Belfast city centre. The Stormont government buildings are nearby and overall the area could be regarded as middle-class, occupied by professional people such as doctors, bank managers and successful businessmen. In comparison to other parts of the city the area was relatively untouched by the troubles.

On the late evening of 5 March 1984, about a month after the television interview, William McConnell and his wife retired to bed, unaware that in number 6 Hawthornden Drive, a large detached house opposite theirs, a drama was unfolding which would shortly end in his murder. That address was occupied by an elderly, genteel couple, Mr and Mrs Gilliland, aged seventy-seven years and eighty-five years respectively. Events for them began at half past five that evening when a man knocked at their front door and asked for directions to Hawthornden Road. Although it did not immediately strike the Gillilands as odd that a stranger should select the third house along a cul-de-sac to seek directions, it later turned out that his visit was for the purposes of assessing what resistance would be encountered later that evening when a Provisional IRA assassination team arrived to take over their house.

This occurred in darkness at twenty minutes to ten when the frail Mr Gilliland, who had been sitting in the rear lounge with his wife, answered another knock at their front door and was confronted by a large burly man who pushed him into the hallway. Mr Gilliland, because of his age, could offer only verbal resistance and when he did so the intruder produced a handgun and growled, 'You be quiet or we'll do it our way.' Another man and a young woman then entered the hallway and quickly closed the front door behind them. On hearing the commotion in the hallway Mrs Gilliland rose to her feet to investigate but the gang then appeared in the lounge and ordered the elderly couple to sit down. The venetian blinds were open on the windows overlooking the back garden. The woman hurriedly closed them to prevent the possibility of anyone seeing in.

The smaller of the two male intruders then stood guard over the Gillilands while his two accomplices began to search the house and went through drawers and wardrobes in the bedrooms. When they returned to the lounge Mrs Gilliland asked them what they had been up to and they replied that they were looking for legally held weapons and were not thieves. Obviously, the gang wanted to ensure that their hostages would be unable to have access to perhaps a shotgun with which they could put up resistance should they have occasion to move them to different rooms in the house. The Gillilands were understandably very distressed and confused at what was taking place in their home and asked the intruders for an explanation. The large man who appeared to be the leader then said, 'We are UVF on the run from the police. They have road blocks all around the place.' He continued with his ruse by saying, 'I come from the Shankill Road. Have you any idea what it's like there with the police coming into the houses? Out at this end of the town you really don't know anything about the troubles.' Mrs Gilliland then told the gang she was feeling unwell. They offered to get her a glass of water. Just at that point Mr Gilliland stood up but was ordered to remain seated with the threat that if they did not do as they were told they would both be tied up.

The leader of the gang then stood guard over the Gillilands and told them that his two friends were going to leave the house for a short time to see if the police road blocks had been lifted. The smaller male and his female accomplice left the house by a side kitchen door but returned a short time later carrying a black coloured briefcase. Subsequent events revealed it contained a sub-machine gun and a radio scanner which in addition to the handgun were in the possession of the large man. The briefcase had probably been hidden nearby. The gang was not going to produce such damning evidence until they were sure that they could retain control of the house unobstructed.

After an hour or so had passed Mrs Gilliland was beginning to regain her composure and, despite threats from the gang determinedly went to the kitchen announcing that she was not going to be prevented from making a cup of tea in her own home. As she entered the kitchen Mrs Gilliland saw the woman attempt to conceal the radio scanner. It was apparent that she was monitoring the police radio network, listening out for calls to Hawthornden Drive. Mrs Gilliland made tea for her husband and herself and returned with it to the lounge where the smaller man had now taken up guard duties. Mrs Gilliland attempted to engage him in conversation by asking if he had a mother and father of his own, but the larger man overheard and rushed into the room warning her to be quiet.

A short time later the same man produced a piece of paper from his pocket and began to quiz the Gillilands about the occupants of each of the houses in Hawthornden Drive. He warned them not to tell any lies as he would catch them out by checking against the details already on his note. He specifically asked them if any members of the security forces lived in the area and Mrs Gilliland evasively replied there was none. He then produced Mr Gilliland's car keys which had been in the kitchen and asked him what sort of car he had. Mr Gilliland replied that it was a Mini Metro with an automatic gearbox. This seemed to temporarily throw the terrorist as automatic cars were still relatively uncommon in the United Kingdom and not everyone had the experience of having driven one. The same man then announced that they would be taking it but would leave it in Holywood, a town some five miles away. Perhaps in the vain hope that he could encourage them to leave soon Mr Gilliland informed him that his garage door was difficult to open, but the man responded that he would call on him for assistance when the time came.

As midnight approached the elderly couple were beginning to feel the strain of the traumatic events which had suddenly descended upon them and asked the leader if they could go to an upstairs bedroom to lie down. He agreed on condition that they left the bedroom door open so that one of them could maintain a watch on their movements. The Gillilands then made their way to a rear bedroom and lay down on two single beds. On checking the room the leader noticed a telephone extension and ordered Mrs Gilliland to unplug it and give it to him. He then left taking with him a chair which he placed on the landing just outside and sat down in a position where he could observe what was going on in the bedroom.

As the hours wore on the Gillilands were still uncertain what the gang were up to but it ominously crossed their minds that the take-over of their home was a prelude to an attack on William McConnell across the street. From where they lay they could hear the three whisper to each other and the sound of the police radio transmissions being picked up on the scanner downstairs. Occasionally Mrs Gilliland needed to visit the toilet and when she ventured onto the landing she was always confronted by one of the male intruders who would summon the young woman to accompany her to and from the bathroom.

At around half past five in the morning the leader of the gang came into the bedroom and ordered Mr Gilliland to come with him to open the garage door. The elderly man did as he was ordered and on the way collected a torch from the kitchen. He opened the garage door under the watchful eye of the terrorist who then escorted him back to the bedroom. An hour or so later the Gillilands heard their car being started followed by the engine revving loudly. It was apparent that the members of the gang were familiarising themselves with its controls in preparation for their eventual getaway. At around this time Mrs Gilliland asked the leader if they hoped to get away with the crimes they had so far committed. He answered, 'Yes. I have a good driver and tell the police they needn't bother fingerprinting because we have worn gloves. We are going towards Holywood and will leave the car there'.

The McConnell family across the street, which included their three-year old daughter, Gail, stirred from their beds at around half past seven to begin their daily routine. William McConnell got washed and dressed and at about eight o'clock sat down to his breakfast in the kitchen. Meanwhile, in the Gillilands' house the terrorists were now displaying signs of greater activity. Their leader came into the bedroom and warned the Gillilands to stay where they were. If they heard shooting they were not to worry as it would only be them defending themselves against the police. When William McConnell had finished his breakfast he collected his overcoat and kissed his wife and daughter in the hallway, totally unaware that this was the last time he would ever do so. He opened his front door and walked to his Vauxhall Cavalier car parked in the driveway. He began to check it for a booby-trap bomb, a normal procedure for many people in Northern Ireland. His wife too had a look round the car while little Gail stood on the doorstep.

Mrs McConnell was the first to notice some unusual movements at the Gillilands' house and saw that their Metro car was parked in the driveway facing towards the street. She also saw a young woman just getting into the driver's seat of the car. Initially she presumed she was a relative of the elderly couple. The Metro car emerged onto the street and suddenly Mrs McConnell saw two armed men dart from the Gillilands' driveway and run towards them with their eyes firmly fixed on her husband. She shouted a warning but one of the men had already begun to fire a handgun at William McConnell. He managed to run a few yards along the side of his house in a vain attempt to escape but soon collapsed from his wounds. The leading gunman then stood over him and fired bullets into his head and chest while his accomplice covered him with the sub-machine gun. When they had finished their devilish business, they got into the waiting Metro car and the young woman drove them off towards the Belmont Road. Mrs McConnell ran to her husband as Gail stood screaming hysterically on the doorstep. Neighbours who had heard the shots, including a doctor and a nurse, soon appeared and joined Mrs McConnell but it was apparent that William McConnell was dead. The Gillilands too heard the shots and emerged from their bedroom deeply distressed at their ordeal. Their worst fears were confirmed when they looked across the street and saw the group of people gathered in the driveway of the McConnells' home.

The police were immediately alerted and a uniformed patrol of officers soon arrived at the scene. When they discovered the nature of the crime they began to move people out of the McConnells' driveway to preserve as much evidence as possible. Mr Gilliland now appeared in the street and disclosed that the killers had taken over his house all night. The officers asked the elderly couple to vacate their home and stay with relatives for a while, pending expert forensic examinations of it. A wider area was then cordoned off with tape. I and several other detectives arrived a short time later and already a battery of pressmen were starting to turn up. A police doctor joined me at the scene and I assisted him in carrying out a preliminary examination of William McConnell. It was obvious from powder burns on his face that the victim had been shot in the head at close range and could not possibly have survived such ghastly wounds.

A well practised investigation system then swung into action. Before long we were joined at the scene by forensic scientists, police scenes of crime officers, photographers and mappers. The immediate requirement was to have the body photographed where it lay and then removed to the mortuary to minimise distress to the victim's immediate family and neighbours.

A ballistics expert examined the driveway and recovered some fragments of bullet heads. There were no spent shells which indicated that a revolver as distinct from an automatic weapon had been used in the murder.

Another forensic scientist began an inch-by-inch search of the Gillilands' home. In the kitchen area, close to a table and chairs, he found a small pile of cigarette ash on the floor, giving the impression that someone had been seated there for a considerable period. This was probably the female terrorist as she monitored the police radio. The expert then moved into an adjoining utility room. The floor here was partly covered with mats, but a centre area of light-coloured vinyl tiles was exposed. Interestingly, on these tiles the scientist thought he could see footwear marks, perhaps caused by the damp soles of shoes. When he chemically treated these imprints a distinctive pattern became more clearly visible and these were photographed with a special camera.

The scientist continued with his painstaking work, and on the basis that every physical contact leaves a trace, examined all of the seating areas on the ground floor in the hope of recovering fibres from the clothing worn by the gang. He also took fabric fibre samples from the chairs, settees and carpets as, conversely, some of these could have been on the terrorists' clothes as they moved around the house and would prove useful if early arrests of suspects were made. The examination extended to the upstairs and the chair on the landing was of particular importance. The Gillilands had already stated that the terrorists had sat on it in turn during the night as they kept guard on them in the bedroom. As an indication of how careful this examination was the scientist detected a single minute red coloured acrylic fibre on the back rest of the chair. This he placed in a plastic container for further analysis when he got back to his laboratory. He completed this stage of his work by taking fibre samples of the remaining furniture and carpets in the bedrooms.

When I had gathered all of the information that I possibly could at the scene I went to Strandtown police station and called in detectives from other stations in the Division. I also received a boost of manpower from the Belfast Regional Crime Squad. A major incident room was set up and staffed. When this had been done I was left with a team of around twenty detectives to work on the investigation. In comparison to a mainland force this would be regarded as a small number of detectives to work on a murder but for the RUC it was actually quite generous considering the number of killings we were faced with each year.

I held an initial and very comprehensive briefing in the main CID office. It was very important that every detective working on the case knew as much about it as possible. At its conclusion they asked pertinent questions on matters they were unsure of. It was abundantly clear from their attitude that they were incensed at the cruel manner in which William McConnell had been gunned down in front of his three year old daughter and I knew they would leave no stone unturned in seeking clues to the killers. I then detailed them for the various tasks, the most important being in-depth house-to-house enquiries in Hawthornden Drive and beyond. Also, all available uniformed staff were assigned to me. I asked them to commence a systematic search of the streets of east Belfast to look for the Gillilands' car which had no doubt long been abandoned by the killers. A short time later, despite the gang's claim that they would leave it in Holywood, they reported back that they had found the car in Eastleigh Drive, off Upper Newtownards Road and about one mile from the scene of the crime. I drove immediately to that area. The uniformed officers had sensibly cleared the street of people and had sent for the services of the army bomb disposal officer to check out the vehicle for booby traps. It took several hours for the bomb disposal officer to complete his strict procedure of checking out suspect cars. He finally gave the all-clear when he blew the boot lid open with a controlled explosion of a few ounces of commercial explosives. The car was then placed on a trailer and delivered to the forensic science laboratory for examination while some of my detectives were diverted to Eastleigh drive to commence house-to-house enquiries.

In crimes of this nature the major incident room is the nerve centre where all of the information gathered by the investigation teams on the ground is fed in by a strict procedure. It is then entered into computers in such a manner that the senior investigating officer can keep his finger on the pulse at all times and be in a position to identify relevant pieces of information and bring them together to form a picture of events.

Also, all members of the investigation team meet twice daily, at nine o'clock in the morning and seven o'clock in the evening when the officer-in-charge of the case brings everyone up-to-date. It is important that these meetings are held in a non-dictatorial manner so that those working on the case can raise matters of interest and suggest lines of enquiry which could usefully be pursued. I have always found that working detectives thrive in such an open atmosphere and it certainly brings out the best in them. At the conclusion of these meetings fresh lines of enquiry are agreed upon and then issued to each of the detectives in the form of written instructions, or action sheets as they are officially known. At the next meeting they would be required to give a situation report on these and so the process continues.

The first of these meetings was held in the main CID office at Strandtown on the evening of the murder. The enquiries to then had established that, after the crime, the Gillilands' car containing three people had been seen heading citywards along the Belmont Road and after about half a mile had turned left into Belmont Church Road. This route would have taken them through a number of side streets to Eastleigh Drive where the car was eventually found. But a number of witnesses had seen the car being parked there a short time after the murder and were emphatic that it was being driven by a lone woman without any passengers. She was then seen to walk off briskly towards the busy Upper Newtownards Road and witnesses lost sight of her after that. The woman had a number of options open to her. She could have been met by someone in a 'clean' car or could have simply caught a bus into the city centre. The main question now was, where had the two men got to? Once again there were a number of options open to them. They could have been dropped off somewhere between Belmont Church Road and Eastleigh Drive and collected by a waiting car. But this was risky as vehicle checkpoints are quickly set up after a terrorist outrage and they would easily be spotted since they were encumbered with the briefcase containing the firearms and the radio scanner.

In any event we had no doubt from the outset of the crime that it was the work of the Provisional IRA. I wound up the meeting by making the investigators aware that the republican press centre in

Belfast, an adjunct of Sinn Féin, the political wing of the republican movement, had issued the following statement, 'Belfast Brigade of the IRA claims responsibility for the execution of H-Block Governor William McConnell who organised and directed beatings in the jail and who was selected by the administration to break republican opposition to the allocation of menial and degrading tasks. This attack does not herald a new campaign against prison officials but it should come as a salutary lesson to those in the administration presently advocating a return to a policy of beatings as a means of controlling political prisoners.'

I spent the remainder of that evening in the major incident room reading the witness statements which were now beginning to accumulate. The phones were also busy, with members of the public calling in to give us information which they believed might be of help to the enquiry. I kept abreast of these until around eleven o'clock when I went home to catch some sleep.

At eight o'clock the following morning I returned to the incident room and before long the station duty officer at Mountpottinger police station telephoned me. This station is also situated in east Belfast in a small but densely populated and predominantly Roman Catholic area, about one mile from Strandtown. The vast majority of people living there are decent and hard working but there is a small element who would be sympathetic to the activities of the PIRA. Unfortunately the local police station bore testimony to this as it had been subjected to attacks from bombs, rockets and firearms. As a result it now resembled a fortress. The station duty officer informed me that at ten minutes to one that morning, the Ulster Defence Regiment was operating a vehicle checkpoint on the Albert Bridge, one of several such crossings of the River Lagan which flows through Belfast, when a Fiat car with three males on board emerged from Short Strand and turned onto the Bridge. On seeing the checkpoint the driver slowed down, almost hesitating, before continuing slowly on to where the first soldier stood. It stopped there. The soldier asked the driver for identification and he handed over his licence which bore the name Eugene Gilmartin with an address in west Belfast. There were two male passengers in the car and when they were asked for identification they replied that they did not have any. The soldier noticed that Gilmartin was sweating and appeared fidgety. He was not at all satisfied with the three men in the car and consequently directed it off the main traffic lane towards a number of other soldiers whose task it was to more closely investigate suspicious vehicles and their occupants.

The corporal-in-charge of this team immediately recognised Eugene Gilmartin and knew he was a suspected member of the PIRA. As a consequence he asked all three to step out of the car. The two male passengers, who I shall hereafter refer to as Mr A and Mr B, were again asked for identification but still refused to give it. It was then noticed that all three had been drinking. This only served to compound their awkwardness and it made them more difficult to deal with. Mr B eventually gave a name which turned out to be false. The soldiers began to search the car at which point he shouted 'UDR murderers', an apparent reference to an incident in Armagh city where members of the regiment were charged with killing a man. The soldiers then began to quiz Mr A as to his name and address. This made him more aggressive and he threw a punch, striking a soldier on the ear. He had to be subdued and after a brief scuffle with the soldiers this was achieved. The members of the patrol then decided to send for one of their officers and when he arrived and assessed the situation asked for police to come to the scene. Two uniformed constables responded to the call and when they heard of the events arrested Mr A and Mr B for failing to identify themselves and assaulting the soldiers. They were moved to Mountpottinger police station and lodged in the cells. The personal property of the prisoners was removed and this included an 1984 pocket diary found in the possession of Mr B.

Meanwhile Gilmartin, who had behaved himself at the checkpoint, was ordered by the soldiers to drive his car under escort to a military vehicle search centre near Lisburn, about fifteen miles from Belfast. The army staff at this centre were specially trained to more or less take vehicles apart in the search for items of a paramilitary nature, e.g. documents, explosives or firearms which might be concealed in car door panels, false fuel tanks etc. They had the expertise to put the vehicle back together again. Nothing of interest was found in Gilmartin's car and at around five o'clock in the morning he was allowed to leave the search centre in his car. He set off in the direction of Belfast. However, he again came under notice, this time by a police mobile patrol who saw him drive erratically, perhaps because he was in a jubilant mood at being released. Unaware of the events to date, the policemen stopped him. They detected the smell of stale drink on his breath and decided to arrest him and take him to Lisburn police station where he was routinely processed by a police doctor on suspicion of being drunk in charge of a motor vehicle. His Fiat car was impounded and at half past six in the morning he was released and took a taxi home.

The true identities of Mr A and Mr B were eventually established by the police at Mountpottinger and it turned out that they also had addresses in republican west Belfast. Considering all of the circumstances, I wondered if these men could be the elements of the PIRA assassination team who had murdered William McConnell making their way back to west Belfast via The Albert Bridge, after having lain low all day in some drinking den in Short Strand. If they were I wasn't going to miss an opportunity so I despatched some detectives to Mountpottinger to re-arrest Mr A and Mr B under terrorist legislation and take them to Castlereagh for interview. Also, I contacted the CID at Lisburn police station and asked them to similarly arrest Gilmartin if and when he returned to collect his impounded car.

On arrival at Castlereagh, police scenes of crimes officers took possession of the outer clothes worn by Mr A and Mr B for scientific examination and the prisoners were given immediate replacements. Then, just after half past one in the afternoon of that same day, Gilmartin, who was now completely sober, returned to Lisburn RUC station to collect his car. He was wearing a red coloured pullover, cream coloured trousers and black leather shoes with moulded rubber ridged soles. He was re-arrested and conveyed to Castlereagh where his clothes were also seized. A team of detectives then began to question Mr A, Mr B and Gilmartin. But these three suspects were no strangers to Castlereagh and said absolutely nothing during their subsequent seven-day period of detention, as was their legal right.

It was therefore important for my investigation team to concentrate their efforts in other directions which might connect the suspects with the crime. One of the detectives on the case carefully examined their personal property and when he had a close look at the 1984 diary belonging to Mr B it was blank except for entries on the spaces dated 28 and 29 February and 1, 2 and 3 March. These had been heavily obliterated by means of a black ballpoint pen. As these dates just preceded the crime they became of great interest to us so I decided to take the diary to the forensic science laboratory to see if they could, by some means, identify just what had been written to cause Mr B to so urgently conceal it. When I showed it to a documents examiner at the laboratory he was not too optimistic that the writings could ever be deciphered because they had been so heavily concealed with the black ink. But he felt that the best way forward was to have it sent to a Home Office laboratory in London, equipped with laser technology which could possibly bring up anything that had been written.

When I was at the laboratory I also took the opportunity to speak with the other scientists working on the case. I consulted with the ballistics expert and he informed me that he had completed his examination of the bullet fragments recovered from the scene of the murder and also the undamaged bullet heads found in the deceased's body during the post-mortem examination. He told me that the weapon used was a .357 magnum Ruger revolver and when he carried out comparison tests he found it was the same weapon used to kill a County Court judge, three soldiers, two policemen and a civilian, all of which were separate assassinations by the PIRA. The tests which led the scientist to this conclusion are carried out using a twin-lens microscope. When a bullet head is seen under magnification its surface is clearly marked with striations and they do indeed represent the appearance of a ploughed field. These furrows are caused by the bullet leaving the barrel of the firearm. As with fingerprints, no two barrels are identical. The twin lenses of the microscope allow two bullet heads to be examined simultaneously and, if fired from the same gun, the heads can be slowly turned until the striations make a perfect match.

This particular Ruger revolver had been lost from a uniformed police officer's holster during a riot in west Belfast and the paramilitaries were obviously making a special point of continually using it.

The ballistics laboratory had also been working on the clothes of the three suspects now in Castlereagh. Interestingly they found firearms residues on the cuffs of Mr A's jacket and on his trousers. Mr B's jacket also showed traces of gunpowder on the cuffs but Gilmartin's were clear of residues. However, this evidence unfortunately could not help to link them to the murder of William McConnell as the description of the clothes worn by the principal gunman was at variance with the clothes worn by Mr A and Mr B when arrested, so these two suspects must have picked up the residues in some other circumstances.

When I had finished discussing the case with the ballistics scientist I called at the biology department and spoke with the expert who had located the footwear marks in the utility room of the Gillilands' house and the single red fibre from the back rest of the chair on the landing. He had more news for me. He had just completed an examination of the Gillilands' car and had found red fibres on the back rest of the rear seat.

The Gillilands had of course already been asked if they owned a red garment which could have deposited such fibres. They replied they did not, so it seemed highly probable that such came from an item of clothing worn by one of the killers. Gilmartin's pullover was still with the ballistics department and a biologist informed me that as soon as it became available to him he would commence an examination to see if the red fibres could have come from it.

While we were there the scientist showed us the photographs of the footwear prints which had just been developed. To the inexpert eye the prints appeared as a jumbled mass of lines, ridges and smudges but the scientist carefully pointed out the outline of the sole and heel of a left shoe with a very distinctive wear pattern almost in the shape of a large question mark. He then unpacked Gilmartin's shoes from their plastic exhibit bags and, in the presence of another CID colleague, the three of us began to compare the photograph with the sole of Gilmartin's shoe which showed signs of heavy wear. At first glance the ridged pattern seems similar. We counted the number of ridge marks on the heel of the shoe and they matched exactly the number appearing in the photograph. We carried out a similar process with the sole and it too matched so, as one can imagine, we were by now becoming quite excited. However, the scientist urged caution at that early stage although I could detect that he too was becoming very interested. At that point he decided to take the examination a stage further. He obtained a large piece of white cardboard which he placed on the floor of the laboratory. He then took Gilmartin's left shoe and inked the sole of it, using a roller. The scientist removed his own left shoe, placed a plastic bag over his foot and put on Gilmartin's shoe. He then trod on the white cardboard and the inked sole left a clear impression. The scientist compared it with the photograph and they were identical. However, he told us that this examination was still very preliminary and that he would have to do a lot more work on it by microscopically comparing other defects in the sole of the shoe, such as cuts and other damage caused by everyday wear and tear, before arriving at a positive conclusion.

I returned to the incident room at Strandtown quietly confident that as a result of the forensic evidence which was now evolving we would probably be in a position to connect Gilmartin with the killing. I addressed my team of detectives at the evening meeting that same day and when I had received a progress report on the various tasks allotted to them I informed them of the developments in respect of the footprint. This, understandably, raised their morale and a highly motivated team left the conference room to continue with their work.

Over the next number of days, while the three suspects in Castlereagh remained silent, I kept in close touch with the scientists and eventually the case against Gilmartin became stronger when the biologist reported that the red fibres found on the chair and in the car could have come from Gilmartin's pullover. This was not simply a matter of matching their colours but involved a chemical analysis of the red dye used by the manufacturers. The process revealed that the suspect fibres were identical to those used in the make-up of the pullover. Although this may seem quite strong evidence it cannot be regarded as conclusive proof that Gilmartin's pullover deposited the fibres on the chair and car. The manufacturers probably produced thousands of similar such garments all coloured with the same batch of red dye and there could be any number in circulation in Northern Ireland. Nevertheless, it was another useful link in what would turn out to be a lengthy chain of evidence.

The same scientist who was also working on the footprint soon contacted me again and stated he had now completed his comparison tests and the footprints on the utility room floor had definitely been made by Gilmartin's left shoe. Furthermore, he told me that the wear on the left shoe was much greater than on the right which may be indicative of some physical deformity. This was an interesting point to note. I went to Castlereagh Detention Centre and consulted with the late Doctor Alexander M.C. who had carried out a medical examination of Gilmartin. He informed me that Gilmartin had a deformed left leg apparently caused by an explosion. This indeed could have resulted in the distinctive wear pattern on the sole of the left shoe.

Several days had now elapsed since Mr B's diary was sent to London for examination but the laser technique had failed to highlight the writing underneath the heavy black ink. It was returned to Belfast on 12 March, some five days after the arrests, and the local forensic document examiners had only one option left open to them and that was to use a solvent to dissolve the black ink. In doing so the experts ran the risk of also removing the writing underneath so they worked with great care and slowly some words began to appear. On the space dated 28 February 1984 they could read '10 am Christines for scale map' and on the entry for the following day, the 29th, was 'Make another arrangement', along with some words which were indecipherable. The solvent failed to uncover any of the entry dated 1 March 1984 but the space for 2 March was very interesting and read '9.00 ETS Camels .... 5 ..... Dene 20 CPA', the dots representing writings which existed but could not be deciphered. Some words also appeared on the entry for 3 March but these made little sense.

The examination of the diary was not concluded until 13 March. The full details of what had been found were then passed to me at Strandtown and I sat down with some of my colleagues to see just what interpretation could be put on the evidence with special emphasis on the 2 March entry. Could the '9.00 ETS' mean the 'estimated time of shooting'? 'Camels' made no immediate sense but the '5 ..... Dene' possibly represented a misspelling of 5 Hawthornden, the scene of the murder. '20 CPA' was most intriguing and could perhaps be an abbreviation of an address. We studied a map of the general area of the crime and there was a street of terraced houses named Campbell Park Avenue, just off the Belmont Church Road, the route the killers had been seen to take. It lay approximately mid-way between the scene of the murder and Eastleigh Drive where the Gillilands' car had been recovered. If we were correct in our deductions then this could explain why the getaway car had been abandoned by the lone female terrorist as the killers had perhaps left the car at Campbell Park Avenue and gone to number 20. We quickly researched this address and discovered it was occupied by a quiet elderly couple, Owen and Margaret Connolly, together with their daughter Carmel. The word 'Camels' appearing on the diary could now possibly be interpreted as a misspelling of her name.

I felt sure we were onto something here and had probably identified a PIRA safe house right in the middle of residential east Belfast. It was imperative that we move as quickly as possible but I also wanted to be reasonably sure that we would net all three members of the family in one swoop. We timed the operation to commence at seven o'clock that evening when the Connolly family should all be home from work. There was no knowing what we would find in the house so we took the precaution of having uniformed personnel set up roadblocks in the adjoining streets as an outer ring of security in the event of someone trying to escape. A section of armed officers was instructed to move stealthily into the alleyway at the rear of the Connolly house. When all was in place several teams of detectives began knocking at doors in the street on the pretext of doing routine house-to-house enquiries. I joined in the subterfuge in the company of a detective inspector who was my deputy and it was pre-planned that we would eventually knock at the door of number 20. It was answered by a small white-haired man aged about sixty years. I introduced ourselves to him and said we were making routine enquiries into the murder of the assistant prison governor and asked if we could come in. He agreed and led us into the rear downstairs living room where a woman was seated. When asked the couple identified themselves as Owen and Margaret Connolly.

I began a conversation with the Connollys and asked them if they had noticed anything suspicious on the morning of the murder which by now was almost a week past. They said they hadn't but I could sense that they were distinctly ill-at-ease with our presence. Owen Connolly then asked me if we were calling at other houses in the street and I told him we were. Without prompting he suddenly declared that he was a retired civil servant and had been a wartime RAF officer. Such a statement made completely out of context only served to convince me that he was making a desperate effort at portraying himself as a man who was a model citizen and should be above suspicion. When asked who else lived in the house he replied his twenty-three years old daughter, Carmel, resided with them and she was presently upstairs. Carmel eventually appeared in the living room and I then announced to the family that they were all under arrest on suspicion of having been involved in paramilitary activity. I already had a fleet of three CID cars on stand-by in an adjoining street with policewomen in them. They were called forward by radio and each of the Connollys was driven off separately and lodged in Castlereagh Detention Centre. A fully trained police search team then entered the Connollys' home and with the help of scientists began to look for evidence which might confirm that it was indeed a PIRA safe house.

Teams of detectives were allocated to interview each of the Connollys and after some initial denials Carmel admitted that their house had been used by the killers of William McConnell. Owen and Margaret Connolly also soon began to confess to their part in the crime. It transpired that initially 20 Campbell Park Avenue had been used by the PIRA only as a place where fugitives wanted by the police could temporarily hide out.

Owen Connolly was asked by his interviewers to describe in detail the events surrounding their part in the murder. He said that in the months preceding the crime he had been asked by the PIRA to intensify his support and to gather intelligence on police officers and other potential assassination targets in east Belfast. As he had comparatively recently taken early retirement from the civil service at Stormont he had time on his hands. He managed to identify cars belonging to police officers and passed their registration numbers back to the PIRA. Owen Connolly went on to say that in early February 1984 a young man who he presumed was a Provisional IRA intelligence officer called at his house and asked him if he would start targeting a prison officer who lived at 5 Hawthornden Drive and also find out what he could about the house opposite. Connolly explained that, as a result, on about five different occasions he walked to Hawthornden Drive. He hung around there, and established a pattern of movements of the McConnell family and details of the occupants of number 6 which he passed on to his contact.

On the morning of 5 March 1984 the intelligence officer called to him again and revealed that the operation to assassinate William McConnell was planned to begin that evening. He asked him if he would allow the PIRA team to use his house. Owen Connolly agreed and was instructed to leave his back door unlocked to facilitate their entry. As that day wore on his wife and daughter both arrived home from work but he did not tell them what was to happen until half past six in the evening when the door bell rang. Owen Connolly answered it to find a man wearing a peaked cap on his doorstep who asked him if it was still all right to use his house in the operation. Connolly told him that everything was okay and the man walked off saying he would be back later. I have no doubt that this was the same man who called to the Gillilands seeking directions at roughly the same time. He was probably the leader of the assassination team thoroughly checking out his final plans for the killing.

When the caller had departed Owen Connolly returned to his rear living room where his wife and daughter asked him who had been at the door. He explained to them that a unit from the Provisional IRA would shortly be coming to their house as part of an operation to kill a prison officer. They allegedly protested at this but to no avail. Then they said that when the assassins arrived they would disappear upstairs and occupy themselves in one of the bedrooms.

According to Owen Connolly about an hour and a half later someone knocked at his rear kitchen window and when he opened the back door into his small yard he found a woman carrying a black briefcase standing there. He knew she was the first of the assassination team arriving. He brought her into the house and showed her into the front downstairs room while his wife and daughter made their way upstairs. They came back down again when they were sure the visitor was out of sight. Some half an hour later they heard other people coming into the yard. Owen Connolly opened the back door again and admitted two men who were also led to the front room while his wife and daughter returned to the bedroom. Owen Connolly joined the three in the front room and watched as they began to disguise themselves by putting on wigs and make-up. After about fifteen minutes they had completely altered their appearances. The three of them left the house by the back door, taking with them the briefcase. Owen Connolly saw them safely off down the back alleyway and on to Belmont Church Road where they disappeared on foot towards the Belmont Road. It would have taken them about fifteen minutes to walk to the Gillilands' house.

While the elderly Gillilands were being terrorised in their own home Margaret and Carmel Connolly retired to their beds at around eleven o'clock in the knowledge that a man was about to be put to death. Owen decided to spend his night in the rear downstairs living room of 20 Campbell Park Avenue to await the return of the killer gang when they had finished their 'work'. He dozed on a chair and occasionally read by the light of a small table lamp which he had dimmed by covering it with a newspaper so that neighbours would not notice anything unusual.

At around half past seven in the morning he could hear his wife and daughter rising from their beds. After breakfasting Carmel left to go to her work as a civil servant in the Stormont government buildings where her father had also once been employed. Margaret Connolly was due to leave home at about half past eight to go to her place of employment in a downtown office. Just before she left the two men who had come to her house the previous evening reappeared in the back yard, excited and carrying the briefcase. Owen received them into the house and anxiously said, 'Was it all right? Did you get him?' The men answered, 'Yes.' Margaret Connolly still maintained her composure and left her home to catch a bus into the city centre. During the journey the driver had a transistor radio turned on and she overheard a local news bulletin to the effect that a man had been shot dead in east Belfast. But she still managed to continue on to her office and carry out a normal day's work.

Meanwhile, her husband was assisting the killers by helping them remove surgical rubber gloves which they had worn to avoid leaving fingerprint evidence in the Gilliland home. The two men removed their wigs and Owen placed them in a plastic bag. One of the assassins opened the briefcase and took out the revolver and sub-machine gun, checked that they were in the 'safe' position and laid them on the floor. They both made their way to the bathroom, stripped themselves to the waist and began to wash, using a bottle of washing-up liquid from the kitchen. They asked Owen if he had any razors as they wished to shave off their moustaches. He told them that he didn't as he used an electrical shaver. But at their request he walked to a nearby corner shop and purchased a packet of plastic disposable razors. The two men removed their moustaches. As they continued to clean themselves up Owen lifted the weapons, put them back in the briefcase and, along with the plastic bag containing the wigs, took them to an attic room for safekeeping after which he came back downstairs and provided the two men with coffee and toast.

It was obvious they were not going to leave the refuge of the house yet so they settled down to watch television in the rear living room in the company of Owen. As lunchtime approached they asked him to go to a nearby fish and chip shop to get some hot food and he readily agreed. They were enjoying their meal when the television news came on. The main item was the murder of William McConnell, to which one of the men callously responded, 'That's him disposed of.' When asked by his interviewers to describe the men who had come to his house Owen gave what details he could recall and significantly said that while watching the television one of them would occasionally rub his lower left leg. He could see that it was scarred as the result of some injury.

At around half past one the two men were becoming restless and were obviously anxious to be on their way. They asked Owen about the times of the buses on the Belmont Road and when they heard that they ran every fifteen minutes or so they decided to leave the house. Owen agreed to walk some distance in front of them so that he could give a signal if there was police activity in the vicinity. He led them down the back alleyway onto Belmont Church Road and then onto Belmont Road. The men separated at that point and went to different bus stops. Owen kept a fatherly eye on them until a bus came along. They both got on board and probably travelled to the Short Strand area. Later that afternoon Margaret Connolly arrived home from work and Owen brought her up-to-date with events. He then retrieved the wigs from the attic room and when Margaret went to the bathroom she found a number of towels strewn about with traces of make-up on them. She placed the wigs and towels in the washing machine in a deliberate attempt to remove any remaining traces of firearms and then hung these items to dry on the banisters of the stairs. A little later Carmel arrived into the house after work but she too had already heard the news of the murder.

Over the next few days the Connolly family settled back into their normal routine again. But they were somewhat nervous of still having the basic assassination kit, particularly the firearms, in their attic. Owen made contact with the intelligence officer who told him to take the briefcase and other items to a particular house in another Belfast republican area known as The Markets, situated just across the river from Short Strand. Some four days after the murder Owen rose early, collected the briefcase from the attic, and left his house by the back door. He caught a bus to The Markets. To the casual observer he no doubt looked like a typical businessman making his way to his office instead of an embittered man who had played such a vital role in the murder of a man in front of his wife and child.

The Connollys made their admissions during their first twenty-four hour period of detention but that coincided with the final day in which we could legally hold Mr A, Mr B and Gilmartin without placing them before a court. The footprint and fibre evidence was certainly strong enough to charge Gilmartin with the murder and I also felt the fact that Mr B was arrested with him some seventeen and a half hours after the crime, together with the entries in his diary, also connected him in some way to the killing, perhaps in a background planning role. Mr A had firearm residues on his clothing although these did not match the description given by the witnesses. But, circumstantially, I believed the evidence against him was just strong enough to link him to the crime and so on the morning of 14 March 1984 all three appeared at Belfast remand court which was presided over by Resident Magistrate Mr Tom Travers. As the three men entered the dock I made my way to the witness box and made a sworn deposition to the effect that I believed I could connect them with the killing. The case attracted quite a lot of public attention and the court was crowded with onlookers and a large turnout of pressmen. When I had finished my deposition a defence solicitor then began to cross-examine me on the strength of the evidence and there followed an acrimonious verbal exchange, but Mr Travers over-ruled the solicitor and remanded the accused in custody.

The forensic and police search team completed their detailed examination of 20 Campbell Park Avenue that same day but the only item of interest found was a torn piece of paper. When it was put together it revealed what appeared to be a rough sketch of the Belmont Road area and may well have been drawn by the gang, as part of their planning of the murder.

In Castlereagh Detention Centre the interviews of the Connolly family continued for several more days as we wanted to elicit from them every scrap of information. This was productive insofar as Owen Connolly admitted having passed details to the PIRA of the home address of a serving policeman who lived near him. We were able to take appropriate measures to ensure the policeman's safety and security.

As a result of the evidence we had against the Connolly family their future was now very bleak indeed and they faced possible lengthy terms of imprisonment for their involvement in the murder. I had some sympathy for the circumstances in which Carmel found herself. I believed she was very much under the influence of her father although she could have taken some steps to prevent the killing because she had known of the plans for at least fourteen hours before it actually took place. However, this would have necessitated her also betraying her parents, so she took the line of least resistance and hoped the truth would never be uncovered. Margaret Connolly too could have prevented the killing but her complicity went beyond that of merely keeping silent. She washed the wigs and towels to remove any incriminating evidence but she perhaps acted in the interests of her own preservation and that of her family.

Nothing could excuse the part played by Owen Connolly. He offered the gang every form of assistance and without his help the PIRA would have faced a more difficult task in seeking out their prey and killing him. It was later confirmed that Owen Connolly did in fact serve with the RAF during the second world war and thereafter had worked for the Northern Ireland civil service for a number of years until his early retirement around 1983. It was difficult to understand just what had now brought him to this point and I explored the issue with him. He explained that he had spent his childhood in the south Armagh area where he had been brought up in the republican tradition. He had joined the RAF not so much to support Britain during the war but as a means of making some contribution in the fight against Hitler's aggression in Europe. He added that when he joined the civil service after the war he felt he could have climbed the career ladder to some extent but that he had been held back because of his religion. He gradually became angry and embittered, so-much-so that when the troubles broke out in 1969 he was ready to actively support the cause of republicanism. Events carried on from there.

He knew he now faced a possible term of life imprisonment which was not a happy prospect for a man aged over sixty years. He searched for a way to ease his situation and I was not surprised when he offered to give evidence against the gang who had carried out the killing. Once more I found myself facing a case involving accomplice evidence. We decided there was little to lose from adopting such a course but, as in other cases, I made it clear to Owen Connolly that I would be making no representations to the Director of Public Prosecutions to ease his culpability or that of his family. He accepted this and some few days later I arranged for Mr A, Mr B and Gilmartin to be produced at Castlereagh from their prison cells so that Owen Connolly could go through the ritual confrontations. He had no hesitation in identifying Gilmartin as one of the men who had been in his house before and after the killing and confirmed he was the one who had displayed the damaged lower left leg. He viewed Mr A face-to-face but said he could not be certain that he was the second man involved in the murder and in respect of Mr B said he may have seen him at some stage during the operation. The case against Gilmartin was now steadily strengthening and another piece of useful information came to hand when a uniformed police officer contacted us to report that on 1 March 1984, some five days before the killing, he had sighted Gilmartin in the Short Strand area. At that time Gilmartin was sporting a heavy moustache and this tended to bear out Owen Connolly's statement that on the morning of the murder he had shaved it off at 20 Campbell Park Avenue.

On 21 March 1984 I charged Owen Connolly with the murder of William McConnell. In view of the lesser involvement of his wife and daughter I charged them with assisting the killer gang and withholding information. All three appeared before Belfast remand court. Margaret and Carmel subsequently made bail applications in the High Court which were granted while Owen, who was still intent on giving evidence, was placed in the secure annex of Crumlin Road Prison for his own protection.

It was clear from an overall assessment of the arrests and discoveries made following the murder that we had disrupted an important assassination gang, but from their past record we knew that the PIRA would be keen to demonstrate they were still very much in business. This became all too true on a quiet Sunday morning in early April 1984, just about a month after the death of William McConnell, when the PIRA stalked Mr Tom Travers, the resident magistrate who had taken such a firm stand at the first remand of Mr A, Mr B and Gilmartin. He had gone to mass at a Roman Catholic chapel in the middle-class Malone Road area of Belfast in the company of his teenage daughter, Mary. Afterwards, as they were making their way home on foot, no doubt looking forward to a family Sunday lunch, the terrorists struck and gunned both of them down, killing Mary and grievously wounding her father.

Following the attack the uniformed police quickly responded and began a sweep of the surrounding streets and roads looking for anyone who might have been involved in the crime. They noticed a well dressed young woman walking along the Malone Road with a small dog on a lead. To all intents and purposes she appeared the epitome of a respectable girl out for a Sunday morning stroll. The police officers stopped and questioned her but were not satisfied with her answers. As the officers were all male they were obviously unable to physically search a woman so they took her to a local police station where they knew a policewoman would be on duty. However, before arriving at the station the young woman confessed that she had two firearms concealed on her person and was in fact acting as courier for the murder team. During the subsequent investigation it was established that the dog she had been walking was stolen from a house in west Belfast.

The two guns were later examined by a forensic scientist and he established that one of them was the lost police Ruger revolver used in the murder of William McConnell. By using this gun on the Travers, the PIRA had made their point. In a sense this latest attack was a repeat of history because some fifteen months earlier they had also used the revolver to kill County Court Judge William Doyle after he had left the same chapel following morning mass. Initially I thought the arrested young woman may have been the same person who was involved in the murder of William McConnell, but other events later proved otherwise and she has not been located and charged.

On the morning of 19 March 1985, about a year after the McConnell killing, Owen Connolly and his family appeared for trial at Belfast Crown Court before Lord Justice Kelly. Owen pleaded 'Guilty' to the murder and was sentenced to the mandatory term of life imprisonment. Margaret and Carmel also pleaded 'Guilty' to the lesser charges and were given suspended prison sentences.

A few days later I visited Owen in prison. I converted what he had to say about the murder into a witness statement and submitted it to the Director of Public Prosecutions. He re-assessed the case and decided that there was insufficient evidence on which to proceed against Mr A. The latter was duly released from custody while the case of murder against Mr B and Gilmartin continued. Their trial was heard some months later before the late Lord Justice Gibson. Mr B's senior defence lawyer argued that the entries in the diary were open to a number of interpretations and that no court could be satisfied that such evidence was strong enough to prove the charge beyond a reasonable doubt. Owen Connolly gave evidence on behalf of the Crown but he was wily and evasive in the witness box and did not impress the judge with his honesty. Accordingly, Mr B walked free but, based entirely on the footprint and fibre evidence, the judge convicted Gilmartin of the murder and sentenced him to life imprisonment. Mr A's freedom was short-lived. Within a number of months he was captured in another situation after a shoot-out with police and was later sentenced to a lengthy term of imprisonment.

Owen Connolly's health steadily deteriorated in prison. Some seven years into his sentence he suffered a major heart attack and on compassionate grounds, the Secretary of State released him early from prison. Margaret Connolly's health also failed and she sustained a stroke. As I write, the couple are living quietly out of harm's way while Carmel married and began to put her life back together again. The McConnell family have recovered as best they can and when I last saw Mrs McConnell she was coming to terms with her loss. Mr Travers too has re-built his life and I am pleased to say that he recovered well from his physical injuries.

10

GETTING EVEN

When the McConnell case was concluded it enabled me to shed my involvement with investigations in which accomplice evidence played a part and to concentrate fully on my post at Strandtown as the detective chief inspector-in charge of the CID in east Belfast. This area was regarded as comparatively quiet and the style of policing was as close as one could get to that of a United Kingdom mainland Constabulary. Just prior to my transfer RUC headquarters had undertaken a review of divisional boundaries and, for some illogical reasons which were never fully explained, decided to bring the large seaside dormitory town of Bangor, situated some 15 miles from Belfast and on the shores of Belfast Lough, into the east Belfast division. So I had responsibility for crime investigations there too. In the early 1970s the loyalist paramilitary groups had been quite strong in many of the working class areas of the division but by the mid-1970s these had largely been dissolved through lack of interest. There remained only a hardcore of extremists who had now turned to general gangsterism and, in between spells in prison, were enjoying a good lifestyle from racketeering, robberies, drugs and hijacking of cigarette and drinks delivery vehicles.

Apart from paramilitary and sectarian murders, we alo had to deal with 'ordinary crime' murders and these tax the investigator's skill as much, if not more, than the paramilitary and sectarian crimes. On the evening of Sunday, 4 October 1987, I was presented with just such a challenge when I answered my telephone at home and a detective sergeant from Strandtown informed me that the body of a young woman, bound and apparently hooded, had been found in a small terraced house at 39 Colvil Street which is situated in a quiet and respectable area about a quarter of a mile from the police station. The detective sergeant told me that the woman appeared to have been severely battered around the head. The scene had been sealed off by the uniformed patrol who had first responded to the '999' call. I told the detective sergeant to ensure that in the interests of the preservation of evidence no one, under any circumstances, should re-enter the house. I asked him to contact the pathologist and the forensic science laboratory and ask them to come to the scene.

I immediately got into my own car and set off for Colvil Street. Although at that stage in my career I had been called from home to the scenes of murders at least a hundred times I always took the opportunity on these journeys to mentally remind myself of the correct investigative procedure to adopt. On arrival I would be expected to take control of the scene and direct the course of the enquiry.

As I turned into the street I could see small groups of local people huddled together, no doubt wondering exactly what had occurred to cause so much police activity at number 39. I was pleased to see that the uniformed officers had cordoned off the area of the house with white tape and that a number of constables had positioned themselves to prevent unauthorised access to the scene.

I got out of my car and the detective sergeant who had phoned me at home appeared out of the darkness. I took him aside and asked for a full briefing on events so far. He explained that number 39 was the home of a twenty-two year old woman named Carol Gouldie. In recent weeks she had taken in a lodger, a young woman student, Valerie Kerr, who was attending the Belfast College of Business Studies. Valerie stayed at the house from Sundays to Fridays when she would then take a bus to Dungannon, County Tyrone, some 40 miles from Belfast, to spend the weekend with her parents. On this particular Sunday evening she had arrived back at 39 Colvil Street at around a quarter to nine. On entering the house she switched on the hall light and then opened the door of the rear downstairs living room which was in darkness. She turned on the light there and was met by the horrific sight of the body of Carol Gouldie draped face downwards over the arm of a large soft velvet chair. Her hands were tied behind her back and her head seemed to be covered with some form of hood which was bloodstained.

The detective sergeant informed me that as instructed he had requested the services of a pathologist, a forensic biologist in addition to the police fingerprint and scenes of crime officers, a photography/video team and mappers. Some of these were now beginning to assemble at the cordon. It was important that I assess the crime myself and be in a position to brief these other agencies and agree on the most productive way to examine the scene for evidence. Consequently, I gave my details to the scene log officer whose responsibility it was to record the movements of all authorised persons now entering and leaving the house. I walked into the hallway and went as far as the rear living room door where I saw the body of the young woman in a kneeling position on the floor with her trunk and head face downwards over the armrest of a large soft chair. Her hands and wrists were very tightly bound together behind her back with what appeared to be a pair of ladies tights or nylon stockings. Her head and face were covered with some form of cloth bag which was heavily bloodstained. I noted that she was well dressed in a grey blouse, black skirt, red high-heeled shoes and that her fingernails were well manicured. There was considerable blood staining on the walls and an area of carpet next to the fireplace was very heavily saturated with blood. Interestingly, the deceased's knees rested on a copy of the *Daily Mirror*, dated Friday, 2 October 1987. As Valerie Kerr had not seen Carol Gouldie since the previous Thursday, 1 October, this piece of evidence indicated that the crime must have occurred sometime from that date onwards. A handbag, apparently that of the victim, was positioned on the floor. From where I stood it did not appear to have been rifled as one would expect in a robbery. I could also see a loaf of bread and a small carton of milk in a plastic bag on a settee.

I completed my cursory examination and had no doubt from what I had so far seen that the crime was sexually motivated. I returned to the street and was pleased to see that the pathologist and forensic scientist had now arrived. I brought everyone together and told them the facts of what lay inside the house. It was agreed that the pathologist and the forensic scientist would now enter the scene and carry out a preliminary examination but would not disturb anything until it had been photographed and videoed *in situ*. I accompanied them and watched as the pathologist cast his expert eyes over the body. He agreed right away that the kneeling and face downwards position were indicative of a sexual crime. He felt the hands of the body without moving them and found them to be cold to the touch. He said that death had certainly not occurred within recent hours. The police photography team were then called forward and they recorded everything as it had been found.

The forensic scientist directed his attention towards an interpretation of the blood distribution in the room and carefully examined the saturated area of carpet close to the fireplace. He gave an opinion that the deceased's head had rested there as she sustained a severe battering and the spattering on the wall and fireplace was probably caused by the assailant repeatedly plunging some form of weapon up and down with great ferocity. Some more blood spattering was found on the opposite wall close to the armchair on which the body lay and this too could have been caused by more blows being rained down on the victim, or, alternatively, by the deceased being lifted off the floor and flung over the armchair with a whiplash effect.

Both experts then turned their attention back to the body and beginning with the head noted that the bloodstained hood was actually a cushion cover. There were several cushions on chairs elsewhere in the room but one was minus its cover. It appeared the killer had ripped off the cushion cover, pulled it over the head of the deceased and held it in place by wrapping a pair of black coloured tights twice round it. They noted too that the bound hands were bloodstained. If she was battered to death on the floor in a horizontal position this could not have been caused by a dripping effect so the unfortunate victim must have been able at one stage to raise her hands in an effort to protect her head. The forensic scientist then completed this aspect of his examination by taking blood samples from the floor and walls and by taking fibre samples from the carpet and soft furnishings.

The next logical step was to move the body to examine the frontal area. We brought a large paper body bag into the room and spread it open on the floor. We gently lifted the body and turned it over. We could see that her blouse had been ripped open and her bra pulled down exposing the breasts. This confirmed our view that the crime was sexually motivated. Three buttons from the blouse lay on the cushion of the chair, indicating that the ripping open had probably occurred after she was draped over the arm rest. The pathologist was now able to examine the limbs and stated that *rigor mortis* had set in which does not occur until some 12 hours after death. The deceased was photographed in the face-up position and we then zipped up the body bag and placed it on a stretcher. The deceased's small red coloured Nissan car was parked in the street at the front door so the funeral undertaker's van was reversed as close as possible, we gently eased the body in and it was driven off to the mortuary followed by the pathologist.

I accompanied the forensic scientist as he continued with his examination. The front of the house seemed secure, with no sign of a forced entry, so we began to systematically work towards the rear. A kitchen area led off the living room and it had a metal framed window and wooden door, giving access to a small backyard. This door was locked and both it and the window were undamaged. Leading further back from the kitchen was a small bathroom and it too had a metal framed window which was lying open. We examined the catch on the window and found it to be loose and in a very rusted condition. It would certainly have given easy access for an intruder. This window was just above the bath. The forensic scientist paid particular attention to its white glazed edge and pointed out what appeared to be a distinctive shoe print with a wave-like sole pattern bordered by squares and chevrons. The two of us unlocked the kitchen door and entered the small backyard to find that a black painted door leading into a back alleyway dividing the rears of Colvil Street and Shaw Street had a slide bolt fitted but that it was in the unlocked position. A closer examination of the surface of the yardside of this door revealed a number of scuff marks. As a result of this evidence the most likely scenario appeared to be that the killer had climbed the rear wall separating the yard from the alleyway, had eased himself down the back door, pulled open the bathroom window and stepped on the edge of the bath as he entered the house. He probably departed the same way but instead of clambering back over the yard wall had simply opened the bolt on the doorway leading into the alleyway and had made his exit.

All of these areas of interest, particularly the footprint, were carefully photographed and videoed, and we turned our attention to the first floor bedroom area of the house. There was no sign of ransacking and so far as we could tell everything was as it should be. The fingerprint team then began their examination by dusting the likely route the killer had taken on his entry and exit while members of the police mapping section drew an accurate plan of the scene. Other detectives had now arrived in Colvil Street and I asked them to carry out some preliminary house-to-house enquiries in an effort to pick up any piece of relevant information.

Meanwhile, at the mortuary, the pathologist had begun his post-mortem examination of the victim and again had her photographed front and back. He then turned his attention to the tying of the hands and confirmed that the material used to bind them was indeed a pair of tights which he undid with some difficulty. He next examined the area of the head and could see that the blood-soaked cushion cover used as the hood showed considerable evidence of damage in the form of holes and tears, indicating that it had been in place for at least part of the time the victim was being battered. The hood was loosely held in place by another pair of tights which had been wound round twice but were not tied. The pathologist removed the hood, revealing horrendous injuries to the top of the skull. These he estimated to have been caused by many severe blows from a blunt metal instrument. The victim's right eye was swollen and blackened and her lower lip showed evidence of bruising. Also, considerable bruising was located on the back of the right forearm and this seemed to have been sustained as she vainly tried to defend herself from her assailant.

Apart from the tearing open of the blouse the clothing was intact but the pathologist noted that she was bare-legged and that the sides of her briefs, which were in place, had been rolled over and over, suggesting that they had been pulled up roughly or in haste. A police scenes of crimes officer was in attendance at this examination and as each item of evidence was removed he carefully placed it in a plastic exhibit bag for closer examination at the forensic science laboratory. In view of the apparent sexual motive for the killing the pathologist took a vaginal swab and it too was submitted to the laboratory for analysis.

The post-mortem and forensic examination did not finish until around 4 a.m., some 7 hours after the body had been found. We kept the house under police guard as we would no doubt want to return to the scene during the course of the murder investigation. The victim's family, who lived in Holywood, about 5 miles from Belfast, had of course by now been told of the tragic news and it hardly needs stating that they were totally devastated.

I sent the detectives who had assisted at the scene and at the mortuary home to catch a few hours sleep. I would require their services again at 9 a.m. on Monday when I hoped to have sufficient facts in my possession to place a full-scale murder investigation on a proper course. A major incident room was set up at Strandtown. I contacted the other stations within the division and the Belfast Regional Crime Squad seeking all the staff that they could spare.

At 9 a.m. I had around 30 detectives at my disposal and I carried out a full briefing using the video tape of the scene to convey the full horror of the crime. Many of the staff were moved to tears by what they saw and once again I knew they would put maximum effort into catching the killer. A lengthy debate then ensued and we discussed all aspects of the crime. At its conclusion all were in agreement that whoever had carried out the murder must have known Carol and have some knowledge of the comings and goings at her house. It was therefore decided that we would have to learn as much as possible about the private and working life of the victim. I thus directed some of the detectives to interview her family, friends and employer. Others were to concentrate on thorough house-to-house enquiries in the streets around the murder scene. I wound up the conference by telling everyone to be back in the main CID office at 7 p.m. when I would bring everyone up-to-date with developments.

I spent the next hour or so in the major incident room ensuring that the complex system of collation of evidence and information was operating smoothly. Then, accompanied by a colleague, I returned to 39 Colvil Street which was still under guard, to begin a careful examination of all of Carol's personal possessions, particularly diaries, notebooks etc, seeking information such as names, addresses, telephone numbers and so on which would give us some insight into her friends and acquaintances. We found a number of documents containing such details and I brought them back to the incident room where, during my absence, a considerable number of facts had started to feed into the system.

The most significant information came from the forensic scientist who had telephoned to report that tests on the vaginal swab had revealed traces of semen. This was not surprising. Also, a footprint expert had examined the shoe print from the edge of the bath and, using his database of footwear impressions, was able to say that it had been left by a basketball type boot brand named Puma Hi-Cut. He even went so far as to send me across a manufacturer's colour brochure on it.

At 7 p.m. I went to the main CID office and as I approached along the corridor I could hear the buzz of conversation from the detectives who had re-assembled following their day's work on the streets. I called the meeting to order and asked each of the team leaders in turn to give me an account of how their enquiries were progressing. I listened carefully and at the end of the conference it was clear that everyone had put maximum effort into the investigation so far. A picture of Carol's life and her movements immediately preceding her death was now coming together.

It transpired she was a very attractive woman with a bubbly personality and worked as a receptionist for a computer company in Holywood, a town where she had gone to school and grown up. In addition to her daytime job she also worked Monday and Friday evenings as a waitress at the Priory Inn, also in Holywood. It was established that she had lived with her parents in Holywood until February 1987, some 6 months before her murder, when she had taken out a mortgage to buy 39 Colvil Street. She lived alone there until September when she had taken in Valerie Kerr as a paying lodger to help ease her finances.

On Friday, 2 October 1987, 2 days before her body was found, Carol had travelled to work as usual in her red car, arriving just before 9 a.m. Valerie Kerr had left the house sometime earlier to attend college in central Belfast and, although she had not seen Carol, was aware she was in the house.

At lunchtime Carol met a friend in Holywood and both went to the Priory Inn for a snack lunch before returning to their respective offices at 2 p.m. Carol finished work at 5.30 p.m. She and a woman colleague locked up the offices and both walked to their cars which were parked at the rear of the premises. At that time Carol was dressed in a grey blouse, a black skirt, red high heeled shoes — the clothes she was apparently murdered in — and was carrying only her handbag. She merged onto the traffic flow on Main Street, Holywood and, followed by her work colleague, travelled along the Sydenham by-pass in the direction of Belfast. At the major Knocknagoney intersection she turned left onto Holywood Road which is the most direct route to Colvil Street while her friend continued along the dual carriageway towards Belfast. Carol was seen parking her car in Colvil Street at around 5.50 p.m. She entered her house alone, carrying her handbag and a small plastic bag probably containing the loaf of bread and the milk, so she must have stopped at a shop along the way and also purchased the newspaper found under her knees. We learned that at 4.15 p.m. that same day Valerie Kerr had briefly called back to 39 Colvil Street to collect some items of clothing. She found everything in order. She then caught her Friday evening bus to Dungannon.

The staff at the Priory Inn had been interviewed. They held Carol in very high regard, considering her to be a reliable, honest and popular employee. They were therefore surprised that she did not turn in for work that busy Friday evening. They telephoned 39 Colvil Street several times but got no reply and were now obviously very distressed at the news of her brutal murder.

Another female friend of Carol's lived further along Colvil Street. She had noticed with some concern that Carol's car had not moved from its usual parking spot all weekend, particularly on the Friday evening. In addition, she had also observed that Carol's bedroom curtains remained open through Saturday and Sunday. She too telephoned the house on several occasions but each time got no reply and presumed that she had gone away for the weekend.

The house-to-house enquiry team was also making good progress. The detective sergeant leading it informed me that in Pimms Avenue, which runs at right angles to Colvil Street, they had located a man who appeared to be a vital witness. On the afternoon of Friday, 2 October this man had been in his front upstairs bedroom. From his window he could see right along the rear alleyway separating the backs of Colvil Street and Shaw Street. Sometime between 4.30 p.m. and 5.30 p.m. he had witnessed a man clamber over the rear wall of a house. When questioned more closely he was able to say that the man appeared to be on the wall of the last house on the left of the alleyway. This was indeed 39 Colvil Street and there seemed little doubt that this was the killer making his entry.

In summary, all of the evidence we had gained to that point, particularly the fact that Carol, when murdered, was still wearing her office clothes, and had not changed into the uniform she wore as a waitress at the Priory Inn, together with the position of her handbag on the floor, the newspaper dated 2 October and the loaf and the milk in the plastic bag on the settee, tended to show that she had been set upon as soon as she opened the door leading into her rear living room. The killer had therefore put considerable planning into the crime and must have had a knowledge of the layout of Carol's house and the movements of both Carol and Valerie Kerr. The next issue was who would want to kill and rape such a lovely young woman. We felt that only a rejected lover or someone with a perverse infatuation or grudge against her could possibly carry out such a dastardly crime. Needless to say the detectives working on the case had found a great fear among the many young women they had so far spoken to during the investigation, in case the killer would strike again. I wound up the conference by revealing the forensic developments to date with particular emphasis on the Puma Hi-Cut basketball boot. The investigation team filed out of the office to continue with their allotted enquiries.

In any murder investigation house-to-house enquires are often the most productive method of obtaining evidence and this was again being borne out in Carol's case. The system we adopt is quite thorough and begins with the senior investigating officer prescribing the areas to be covered. This normally extends to at least the half dozen streets branching out in every direction from the scene of the murder, although this can be adjusted as events develop. A detective sergeant is placed in charge of the enquiry team, sets up office and from there controls the operation. Every house within the given area has to be visited and each of the occupants interviewed. A pro forma is used to list the names and ages of the persons resident in the house. To ensure that the detectives are not being misled this is cross-referred and confirmed by asking the neighbours on each side who lives next door, and so the process continues. It is rare to find every occupant of a house at home when it is first visited so officers have to call back, perhaps several times, until everyone is interviewed. In effect, no one should be overlooked.

It will be remembered that on the evening of the discovery of the body detectives carried out some preliminary house-to-house enquiries at Colvil Street. One of the houses they called at was number 23, just 7 doors from the murder scene, which was the home of a Mr and Mrs Callaghan and their twenty year old son, Kenneth. They were asked if they had seen or heard anything suspicious which might be connected to the murder. Kenneth said that on the previous Friday afternoon he had seen a white coloured Opel Manta car driven by a lone male in the vicinity of Carol's house but that it moved off after a short time. No written statement had been recorded from him at that early stage as the events surrounding Carol's death were still far from clear. But the information was logged in the major incident room and a written direction, or action sheet as it is officially known, was raised to have Kenneth Callaghan re-interviewed and a full witness statement taken from him. Two detectives had called at the Callaghan house several times since but on each occasion had just missed him. On Tuesday, 6 October they made a firm appointment to see him around 6 p.m. When the officers called back at this time Kenneth was present and informed them that he was a night shift worker in a local factory. He stated that on the afternoon of Friday, 2 October he had spent several hours walking his dog in and around

Colvil Street and that at approximately 4.30 p.m. he had observed the white Opel Manta car, driven by a lone male, stop at Carol's house for about 30 seconds after which it moved off.

The two detectives felt it somewhat odd that Kenneth Callaghan should have walked his dog around the area for so long, particularly when there are a number of public parks not too far away. However, they shrewdly said or did nothing to alert him to their unease and merely wrote down a simple witness statement which he signed. They returned to the station and made me aware of their views. When I read the statement I shared their feelings of disquiet. I felt too that he had indeed probably been wandering with his dog as claimed and, reasoning that several people were bound to have seen him, he would have been foolish to draw attention to himself by not coming forward. I also sensed that he had an ulterior motive for spending so much time in Colvil Street and the more I thought about him the more concerned I became. After all, here was a man who lived only a short distance from Carol. He would have known the layout of her house as it was similar to his own. In addition, he would be in position to study the times Carol and her lodger came and went and his wanderings with the dog would give him an opportunity to ensure that Valerie Kerr had left the house for the weekend.

At 9 a.m. the following day, which was Wednesday, I held the routine conference with the investigation team and after the usual progress reports I raised the subject of Kenneth Callaghan. This prompted the two officers who had first spoken to him on the night the body was found to reveal that, in hindsight, he had acted oddly on that occasion. While being routinely questioned he had kept his eyes fixed firmly on the television and fidgeted with the leather strap of his watch to such an extent that it actually snapped.

The suspicions that Kenneth Callaghan was our man were now growing stronger by the hour. If he was the killer he had been cool enough to brazen out the interview with the two detectives who had recorded his witness statement so we had to plan each further move in connection with him with great care. Also, we were very conscious that the law in Northern Ireland at that time allowed us to hold a non-terrorist suspect in custody for only 24 hours. This could be extended to a total of 48 hours provided he was charged and placed before a remand court within that same period. Therefore, in view of the limited time we could hold him it was vitally important that we should have as much work done as possible on our suspect prior to his arrest. Incidentally, the Police and Criminal Evidence Act has changed the law somewhat and we can now apply to a magistrates court to have a prisoner remanded back into police custody for continuing investigation.

In reality the only physical evidence we would have to connect Callaghan with 39 Colvil Street, if he was the killer, was the footprint on the edge of the bath. It would be a major advance in the investigation if we could get possession of his footwear. We decided to take a calculated risk so often necessary in CID work and arranged for a detective sergeant and a detective constable to return to Colvil Street on the pretext of tidying-up the house-to-house enquiries, eventually to call with the Callaghans, and surreptitiously try to see what footwear Kenneth had. Also, in the event that this plan would go wrong we placed covert surveillance on his house lest he should catch onto our suspicions and attempt to flee.

The two detectives chosen to carry out this ploy then went to Colvil Street and made their presence known by calling again at several houses, eventually arriving at the Callaghans in number 23. The door was answered by the father of the household and the two detectives managed to get themselves invited in. When asked where Kenneth was Mr Callaghan said he was upstairs in bed as he was still on night shift. The detectives asked if he could be aroused. He eventually appeared downstairs and a few pleasantries were exchanged to put him at ease. The detective sergeant then explained to Kenneth that he was tying up some loose ends in connection with the murder of Carol Gouldie. He said that a witness had reported seeing a young man wearing white boots with red flash on the sides walking a dog in Colvil Street on Friday afternoon and he wondered if it was him she had seen. Callaghan responded that it sounded like him only his white boots had a grey not a red flash on them. The detective sergeant asked Callaghan if he could see the boots for the purposes of elimination and he disappeared upstairs to fetch them.

After what seemed an excruciatingly long period but was in fact only minutes, he returned carrying a pair of white Puma Hi-Cut basketball boots. There now seemed little doubt that we were on the right track but the two detectives remained cool and asked Callaghan if they could borrow the boots to show to the witness. He agreed. On their way out of the house Kenneth Callaghan asked if he and his father were suspects for the crime. The detective sergeant made light of this by saying every man in Belfast was a suspect.

Meanwhile, back at the major incident room in Strandtown, I and others were anxiously waiting for the return of the two officers from their mission. As soon as they appeared I could detect a satisfied look on their faces and I soon saw the reason when they handed me the pair of boots. We examined the soles and sure enough there was the wave-like pattern bordered by the squares and chevrons. Under good light we thought we could see blood stains on the ridge of the soles and on one of the tongues. We immediately placed each in a plastic exhibit bag and despatched them to the forensic science laboratory. I telephoned ahead and spoke to the scientists working on the case and I made them aware of the urgency of our situation, letting them know that we had the home of the suspect under observation. They agreed to look at the boots right away and within an hour I received a call from the laboratory to say that the pattern on the soles was similar to the imprint found on the edge of the bath but that considerable microscopic work would have to be done before arriving at a positive conclusion. However, they did say that the stains on the boots were indeed caused by human blood which had since been grouped and it matched that of Carol's.

The investigation was now coming steadily to a head and as on other similar occasions I was becoming high on the adrenaline created by the excitement of seeing so much hard work beginning to show results. I called all of the available detectives together and asked for two units of uniformed staff to come to the main CID office. I briefed them on the developments in the case and explained that we were now going to proceed with the arrest of Kenneth Callaghan. I had kept in touch with the team who had the house under observation and they reported that there had been no movement since the two detectives had left. I instructed the uniformed staff to seal off both ends of Colvil Street to ensure that Kenneth Callaghan did not escape and I gave the two detectives who had so skilfully obtained the boots the privilege of now executing the actual arrest. We left Strandtown station in convoy and within minutes the street was cordoned off by uniformed police. Some of them had also quietly moved to the back of the Callaghans' house. I watched from a distance as the detectives re-entered by the front door. After a few minutes Kenneth Callaghan emerged handcuffed and wearing a police overall. All of his clothes had been seized for forensic examination. Two scenes of crimes officers then entered the house and Mr and Mrs Callaghan were asked to vacate it for a few days. We would require to work there undisturbed in a relentless search for further evidence. They co-operated and went to stay with relatives for a few days.

On arrival at Strandtown police station Kenneth Callaghan was taken to the cell block where he was examined by a police doctor for a number of reasons, the principal one being that we wanted to establish if he sustained any injuries such as scratches consistent with the attack on Carol. Also, we wanted some body samples from him in the form of head and pubic hair together with blood and saliva which could be used in comparison tests with the semen detected on the vaginal swabs. Callaghan submitted to all of these requirements and at the conclusion of the examination the doctor told us that he was uninjured. But he advised us to be wary of the young man if he turned aggressive as he was into body building and was immensely strong.

I then detailed a team of four detectives to interview the prisoner. The first two officers took him from the cells around mid-afternoon and began to question him about his movements on the Friday of Carol's murder. He said that because of being on night shift he did not get out of bed until 12 noon after which he washed his car. He repeated that from around 2 p.m. onwards he walked his dog for two or three hours in the area of Colvil Street to pass the time. He again mentioned that he had seen the white Opel Manta car near Carol's house and said that about 4.30 p.m. he did some shopping after which he returned home, went to his bedroom, put on his CD player, lay on the bed and fell asleep. He continued by saying that he awoke a short time later, around 6 p.m., got washed and dressed and drove to his girlfriend's house in another part of east Belfast, arriving at 6.30 p.m. According to Callaghan he took his girlfriend to the cinema and afterwards brought her back to his parents' house in Colvil Street.

The interviewers listened patiently to what Callaghan was saying and then asked him if he had known Carol Gouldie. He said he did and was actually on first name terms with her. He went on to explain that he had originally met her one evening in the Priory Inn. She had waited on his table introducing herself by saying, 'Good evening. I'm Carol, your hostess for the evening.' Callaghan said that about a week later he was walking his dog in Colvil Street when he unexpectedly met Carol. After they exchanged greetings she explained she lived in the end house which was a surprise to him.

It was then decided to raise the tempo of the interview and the two detectives suggested to Callaghan that he was lying about events on the Friday afternoon. They put it to him that a man answering his description had been seen climbing over the rear wall of 39 Colvil Street. He denied that it was he, so the interviewers pressed him harder and told him a footprint similar to his own had been found inside Carol's house. Callaghan was visibly shaken by this disclosure. As he appeared to be now weakening, the interviewers verbally pursued him and told him that in addition to his footprint being found, blood had been discovered on his boots. Callaghan tried to retain his composure but suddenly slumped forward over the interview room table and covered his face with his hands. He was then quietly asked to tell the truth and at that point confessed that he had killed Carol. He claimed he was prone to blackouts and on that fateful Friday afternoon, while wandering around Colvil Street, had lost control of himself. In order to get away from people, he had climbed the wall and entered Carol's house by pulling open the bathroom window. He entered her rear living room and hid under the stairs for a while where he found a metal object in the shape of a mallet. He held this tightly in his hands. It was stuffy and cramped beneath the stairs so he emerged back into the living room and hid behind a chair. Carol duly arrived home and when she opened the living room door saw him and shouted, 'What the hell are you doing here?' According to Callaghan, Carol lunged at him and as a result he went 'bananas' and began to hit her around the head with the mallet-like object. She fell to the floor making gurgling noises and he continued to beat her around the head. He found a pair of tights and tied her hands behind her back and then ripped off a cushion cover and pulled it over her head, after which he picked her off the floor, flung her across the chair and raped her.

In any interview with a suspected criminal it is good practice to withhold some minor pieces of information to ensure that he is not falsely admitting to a crime which he did not commit. In this instance the two detectives asked Callaghan to go into more detail of Carol's entry to her house and their initial confrontation in the rear living room. He replied that he had heard Carol coming through her front door and along the hallway to the living room where she undid the small bolt on the hallside of the door. He went on to say that she entered the room and placed her handbag on the floor, then threw a plastic bag containing a loaf of bread and a carton of milk onto the settee. The knowledge and recollection of these simple facts were further confirmation that he was indeed the killer. When asked what he had done with the murder weapon Callaghan said that he could not remember but that after the killing he had gone to his own house, cleaned himself and then driven quickly to his girlfriend's house. He thought he might have thrown it out of the car on the way.

The two interviewers then took down Callaghan's written confession and placed him back in his cell. They joined me in the main CID office where I had been anxiously pacing the floor and they related the details of the interview. It was clear from what I heard that although Callaghan was accepting having killed and raped Carol he was trying to lessen his culpability by claiming he was suffering from blackouts. I did not accept this as his actions prior to the killing showed a high degree of cunning. His lapse of memory over the whereabouts of the murder weapon was also deeply suspicious. As a consequence I decided to explore his behaviour more closely after the killing to see just what his state of mind was. The first matter we wanted to establish was the whereabouts of his parents immediately after the murder as we felt it unlikely he would present himself to them at home in a bloodstained condition and no doubt in a highly excited mood. It turned out that his mother was actually working in a nearby supermarket until 9 p.m. and his father had been visiting a friend until 7.30 p.m. so Callaghan had carefully chosen his time to strike.

We also interviewed his girlfriend and her recollection was that on the Friday of the murder Callaghan had arrived to her place at around 6.45 p.m. Within the space of an hour or so he had killed and raped Carol, gone to his own house and cleaned himself up, and managed to make it to his girlfriend's house probably in an effort to establish an alibi of sorts. She recalled they spent the evening at the cinema and Callaghan then took her to his house at 23 Colvil Street arriving just after 10 p.m. They chatted with his parents for about 15 minutes and Callaghan then suggested they go for a walk. She agreed and as they passed Carol's house Callaghan said, 'I wonder why Carol's not working tonight — she normally works in the Priory Inn on a Friday night.' I have no doubt he was trying to gauge what activity if any was taking place at Carol's house but of course there was none as the crime had not yet been discovered.

Our enquiries also revealed that on the following day Callaghan telephoned another female acquaintance and asked her if she would accompany him to the Priory Inn that evening. She agreed. He collected her in his car and drove along Colvil Street. As they passed Carol's house Callaghan remarked that she must be away on holidays as her car was still there. They continued on to the Priory Inn where they spent the evening. Callaghan may well have been attempting to assess the degree of reaction to the non-appearance of his victim the previous evening. Remembering also that Callaghan had brazened out two interviews with detectives prior to his arrest I felt that all-in-all we would be in a position to refute any defence of mental instability should he raise one at his trial.

As a consequence I charged Callaghan with the murder of Carol Gouldie and when asked if he wished to say anything further he replied, 'I think everybody knows I am sorry. I have told them enough.'

I then travelled to Holywood and brought Carol's parents up-to-date. I advised them that the murder would again be at the forefront of news bulletins the next day when Callaghan would be appearing in court. On that day he was brought into the dock and I went to the witness box where I made a formal deposition. Callaghan was remanded in custody and no doubt many frightened women in east Belfast breathed a sigh of relief. Before Callaghan left the dock his defending solicitor said that he wished to convey his heartfelt sympathy to Carol's family. This was a fitting gesture.

When I had finished at the court I returned to Strandtown police station and thanked all members of the investigation team and the major incident room staff for their dedicated hard work. The enquiry team was then reduced to a small number of detectives who would be required to tidy-up a few loose ends. During the following weeks the forensic scientists continued working on the case. In due course they positively matched Callaghan's boots to the footprint. The biologist was anxious to see if the relatively new technique of DNA profiling, or 'genetic fingerprinting' as it is more commonly known, could be used to match the semen from the vaginal swabs with Callaghan's blood sample. Essentially, this amounted to the analysis of the chemical structure of the semen which should be identical to that of the blood if both came from the same person. At that time the Home Office Central Research Establishment at Aldermaston was pioneering the technique and the samples were delivered to their laboratory. They obtained DNA profiles from the semen and blood and both matched perfectly. The chances of obtaining a similar result from someone other than Callaghan were authoritatively put as being less than one in 10 million, a most compelling piece of evidence.

Within a few weeks I assembled all of the case papers and forwarded them to the Director of Public Prosecutions who ordered that proceedings on the charge of murder should continue. Callaghan was returned for trial to Belfast Crown Court. On Thursday, 23 June 1988, some 9 months after the killing, the case opened before Mr Justice McCollum QC and Callaghan was represented by two senior counsel. Callaghan was led into the dock by prison officers and he kept his head lowered as the judge appeared on the bench. Carol's family was also present and the clerk of the court formally arraigned Callaghan on the murder charge. He whispered, 'Guilty' and no defence of diminished responsibility was raised. The Crown prosecutor briefly outlined the facts of the crime and the judge gave him life imprisonment. Callaghan was taken down the steps of the dock to begin his sentence.

The one aspect never satisfactorily resolved was Callaghan's motive for carrying out such a dastardly crime, but I believe the answer lies in the rape aspect of it. To some people, including some learned judges, rape appears to be a matter of a man having sexual intercourse with a woman against her will as a means of simply obtaining sexual gratification. However, research has shown that rapists carry out their crimes as a means of expressing anger and gaining dominance over women in general. It really is one of the most horrible crimes imaginable and one which has caused consternation in recent years when a few courts have treated it somewhat flippantly. Some British judges have even gone so far as to pronounce that the victims 'Asked for it'. This is an unfortunate misconception and in Carol's case Callaghan perhaps felt put down or shunned in some way by her and the killing and raping was his way of getting even.

11

A BODY IN A BIN

Later in 1988 I was faced with yet another complex murder investigation in my geographical area of responsibility. The events for me began on Saturday, 8 October 1988 when the uniformed sub-divisional commander at Bangor made contact with me at home expressing concern that something untoward may have happened to a local businessman, a Colin Hunter, aged 28 years, who had mysteriously disappeared some nine days previously on Thursday, 28 September 1988.

Bangor is a large seaside town, approximately 15 miles from Belfast and situated on the southern side of the wide entrance to Belfast Lough. There is normally a ship or two in sight as they ply to and from the port of Belfast. On most days one can also see across to the rolling Antrim hills on the far coast. Colin Hunter and his girlfriend, Jennifer McKendry, lived together in a small house overlooking the picturesque harbour of Bangor.

Colin's main business interests were in a small bar on the sea front owned by his father and in larger licensed premises known as Clookie's or C's, situated a hundred yards or so away in a side-street leading from the harbour. He jointly owned these premises with a Ricky Chambers of approximately the same age. Together they also ran a gaming machine business, with several machines installed in premises in Bangor and other nearby towns.

On Thursday, 29 September 1988 Colin had failed to return home, which was something completely out of character for him, and he had also not been seen since in his usual haunts in the town. His girlfriend and family were very concerned and checked everywhere he could possibly be, such as friends' addresses, but there was no sign of him. They even considered the possibility that he might have simply gone away alone for a few days to escape business pressures. As the hours wore on into Friday his family decided to report the matter to the police. They did so at Bangor RUC station and spoke to the uniformed constable on desk duty. Almost every week someone is reported missing and on most occasions they eventually turn up unharmed. As there was no immediate evidence of a crime in this instance the constable took down descriptive details of Colin and circulated them to every police station in the Province.

Over a week had now elapsed and still their was no sign of Colin. The sub-divisional commander informed me that the town was rife with rumours that Colin had been murdered by his business partner Ricky Chambers and that his body had been secretly disposed of, so he asked the CID to now take over the case. On the scant details I had so far learned I certainly agreed that this was not simply a case of a missing person, so I assembled the local detectives and took the precaution of treating the incident as a murder investigation from that point. If Colin Hunter eventually turned up unharmed it would be an easy procedure to wind down the investigation, but if we later found his body and had not treated it as a murder enquiry from the outset then we ran the risk of losing valuable evidence.

Once the major incident room had been set up I detailed a number of detectives to interview the missing man's girlfriend and family in order to begin to build up a picture of his private and business life. The most revealing information came from Colin's girlfriend, Jennifer McKendry. When interviewed she stated that Colin and she had worked together in his father's bar, simply known as Hunters, on the evening of Wednesday, 28 September 1988. At 10.45 p.m. or so Colin had left to walk the short distance to C's where he intended to close up, count the day's takings and empty the gaming machines. Meanwhile, Jennifer closed up Hunters, cleared up the glasses and bottles and sat down alone in the bar to watch the Olympic Games on television and await the return of Colin. At 2.40 a.m. Colin had still not re-appeared so Jennifer walked over to C's and knocked at the door. After a few minutes delay Colin answered it. When Jennifer asked if he would soon be finished he replied that he wouldn't as he was talking to Ricky Chambers in an effort to get things sorted out.

Jennifer explained that she was aware that business relationships between Colin and Ricky were becoming strained. In general Colin felt Ricky was not pulling his weight and the proceeds from the gaming machine operation were steadily dropping off. Colin had gone so far as to say to her on an earlier occasion that he planned to have Ricky's name taken off the lease of C's. This was an indication of how their relationship had deteriorated.

Jennifer then asked Colin how long he expected to be and he said it would probably take another half an hour, so she returned to Hunters and resumed watching television. By 3.30 a.m. Jennifer was understandably becoming bored at having to hang around waiting for Colin so she returned to C's and knocked at the door. It was again answered by Colin who repeated that he was still talking to Ricky. Jennifer then left and walked to her flat and went to bed. She fell asleep but awoke at 7 a.m. to find Colin had not come home so she dozed on and off, finally arising at 11 a.m. with still no sign of her boyfriend. Jennifer remained in her flat until around 1.30 p.m. when she decided to walk to Hunters bar. She asked the day staff if they had seen Colin but they said they hadn't. From there Jennifer went to Colin's parents house but they too had not seen him. She decided then to telephone Ricky Chambers' house where she spoke to his girlfriend, Susan Potts, who told her that Ricky had come home around 12.30 to 12.45 a.m. and that she hadn't seen Colin recently.

When the detectives now working on the case returned to the police station on the evening of that first day of the CID involvement in the case we pooled all of the information we had so far gleaned. In addition to what Jennifer had told us some of my officers had picked up intelligence to the effect that Colin had been stabbed to death somewhere in C's bar by Ricky Chambers shortly after the last visit by Jennifer in the early hours of that Thursday morning; that later he had obtained the help of a close friend, Stephen Millen, and together they had discussed the best way to dispose of the body.

Due to the lapse of time since the alleged occurrence of the crime it was imperative that we move against Chambers and Millen as quickly as possible and forensically examine C's bar in the hope of obtaining some evidence if indeed a murder had occurred. Consequently, I arranged for both suspects to be arrested at their homes the following morning, a Sunday, and brought into Bangor police station for questioning. I also contacted the forensic science laboratory and requested the services of a biologist. It was planned to co-ordinate the examination of the bar and the arrests.

The arrests went according to plan. Both men were picked up at their homes and teams of detectives began to question them about the disappearance of Colin Hunter. As this was being carried out I went to C's bar accompanied by a forensic scientist and a police scenes of crimes officer. We let ourselves in, using Ricky Chambers' keys which had been seized during his arrest. The premises consisted of a large ground floor bar which was carpeted and furnished in the style of open plan cushioned seating areas. The carpet was heavily stained most probably through the spillage of drink and contributed to the rather sleazy atmosphere. We moved upstairs to the first floor. It was sparsely furnished and had a number of gaming machines, a juke box and some pool tables to entertain the clientele. It too had a somewhat grubby appearance with shards of broken glass, empty beer cans, and unwashed glasses. Obviously the premises had not been cleaned from the previous day's business. There was a narrow set of stairs leading from this area to a locked room on the second floor and when we opened it with a key found it to be an office of sorts with receipts and other documents carelessly scattered about.

The forensic scientist and the police scenes of crimes officer then began to swab the floor of the office with a special chemical which would react against the presence of blood. None was found in the office so they slowly worked their way down the carpeted stairs, testing each one in turn. But again the swabs failed to respond to the presence of blood. They turned their attention to the large first floor pool room and laboriously swabbed it too but no evidence of bloodstaining was found. A similar procedure was carried out on the ground floor but it too proved negative.

We then returned to the first floor of the premises and towards the rear we unlocked and examined a beer chilling room. Nothing of interest was found there. Close to the chilling room was a door which opened onto a set of steel fire escape doors which led down to a large open rear yard. The yard seemed to be shared by other nearby premises such as an Indian restaurant. Situated in the yard was another storeroom belonging to C's. We opened it with a key and carried out a detailed examination but nothing of evidential value seemed apparent.

The forensic scientist then turned his attention to six large heavy duty refuse bins lined up against a wall in the yard. Each bin was about 5 feet in height and 3 feet in diameter and all contained a considerable amount of bar and restaurant waste. The exteriors of the bins were minutely examined for traces of blood but again none was found. However, on the interior wall of the fourth bin was a reddish coloured smear about 12 inches down from the rim. The forensic scientist tested the smear and it gave a positive response for blood. This was interesting, but it could also prove insignificant, bearing in mind the fact that the bins contained restaurant waste. It was a probability that it would turn out to be animal blood, caused perhaps by the dumping of remnants of animal meats.

The forensic scientist informed me that he would have to take a sample of the smear back to the laboratory where he had more sophisticated equipment which could distinguish between animal and human blood. Obviously it was vital to the investigation to find out either way so the scientist set off for the laboratory and I arranged for uniformed police to guard the premises and rear yard in the meantime.

I returned to Bangor police station and was brought up-to-date with the progress of the interviews of Chambers and Millen. Needless to say they were denying any involvement in Colin Hunter's disappearance. Despite what Jennifer McKendry had stated about calling at C's on two occasions on the morning of his disappearance, the last time being 3.30 a.m. when Colin told her he was still talking business with Chambers, the latter denied that he was actually present and said he had arrived home some three hours earlier at 12.30 a.m. His live-in girlfriend, Susan Potts, was also supporting this story. It was obvious that Chambers and Millen had used the 10-day interval between the suspected crime and their arrest to good advantage by preparing their alibis and fortifying themselves for the inevitable interviews.

A short time later the forensic scientist telephoned me from the laboratory and reported that his analysis of the blood sample from the bin had proved it to be of human origin. Any lingering doubts in my mind about the crime having occurred now dissipated. The scientist asked that we arrange for the bin to be delivered to the laboratory, as he wished to carry out a more detailed examination of it to see if he could come up with some more clues. This we did by arranging a van and trailer. The bin, covered with a tarpaulin, was transported to the laboratory.

The interviews of Chambers and Miller continued on throughout that day and although the crime was later proved to have some terrorist connotations, we were bound at that early stage by the ordinary criminal law and therefore could only detain them for 24 hours without bringing criminal charges. I knew we certainly had a long way to go in the investigation so with some reluctance I ordered the release of Chambers and Miller. They were still denying any complicity in a crime when their period of detention expired.

The following morning I sat down with my investigation team to again assess our situation. After a lengthy analysis of the information and evidence to that point we agreed to concentrate our enquiries in two main areas, the first being the location of the body of Colin Hunter and the second an in-depth investigation into the business relationship between the missing man and Ricky Chambers.

The most compelling evidence of a crime having occurred was of course the bloodstaining in the bin so a small number of detectives were detailed to interview the local refuse collectors and endeavour to trace the current whereabouts of the contents of the bins since Colin Hunter was last seen alive on Thursday, 28 September 1988. The detectives went to the local council refuse collection depot and were soon put in touch with the team responsible for emptying the large industrial bins in the rear of C's. They had last done so on Monday, 3 October 1988 and they described how they reversed their large refuse truck into the rear yard area of C's. Each of the bins was then hauled to the rear of the truck and thereafter mechanically hoisted until the contents fell out, after which the rubbish was pushed forward by means of a hydraulic ram. On that particular day they had noticed one of the bins was heavier than normal and was difficult to manoeuvre. The man who operated the mechanical hoist heard a heavy thump as the contents were tipped into the back of the truck. Remarkably, he looked inside and saw a hand sticking out of the rubbish but immediately thought it was part of a tailor's dummy. The previous week they had had a similar incident. Some of his workmates had played practical jokes with it and he did not want a repetition on this occasion.

When they had finished their collection round they returned to the local council depot where the waste from their truck was tipped into a large hopper. It was then compressed into blocks with a ratio of 3:1 and transported to the municipal dumping site at Dargan Road, Belfast.

This was a most interesting piece of information, so the detectives set off for Dargan Road in Belfast and spoke to the council officials in charge. The officials were extremely helpful and explained that all refuse collected in Belfast, Bangor and Carrickfergus was brought to what is officially known as Dargan Road landfill site. The site is situated on the shores of Belfast Lough. Like that of any large city the dump was huge and covered an area of several acres. The material being dumped was being used to reclaim a marshy area. The progress of the tip was carefully plotted on a map and each day it moved forward two or three metres and at a depth of some ten feet or so. When asked if they could give an indication of where the refuse collected in Bangor on 3 October 1988 now was the council officials drew a square on a map of the site, representing an area of approximately 50 square metres, and said with certainty that it was within these boundaries.

The two detectives returned to the major incident room at Bangor and brought me up-to-date with this information. I knew it was going to be a formidable task to excavate the area described but I found the challenge of locating Colin Hunter's body irresistible. As a result I went to the landfill site myself to see at first hand the scale of the task. I found it even worse than anticipated with refuse trucks entering or leaving every few minutes or so. But successful crime investigation comes from having the tenacity to take those few extra steps so I took a firm decision that we should proceed with the dig. However, there were literally hundreds of tons of rubbish to be dug up and sifted through and of course this could only be carried out with mechanical excavators. I made contact with my CID authorities at RUC headquarters, seeking financial sanction to hire two machines for an indefinite period. Within a short time I received approval to do so.

I knew also that the police activity at the landfill site would soon attract the attention of the local press. So it was important that the Hunter family should be aware from the outset of what we intended to do and that they be brought up-to-date with the progress of the investigation. As a consequence I asked them to call and see me at Bangor police station on the evening of Monday, 10 October 1988. They turned up as agreed and I took them to a quiet room in the station and gently broke the news that our enquiries to then tended to indicate that their son had most probably been murdered and that we intended to commence excavating the landfill site the next day in an effort to locate the body. They too had sensed for over a week now that they were unlikely to see their son alive again. Nevertheless, being officially told by me caused them considerable distress and I had staff on stand-by to assist in comforting them.

The following morning two mechanical excavators arrived at the landfill site. I had arranged for two police scenes of crimes officers, two detectives and a number of uniformed police to to be present. The working conditions at the site were quite horrendous and the police were suitably attired in overalls, rubber boots, gloves and face masks. The area to be excavated had now been pegged out by the council staff. The police team required little briefing as it was simply a matter of the excavators scooping out large bucketfuls and dropping the contents loosely to one side where it could, if necessary, be raked through for signs of the body.

Meanwhile, other detectives from the investigation team were beginning to learn about the business relationship between Colin

Hunter and Ricky Chambers. It appeared they first began to work together around 1983 when they opened a gaming machine arcade in Bangor which lasted until 1985 when Colin opened a night club named Spooks. It was unlicensed to sell alcohol but the patrons could bring in their own drink and be supplied with glasses and mixers. However, this turned out to be illegal and eventually the premises were closed down. Colin received a conviction under the liquor licensing laws. Around mid-1988 Colin and Chambers decided to purchase C's bar by means of loans from a bank and a brewery and they obtained legal possession of the premises in July. When they applied to the local magistrates court for a licence to sell liquor the court took into account Colin's previous conviction and refused him but allowed Chambers to become the licensee. It transpired that Colin had anticipated such an outcome and that was one of the main reasons why he was anxious to retain Chambers as a business partner in the bar, in addition to the gaming machine operation.

When C's finally opened for business Colin had fully expected Ricky Chambers to concentrate his efforts on running it while he continued looking after his father's bar. Things did not turn out that way and apparently Chambers left the running of C's to the bar staff while he spent a considerable period drinking in the Helmsman Bar next door where Stephen Millen was the doorman. Also, the income from the gaming machines business was beginning to drop off and Colin began to realise he had made an error of judgement in taking on Chambers as a partner. It therefore seemed most likely that it was these matters which they were acrimoniously discussing in C's in the early hours of that Thursday morning when Jennifer McKendry had last seen Colin alive.

The enquiry team also learned from the bar staff at Hunters and C's that at about 9 a.m. on the Thursday we believed the crime to have been committed, Chambers and Millen were up and about at a time which for Chambers was considerably earlier than usual. They were seen to move a gaming machine from C's across to Hunters and one of the staff recalled that Chambers looked drawn as if he had not been to bed, while Millen appeared more fresh. This member of staff also smelled stale drink from Chamber's breath and poked fun at him, saying that he looked like a man who had been on an all-night drinking session. But Chambers brushed this off, commenting that the smell on his breath came from having just eaten some egg and onion sandwiches.

I knew the forensic scientist involved in the case was working on a minute examination of the blood-stained bin so I then decided to call at the forensic science laboratory to see how he was getting on. The reception staff tried to telephone him in his office but were told he was working on the bin in a large garage area of the complex. They directed me towards it. It was obvious that the bin was too large to manoeuvre into the biology laboratory itself so I made my way to the garage where there were several cars connected with other crimes under examination. I could see my bin but there was no sign of the scientist. I called out his name and suddenly his head appeared over the rim. He was actually inside it, working away meticulously. He informed me that in addition to the blood smear he had detected on the Sunday he had now found more stains on the wall of the bin below it. He gave an expert opinion that an object heavily saturated with blood had been deposited in the bin initially causing the smearing and that it had continued to drip, leaving the staining towards the bottom. We both knew in our hearts that this must have been the body of Colin Hunter.

During the remainder of that week the investigation team continued with their work, building up an intimate picture of the lifestyles of Colin Hunter and Ricky Chambers. Each day I called at the landfill site where the excavation was steadily progressing. It was now a deep chasm some 50 metres wide with the excavated material forming a veritable mountain of rubbish to one side. The working conditions for the officers were quite appalling but they had lost none of their enthusiasm, I observed with satisfaction, as they continued examining each excavator bucketful of rubbish.

On the morning of Saturday, 5 October 1988, five days after the dig began, I took a telephone call at my office from the Belfast communications centre who informed me that my presence was urgently required at the landfill site as parts of a body had been found. I immediately telephoned the forensic scientist and we both agreed to proceed to the scene at once. I arrived half an hour later and was met by the excavation team who were in an obviously jubilant mood. They informed me that shortly after the dig resumed that morning most of a human body had tumbled out of the excavator bucket. The head and right arm were missing. The team had laid the remains out on a body bag and together the scientist and I carried out a cursory examination of it. It was in a very advanced state of decomposition. One could distinguish that it was dressed in a jacket, a short-sleeved shirt and a pair of trousers. One of the few parts of the body still in reasonably good condition was the left forearm and we could just decipher a tattoo which simply read, 'Colin'. There was no doubt in our minds that this was the missing man and the excavation team deserved great credit for pulling off such a feat.

However, the head and right arm were still missing and had obviously come apart during the excavation. The forensic scientist was not surprised at this. He explained to me that although Colin Hunter had been missing for just over two weeks, the rubbish in which he had been buried initially heated up for a period and would enhance the process of decomposition. We agreed that the head and arm could not now be too far away so we asked the excavation team to continue with their good work until they found them. In the meantime pressmen had begun to gather at the scene, some equipped with long range camera lenses, but were kept at a distance by uniformed police. I approached them and explained briefly that we had found a body as yet formally unidentified. One of them asked me if it was true that it was headless. I told him that I could not reveal such intimate details at present.

The search for the missing head and arm continued all weekend and after much sifting and re-sifting of the excavated rubbish both parts were found on Monday, 17 October 1988 and removed to the mortuary where the pathologist was able to carry out a full post-mortem examination.

One of the major problems we faced was the formal identification of the body. The forensic scientist cleaned up the clothing which had been removed from the corpse and some members of the Hunter family were able to say the items were similar to those worn by Colin.

He had never received any dental treatment so that option was closed to us. We were forced to rely on the tattoo on the left forearm and steps were taken by the mortuary staff to prevent the body from further deterioration. Reluctantly, we were placed in a position where we would now have to ask Colin's father to come to the mortuary and look at the tattoo. We felt it would have been too distressing for him to view the whole body so the mortuary staff carefully covered the decomposed remains with sheets and exposed only the tattoo. Mr Hunter complied with our request and without hesitation identified it as his son's.

The pathologist had an extremely difficult task in carrying out his post-mortem examination but he thought he could see evidence of stab wounds to the back of the deceased. The forensic examination of the clothing from the body, although torn because of the rough manner in which the body had been located, displayed a series of cuts in the jacket and shirt. When overlaid, one on top of the other, these matched perfectly and corresponded with the position of the suspected stab wounds on the back of the body. Further scientific examination showed these cuts had been caused by a sharp single-edged instrument, probably a knife. There seemed little doubt that Colin Hunter had indeed been stabbed to death. Unfortunately, due to the poor state of the body all blood had drained from it prior to recovery so we could not take any steps to match it with the bloodstaining in the bin. However, we had no doubts in our minds that it was that of Colin Hunter.

While all of this was taking place we of course re-arrested Ricky Chambers and Stephen Millen under the ordinary criminal law. Although they must have been psychologically shaken from our finding of the body they still continued to deny involvement. It was apparent that they had taken strong legal advice and knew in their hearts that the only way we could connect them with the murder was by their own admission. So once again we were forced to release them.

Several days later the funeral of Colin Hunter took place in Bangor. Among the mourners was Ricky Chambers who kept up his charade of non-involvement in the crime by sympathising with the relatives of the deceased.

We continued working on the case for several more weeks in the certain knowledge that Ricky Chambers was the killer but we could do little more until some fresh evidence came to light. Although disappointed I was optimistic that with patience the case would eventually be solved and I was immensely proud of the outstanding work my staff had done to that point.

It was not until some two years later, in the autumn of 1990, that fresh information concerning the crime began to filter through to the police. It was to the effect that some of the proceeds of the gaming machine business run by Colin Hunter and Ricky Chambers had been going towards loyalist paramilitary funds. All of the paramilitary groups in Northern Ireland had several ways of raising finances and many of them did indeed get a rake-off from gaming machines. It seemed a reasonable proposition that the diminishing revenue that Colin Hunter complained of to Chambers was perhaps finding its way into paramilitary coffers.

As a consequence it was decided that Chambers and Millen could now be lawfully detained under terrorist legislation so on 4 December 1990 both men were again arrested but this time under the Prevention of Terrorism Act. This allowed the police to hold them without charge for 48 hours with the possibility of a further extensions of five days with the permission of the Secretary of State.

They were both taken to Castlereagh Detention Centre. Chambers, who seemed piqued by yet another arrest, remained silent until the evening of the third day when he broke down and cried and made his long-awaited confession to the crime. He began by outlining his business relationship with Colin Hunter and confirmed much of what we already suspected. He agreed that Colin had begun to complain about him not spending enough time at C's and the declining revenue from the gaming machines. Chambers went on to explain that at around midnight on 28 September 1988 he had gone to C's to collect his fishing knife and sharpening steel as he intended going sea angling the following day. He said he did not expect to find anyone on the premises and was surprised to find Colin present with a couple of locals in the first floor bar. These people left a short time later, leaving Colin and him alone. Chambers said they had a few drinks together and Colin then brought up the subject of the loss of income from the gaming machines. He tried to explain to Colin that a recent change in legislation had resulted in the police removing some of the machines from certain premises.

According to Chambers the discussion with Colin degenerated into an argument and on several occasions they almost came to blows. He recalled the door of C's being knocked at a number of times as the hours wore on. On each occasion Colin went down the stairs, answered it and when he returned he said it was Jennifer urging him to hurry up. Eventually the argument came to blows and he struck first by punching Colin around the face. Colin reacted by diving on him and hitting him with a bottle or jug and they both fell against the bar counter. Chambers said he reached for his fishing knife and they wrestled against the juke box and then onto the floor where he stabbed Colin several times. When he had finished his hands and knife were covered in blood. Colin was sitting on the floor in an upright position, with his back against the seating close to the juke box, his head hanging loose. He was apparently dead.

Chambers panicked at that point and ran out of the bar. He walked around some of the side streets but returned a short time later to Colin's body. He then opened the back door of the bar close to the beer chilling room, lifted the body, carried it down the steel stairs to the back yard, intending to put it in the outside store and dispose of it later. But on the way he changed his mind and threw it into one of the large bins. Chambers said he returned to the bar and using cloths began to push some of the thick blood from the floor into a cardboard box. He used more cloths to wipe up the remaining blood and then threw the box, cloths and knife into a separate bin, after which he turned off the lights, closed the bar and went home.

He went to bed but understandably could not sleep so he got up around 8 a.m. and went to see his friend, Stephen Millen, to confide in him what he had done. Millen's girlfriend was present so Chambers could not reveal the true reason why he wanted to speak to him. He asked him to come with him to help move a gaming machine. When they were alone in the car Chambers revealed to Millen that he had killed Colin Hunter. At first Millen did not believe him but when the truth sunk in he offered him little comfort, saying he would probably end up getting life imprisonment. They drove to C's bar but on arrival two cleaners were already present so both men acted out the charade of moving around gaming machines. This was to explain their earlier than normal appearance.

Millen eventually left and returned home as he and his girlfriend had planned to do a day's shopping. Chambers was left alone with the problem. He hung around for a while and then returned to the bin where Colin's body was. He tried to lift it out but it proved too heavy and awkward so Chambers left it where it was. Over the following days he gradually worked himself back into a normal routine while the Hunter family wondered where their son had got to.

During the course of interviews at Castlereagh Millen confessed to his limited knowledge of the crime and said that on previous occasions, when arrested and interviewed by the police, he had been too scared to confess. He had simply decided to lie his way out of it in the hope that in due course the events would pass into history.

As a result of the reasonably comprehensive confession by Chambers the investigation team were now able to identify with some certainty the location in the first floor bar of C's where Colin Hunter had been propped against after the stabbing. The forensic scientist was asked to carry out a further examination even though more than two years had passed since the actual killing. He dismantled the seating area beside the juke box and in one of the wooden components found a blood stain which had dried and cracked with age. He took it back to his laboratory and an analysis revealed it to be of human origin and no doubt that of Colin Hunter.

Chambers was charged with murdering Colin Hunter and Millen was accused of a lesser offence of withholding information about the crime. Both men appeared at Bangor Magistrates Court and were remanded in custody. Millen was later granted High Court bail and the extensive case papers were prepared for the Director of Public Prosecutions who agreed to proceed on the charges.

The trial of Chambers and Millen opened at Downpatrick Crown Court on Monday, 20 January 1992 before Mr Justice McCollum QC. Although there had been some suggestion that part of the proceeds of the gaming machines business run by Hunter and Chambers was going towards loyalist paramilitaries, the Attorney General felt that the crime was motivated more by the business dealings between the deceased and the accused. Consequently, he granted Chambers and Millen a jury trial as distinct from a Diplock hearing reserved purely for terrorist cases where a judge would consider the evidence alone. A jury was sworn in and when arraigned by the clerk of the court Chambers pleaded 'Not Guilty' to the murder charge. Millen pleaded 'Guilty' to withholding information.

The Crown opened the case by presenting a brief outline of the crime to the jury and began to call the various witnesses to prove the formal aspects of the case such as the arrests and interviews of Chambers, the finding of the body, the post-mortem examination and so on. Defence counsel of course cross-examined many of the police interviewing officers and suggested that they had duped Chambers into confessing by promising him that he would be charged only with the lesser crime of manslaughter and that he would get bail between his first remand and trial. The officers denied that they had struck such a bargain with the accused and the trial continued.

It took several days for the Crown to finish their evidence and it was then the turn of the defence. They called only one witness and that was Chambers himself. From the outset he conceded to the court that he had killed Colin Hunter but had done so in self-defence in a sudden fight, thereby laying the foundation for a claim that he should only be convicted of manslaughter. Altogether he spent three days in the witness box, most of it under cross-examination by Crown counsel who pursued him on why he had told so many lies to the police, why, if he acted in self-defence he had shown little or no injury while the deceased had sustained multiple stab wounds. The Crown barrister also suggested to Chambers that he was a cold, calculating man given the manner he had disposed of the body and his callous attendance at the funeral. Overall, Chambers gave a poor account of himself in the witness box and several times he broke down sobbing.

When all of the evidence had been heard both Crown and defence counsel made lengthy submissions to the jury and when they had finished the judge skilfully summed up both arguments. The jury retired to consider the evidence and four hours later returned with a unanimous verdict of 'Guilty' to murder. Millen was now brought back to the dock and both accused seemed outwardly composed as the judge sentenced Chambers to the mandatory term of life imprisonment. The judge acknowledged Millen's lesser part in the crime by giving him a suspended sentence. The Hunter family filed out of court satisfied that justice had been done.